Economic Crisi:
THE FULL

What caused Indonesia to experience the largest fall in the value of its currency of any country since World War II? Was it Soros-type speculators stampeding herd-like out of the rupiah after a massive collapse of confidence? Was it a calculated plot by an unknown person, group or power to topple President Soeharto ahead of the Presidential elections? Was it Indonesian Government ineptitude? Was it the reckless borrowing by the private sector? Was it corruption, collusion and nepotism? Did the IMF solve the crisis or make it much worse?

Whatever the causes of the unimaginable downward slide of the rupiah, the consequences have been devastating. Growth down from plus 8 percent to minus 5 percent, many projects and factories on standstill, per capita income slashed by nearly 80 percent down to less than US$300, inflation threatening to skyrocket, unemployment up by almost 10 million, companies and banks technically bankrupt. And, as if this was not bad enough, the country was reeling from scarcities caused by the prolonged drought, not to mention health problems caused by haze pouring off raging forest fires.

For 30 years praise had been heaped on the New Order Government for its macroeconomic management. 'Friendly' countries poured in investment dollars which have increased by many magnitudes since President Soeharto's early days. Abruptly,

Indonesia found that most of its economic 'friends' were fair-weather companions. Except countries in the immediate region, many a door was firmly slammed on its requests for help. Suddenly, Indonesia, its Government and its President found themselves fighting an economic war against an unseen enemy resistant to every kind of 'medicine.'

Day by day, step by step, blow by blow, this book traces Indonesia's unfolding tragedy - a disaster which some say will take three to five years to correct.

Richard Mann is a British economist, author and publisher, specialising in Asian affairs, especially Indonesia. His wife, Jenny, is Indonesian and the couple have two children, Ian and Sarina, based in the United Kingdom.

Economic Crisis In Indonesia

THE FULL STORY

by RICHARD MANN

Gateway Books

CONTENTS

FOREWORD

This study has been compiled monitoring media coverage of the economic crisis in Indonesia from England, Singapore, Malaysia, Australia and Indonesia itself.

It is the story of how market forces sent Indonesia crashing on its face and it has been told by letting it tell itself, event by event. It will be of particular interest to non-Indonesians by being told largely from what I perceive to have happened within Indonesia. Throughout the crisis, Indonesian and foreign perceptions and reactions were widely different.

What emerges it substantially different from the overall public impression of Indonesia's handling of the crisis and even of its causes.

In the beginning, Indonesia was an innocent and unaffected bystander to the crisis in Thailand. Then it was a bewildered participant as the crisis appeared to roll through Malaysia, Singapore and Indonesia, before turning north to South Korea and, at various times, appearing to threaten China and Hong Kong. Next, its economic managers applied every tried and tested financial mechanism to shore up the falling rupiah - with no effect. Finally, as the crisis turned from somebody else's to Indonesia's very own, the country was caught up in the most savagely destructive economic downturn in more than 30 years. Whatever counteractive steps the Government took, failed dismally and, the greater the failure, the deeper the loss of investor and business confidence and the more severe the economic collapse. In desperation, in January, with the rupiah at Rps 17,000 to one US dollar, the Government turned to the International Monetary Fund (IMF).

Fund directors seized the opportunity to try to bring Indonesia to the path of ideological free market purity, instead of focusing on the causes of the crisis. As bad luck would have it (from Indonesia's point of view), just as Jakarta asked the IMF for assistance, the Fund was extending its activities from simple bailouts to wholesale economic and political reforms, including, by implication, even social reforms. Indonesia couldn't cope with its suggestions and demands, though, as the crisis deepened, it

7

tried harder. The result was not immediate help but a barrage of IMF-led international criticism which threatened to turn one of Asia's success stories into a pariah among nations. Swamped by criticism and bereft of the prompt help it needed, Indonesia's economy slipped further and ever more rapidly downhill on the back of a currency that also slid remorselessly downwards. The few concrete, short-term measures suggested by the Fund, such as tightening liquidity and bank closures only made the crisis very much worse. Eventually, the Government of Indonesia felt compelled to look for other ways to halt the catastrophic fall of the rupiah and turned to the idea of a Currency Board, a solution President Soeharto called IMF-Plus. That didn't work either because by this time foreign currency reserves were too low and the banking system too perilous.

It was probably just as well because the Currency Board would have dollarised the Indonesian economy just at a time when it was important for all prices and transactions to be in rupiah. Malaysia had stuck to Ringgit pricing and seemed much better off. Few of its business operators had been forced to close because they could not pay US dollar denominated rents in the heart of Asia.

By April, there seemed no solution for Indonesia, other than to follow the so far unsuccessful advice of the IMF. It really was the last chance. Everything had been tried. If the IMF's medicine didn't work this time, Indonesia was faced with living through the nightmare of letting its economy's now multiple ailments cure themselves, over time.

At the outset, virtually no one had realised the extent of Indonesia's offshore, foreign currency denominated debt. Of course, they should have, especially the Central Bank. But they didn't. Even when it **was** realised, both the Government of Indonesia and international 'rescue' agencies like the IMF turned their backs firmly on paying the corporates' bills. The private sector had borrowed far more than it could ever hope to repay in a very short-term and just trying to do so pushed the rupiah constantly down and the dollar equally constantly up. Worse still, the dollar was on a ride to record highs. Loss of confidence in the rupiah led to a stampede out of the national currency and into US dollars. To varying degrees much the same sort of things were happening elsewhere in the region. In the US, for the first time in 30 years, the

Federal Government was budgeting a surplus. There was a dollar drought.

With official backs firmly turned against paying the private debt, the only solution was for the companies to request roll-overs from their creditors and/or for Indonesia to weather the repayment storm while taking whatever prudent steps could be taken to minimise economic and social damage. The creditors were not keen. The crisis continued.

Because the cause of the crisis was late in being understood and everything the Government tried seemed to fail, more and more Indonesians blamed the Government. There was a massive outpouring of frustrations which had built up over many years related to corruption, collusion, nepotism, lack of Western-style democracy, lack of accountability, lack of transparency and an inadequate legal and regulatory structure, especially for banking and business. In fact, all these things had been true for many years, in Indonesia and elsewhere in the region, but everybody had got by and the so-called Asian economic miracle had rolled on. On January 24, discussing the region, Gwynne Dyer wrote in the 'Jakarta Post: "The cozy "Asian way" capitalism that served the "tigers" so well in the first phase of industrialisation (as it served Japan, too, a century before), suddenly ran out of rope. The flood of money from outside exacerbated all its worst tendencies to over-investment and non-accountability - and then exposed it to a scrutiny it could not survive. Crash."

The opening up of economies and the injection of tidal waves of foreign capital with clear expectations of repayment proved too much for Indonesia, with a still-undeveloped legal and regulatory environment and weak institutions. Because society was suffering, the Afinger of criticism was pointed at the Government by virtually all levels of society. The general tenor of the criticism was that the Government was to blame for all the weaknesses and should be changed. Also, people who had grown up in Indonesia knowing only one President especially wanted change and there was widespread resentment at the way the President, his family and his friends appeared to have benefited from a system that now seemed incapable of guaranteeing even the basic needs of the people for employment and food - a situation made infinitely worse by a long drought which had drastically curtailed domestic food production, threatened water

9

supplies and removed any rural safety net from beneath displaced urban workers.

While the crisis worked itself out, a Government which had become unpopular because of its perpceived failure to deliver, faced the prospect of social unrest over escalating prices and loss of income and mounting political criticism from university students. The so-called middle class remained mostly quiet or backed the Government although there were plenty of frustrations and criticisms, particularly among intellectuals, among those who felt that they had been excluded from power and influence and even among the upper sections of the bureaucracy. In a sense, large swathes of the rural populace and the working people were in the classic position of having nothing to lose if they vented their displeasure on hoarders, shopkeepers who were felt to have unjustifiably raised prices or even the Government. But the middle class, though suffering, were as much afraid of the turbulence from this quarter as they were of the crisis itself. This fear went some way toward guaranteeing the stability of the Government. After the March meeting of the People's Consultative Assembly, the election of a 'new' president and vice-president and the swearing in of a new cabinet, the new Government knew that it had to find a way of stabilising the rupiah or perhaps face the prospect of riot or even revolution.

Understanding of the crisis in Indonesia has not been assisted by continuous prejudiced and even inaccurate reporting, particularly but not exclusively by the Western media and by reportage that was demonstrably incorrect. While it was true that the Government had responded with tragic slowness before Christmas, as it sought to understand what wals causing the crisis, in the New Year and particularly after the signing of the January accord with the IMF, Government action came swift and fast. Yet President Soeharto and the Government were still pilloried in the media for being reluctant to introduce reforms and for not carrying out the agreement with the IMF to the letter. Even one of the New Order Government's staunchest critics, in the end, was forced to say: "What more could President Soeharto do?"

Many Indonesians felt, that far from going slowly, President Soeharto had "given everything away" in his deal with the IMF, such was the Government's understandable panic that its national economy was about to collapse with devastating consequences. It was this panic that led to the picture of President Soeharto apparently obediently signing the IMF agreement with Michel Camdessus standing over him like an angry school teacher!

Only when the Indonesian Government realised that the IMF's measures were ideological and long-term, and therefore incapable of solving the immediate crisis, did the New Order Government's relationship with the IMF and other agencies, such as the World Bank, become turbulent. But the facts spoke for themselves. The rupiah refused to stabilise, bank insolvency was rising, corporate debt was increasing, offshore loans could not be repaid, letters of credit were not being honoured overseas and the economy generally was grinding to a halt.

The markets were not influenced, as was public opinion generally, by misinformation from the media, whether innocent or deliberate. The markets saw only unpaid debts and economic collapse, and, as a result, dwindling grounds for even a shred of confidence. After the March election, the Government squarely faced this issue: how to restore confidence by stabilising the rupiah at a reasonable exchange rate to the US dollar so that business could start to function again.

Asia's currency crisis swept through Indonesia stripping bare all its weaknesses and exposing them to ruthless international scrutiny. The crisis sowed doubts in the minds of Indonesians about their readiness for globalisation and sparked a feverish search for scapegoats to blame for all that had apparently gone wrong. Problems mounted on problems. Blame mounted on blame. Some people were afraid. others said they lived in exciting times, rich with the prospect of change and improvement. Indonesians felt sorry for themselves. Foreigners who knew Indonesia felt sorry. How things would turn out only time would tell.

Richard Mann

Penang, Malaysia

CHAPTER ONE

A Crisis
Far
Away

Few things illustrate more graphically the Government of Indonesia's response to the monetary crisis than President Soeharto's December admission that he was "puzzled." If we look at the early, optimistic forecasts of international financial institutions and economic experts, the President was by no means alone.

As late as November, 1997, even the International Monetary Fund, (IMF) was still forecasting 3 percent GDP (Gross Domestic product) growth for Indonesia in 1998-99! In Vancouver, Canada, the Asia-Pacific Economic Cooperation forum (APEC) was even predicting 6 percent growth! On November 5, Reuters quoted World Bank President, James Wolfensohn as saying: " I believe the worst (of the crisis) is over". Three months later he was quoted in the 'Jakarta Post' as saying: "I think we got it wrong, along with a lot of people." He added that the World Bank had been over-optimistic about Indonesia. He was quoted as saying: " I was caught up in the enthusiasm of Indonesia. I am not alone in thinking that 12 months ago Indonesia was on a very good path. There was no prediction then of an 80 percent drop in the currency."

Some American news commentators have said that there was a power vacuum in Jakarta as the monetary and economic crisis unfolded after mid-1997. There was no power vacuum. What there was, was a great deal of bewilderment and a typically Javanese, if not Indonesian lingering hope that things would soon get better. Knowing Indonesians, we can also be quite sure that there was a lot of prraying. What there wasn't, was any predilection for rapid response.

In early June, 1997, with the elections over and another massive 74 percent win under its belt, the Government felt confident, as it basked in an atmosphere of political security, a rupiah stable at about Rps 2.4 to the US dollar, high and rising forex reserves of US$28 billion plus, low inflation and a trade surplus.

Four months later, as heads of neighbouring states arrived in Jakarta bearing offers of billions of dollars, ostensibly to help bail out the country from an historic crisis of confidence, the smiling general smiled more broadly than ever - in a Javanese, a sure sign of embarrassment. It had never been proud Indonesia's habit to ask for international help - a trait many thought of as a weakness, particularly the victims of Indonesia's uncontrolled forest fires.

As important for the regime as anything else, the drought cast doubt on the Government's ability to adequately help people in serious distress. The drought and the smoke which hovered for months, not only over Indonesia, but over much of southeast Asia revealed that the Government's forestry and environmental protection policies were in shreds. Critics said later that it was hard to motivate Government officials to put out the fires and that too few fire-fighters and too little equipment had been deployed. Even the responsible minister said that it was hard to motivate officials, especially those with power in Jakarta. Punishment did not seem to go beyond name taking and warnings - presumably all largely unheeded by the fire starters.

As with the currency crisis, in connection with Indonesia's drought, the Government had been alleged to be slow to get emergency supplies where they were needed and people began dying in Irian Jaya. the Government seemed to have felt that the rain would come and then the problem would be solved. But the rains didn't come. The drought exacerbated forest fires throughout Irian Jaya, Kalimantan and Sumatra which became so serious that tens of thousands became ill, a jet liner crashed because of poor visibility, ships and boats collided. Tourism plummeted.

Some of the fires were set by farmers as part of their traditional culture of slash and burn agriculture, but 65 percent of them were said by the Government to have been set by private and even Government plantation, logging and development companies. The biggest fire of all was set by the Government in Kalimantan at a site earmarked for transmigration. Putting two and two together, Government critics were later quick to say that the reasons were the same as those underlying the economic crisis - cronyism and corruption.

In June, it was not haze drifting around the region that worried President Soeharto so much as the prospect of 'contagion' from Thailand's 'currency' crisis. Never a man to be unrealistically complacent, June's unfolding events in Thailand were by no means lost on the President. The Bhat was under attack and there was the looming prospect of corporate bankruptcies leading to a slowdown in Thailand's decade-long, non-stop economic growth. Suppose the same virus infected Indonesia?

While in Istanbul, attending the D-8 Summit during the second week of June, President Soeharto took the opportunity to meet American professor, Steve Hanke, a man with a reputation for stabilising currency free falls. Hanke said later that the President expressed keen interest in his systems and methods.

At the onset of difficulties, in June and July, the whole crisis had seemed Thai and Thailand was a long way away. The Thai private sector had run up an overseas debt of US$73 billion out of a total of US$89 billion. Much of this money had been lent to an over-supplied property sector which had crashed. Bad news led to bad news, one crash led to another until, finally, 58 Thai finance companies loaded down with about US$16 billion of bad debt were suspended from trading. In Thailand the crisis was very real. In Indonesia, where everyone thought that the country's fundamentals were very strong, the growing problem of the exchange rate of the rupiah against the US dollar was thought of as a 'currency' crisis rather than anything more sinister. The forex experts said that Thailand's 'currency' problems which had begun in mid-May had rolled south pulling down neighbouring currencies, such as the rupiah and creating a regional crisis of "sentiment."

Naturally, the region hoped that Thailand's 'currency' problems would stay in Thailand. But, the southward roll continued all through July with ever deepening and depressing consequences for Malaysia, the Philippines, Indonesia and even Singapore.

In June, in its report on Indonesia, the World Bank had praised Indonesia's strong economic performance but warned of looming problems relating to the current account deficit and private offshore borrowings - a warning to which all concerned would have done well to have paid very much more attention. Indonesia was also criticised for a slow-down in the deregulation process as well as for inconsistencies in implementation. Perhaps growth had been too good for Indonesia, causing the country, to some extent, to bask indolently in the warm sun of success.

In July, after routine consultations and routine praise of Indonesia's macroeconomic management, the IMF warned the Government of Indonesia that there were serious and growing weaknesses in the country's banking sector. Whatever they saw wrong with the system can only have been a partial picture, and all the more worrying for that, because many of Indonesia's private banks do not even publish annual reports. The Government was urged to take prompt and decisive action to resolve the problems of insolvent banks and to recover non-performing loans.

In theory, the problem of bank insolvency could be addressed either through closures or mergers. In practice minimum bank capitalisation had been set too low removing any financial pressure for voluntary mergers and the laws governing insolvency and bankruptcy were out-of-date and vague. The problem of recovering non-performing loans was one which could only be solved by the exercise of due diligence by bank officers and willingness to take appropriate steps against defaulters proved still to have assets. In a country where deference and connections are everything, enforcing strict banking prudence was fraught with challenges and even risks. When it had deregulated the banking sector in 1988, the Government had left its growth and management to private business and, in 1997, showed no signs of wanting to take on new responsibilities, however prudent and well advised.

Even before the IMF warning, after the June elections, the Government had, in fact, announced its intention of merging the seven state banks, reducing their number to."two or three" and offering them for sale to private buyers. Quite probably the three were the ones selected later to pay out funds to depositors who had accounts with banks deemed to be insolvent or very close. As much as anything, the proposal to merge the

16

state banks formed part of the Government's long standing policy of privatising state enterprises which were, or could be brought to be, not only commercially viable but even profitable. In the case of the state banks, there was also a hope that their capital bases would be strengthened both by merger and through privatisation and investment.

The Government had instantly been encouraged by Indonesia's private banks to take steps to bring about mergers in the private sector. Clearly, some bankers, at least, thought that the time had come to bring out into the open the weakness in Indonesia's banking system, highlighted by the IMF. Clearly also, there was thought to be little chance of substantial numbers of banks merging except under Government fiat.

The President of Bank Central Asia, Abdullah Ali was quoted as saying: "Many private banks are in an unhealthy condition because they extend credits carelessly and, even worse, shareholders are reluctant to improve their condition." Abdullah was also quoted as saying that some healthy banks had run into trouble when their managements were compelled to extend credit to "certain parties" without collateral.

In mid-May, by contrast to the picture painted by Abdullah, as if to illustrate what a good job it was doing, Bank Indonesia had successfully uncovered a 'scam' at Bank Arta Prima and arrests had been made. In early June, Governor Soedradjad Djiwandono had given himself a pat on the back by saying that "banking conditions are better now than four years ago." He was not entirely wrong. A US trained professor of economics, Soedradjad had been appointed to the top banking post in 1993 - in the midst of the banking bonanza which followed deregulation. There were glaring weaknesses which he took calculated steps to remedy - he improved capital adequacy ratios, allowances for bad debt, the loans to deposits ratio and legal lending limits. He tried to promote greater transparency in the banking industry including higher levels of disclosure and more effective internal auditing. Soedradjad could see very clearly that not all of Indonesia's more than 240 banks were sound and, as the IMF was to do later, he argued for mergers. Although there were no restrictions on private borrowing, he also cautioned against borrowing excessively from overseas.

His major problem was that Bank Indonesia was not

independent of the Government and, though a member of the cabinet, Soedradjad was very much a junior minister. Moreover, the banking system was honeycombed with powerful vested interests which it was difficult or impossible for him to challenge. To bring about an achievement as massive as bank closures required the highest level backing from his cabinet colleagues. Other than bank closure, for which he needed cabinet approval, Soedradjad's power was largely only that of persuasion and, in Indonesia, any objective sought through persuasion alone, is almost by definition bound to fail, especially if the objective is not widely or universally shared. His ability to enforce new rules and regulations was strictly limited to the willingness of bankers to obey. Later, when a number of banks were closed, two of them remained defiant - despite family links to the President, who had authorised the closures. Indisputably, private banks preferred to carry on as they were. Banking was a lucrative business and no one wanted to make unnecessary sacrifices. With a banking boom under way, many chose to bend the regulations and ignore Soedradjad's prudential advice. Enforcement was weak or made impossible by the importance of bank owners' connections.

What were some of the realities of the improved banking system he supervised? According to Marike Stellinga, writing in the 'Jakarta Post' on October 10: "As to the state of bank supervision in Indonesia, Bank Indonesia admits that it has problems in enforcing regulations. The share of banks not complying with required ratios - as for instance the ratio of risk-weighted capital to assets - is about 8 percent. In addition the position of 17 banks is unclear as they have not published a report in the past two to four years. Among these is state bank Bapindo.

Stellinga wrote: "Around 20 banking scandals since 1990, involving outright fraud, with commercial paper, cofllusion and connected lending, give the impression that bank Indonesia has a hard time controlling the illegal behaviour of banks. There have even been reports of involvement of bank Indonesia officials in some bank scandals. Since 1988, not one bank .....has actually been liquidated even though about 10 percent of banks have actually crossed the line to insolvency. .... this policy .. signals to the market that the risks of misconduct are small compared to the possible gains......a large number of ....banks seem to be violating the legal lending limit of Bank Indonesia that restricts connected lending to 20 percent of bank capital."

Soedradjad's prudential tinkering with the banking system, while not revolutionary, was, nevertheless, steady and consistent. Bank Indonesia's periodic measures to maintain currency stability or to prevent overheating worked so well as to be unremarked. Neither from words or actions was there any sign of the extent to which Indonesia's banking system might be in trouble. It was this 'business as usual' approach, this phlegmatic unflappability, this quiet certainty, that made the events of October so deeply shocking.

As, what still seemed to be Thailand's currency crisis, dragged through July, in Indonesia, there was little sign of any willingness to act quickly, comprehensively and resolutely on the IMF's warning about the banking system. IMF and World Bank executives characterised much Asian banking as consisting of state banks operating under Government-imposed but often hazy rules and controls and private banks operating on the basis of generally bad banking practices, especially having scant regard for the ability of their borrowers to repay and granting loans on the basis of poor asset quality.

According to the IMF's World Economic Outlook, with notable exceptions, especially Singapore, many regional banks were poorly managed and supervised and lent without proper regard to risks, especially to real estate developers and to the consumer goods industry. Loans were often short-term and made against assets rather than cash flow. The sheer volume of credit available from foreign investment sources worsened many countries current account balances, creating or deepening deficits. Problems were compounded by the presence of corrupt banking officials and pressure from the top on people at the bottom to extend facilities known to be imprudent. And compounded further by the way in which Asia did its business based on connections rather than on hard facts - the so-called crony capitalism. With exceptions, favoured friends of power holders received favoured borrower status.

Despite increasingly public misgivings about Indonesia's banking system, all of the above had long been part of the Indonesian banking scene. Such 'weaknesses' were well known and an 'essential' aspect of banking in Indonesia. Until now, there had been no problem. "Ways" had always been found out of any difficulty. The very murkiness of the system generally enabled workable solutions to be found.

In any case, until July 1997, there had been no sign of any economic crisis blowing up in Indonesia. Despite the known and suspected weakness of the banking system, economic growth remained strong, exceeding all expectations and forecasts. The fact that the current account deficit was widening had been noted but was thought likely to correct itself once a capital goods buying spree was over. Evidence of the buying spree was very tangible. Aside from the US$8.1 billion deficit itself□c, 3.5 percent of Gross National Product, Jakarta's harbour at Tanjong Priok was said to be clogged with containers awaiting inspection by Indonesia's newly invigorated Customs Service. On the other hand, the deficit was the lowest in ASEAN.

In his book 'Currency Crisis in Southeast Asia,' Manuel Montes says that current account deficits of 3 percent were generally recognised as a "benchmark" for developing countries. Indonesia was extremely close. Montes went on: "Because of the region's established export industries, the higher-than-world-average growth of its productivity and its relative success in attracting more stable inflows of foreign direct investment, current account deficits higher than 3 percent, can be sustainable in the region." Everything should have been all right. But....

"It appears, however, that currency markets, whose players seem to be just as laggard in doing their homework during the currency crisis as before it, will not permit high current account deficits at this juncture...... in order to maintain confidence in the currency markets, Southeast Asian Governments are delaying or cutting back on their investment projects, with an implicit objective of attaining current account deficits in the order of 3 percent of GDP." Montes described this as a "tragedy."

On the foreign debt side, from the Government's point of view, a public debt of only US$ 52.4 billion was thought manageable - especially since a great deal of it was in weak Japanese yen and long-term.

Private debt was a matter for the private sector.

Even in early September, Standard & Poor's, E.H.Chan, was still able to say: "Basically, we don't see Indonesian banking as another Thailand because the banks and their customers are not leveraged in terms of short-term external debts. "That's important, because it affects liquidity. If foreign investors stop lending when your foreign debts mature, then you have a liquidity crisis." Chan added that Indonesia's foreign debt was better structured than Thailand's and had longer maturity. He also felt that local banks were protected by the long position they adopted on the US dollar and also by their repricing policy on loans which enabled them to adjust interests rates every three months. It all sounded very cozy and rosy and, in hindsight, could be seen to illustrate how pitifully little was known about Indonesia's private debt. "But", Chan warned: "the banks are all right but what about their customers and borrowers? If borrowers are unhedged or cannot pay high interest rates, then they can default, asset quality drops and it will affect the banks profitability."

These were to turn out to be prophetic words Mr Chan's last anxious comment aside, against a background of generally glittering economic success, to put it mildly, Indonesia's leaders were shocked, surprised and bewildered when negative 'sentiment' drove the market to look ever more closely at Indonesia for signs of a sickness similar to that found in Thailand. And the more they looked, the more negative sentiment became. The more negative sentiment became the greater the fall of the rupiah.

Like so many others, the Indonesian Government believed fervently that its 'fundamentals' were firm. No less a body than the World Bank had said repeatedly that this was the case. Less than a year ago, the World Bank's Country Director for Indonesia, Dennis de Tray, told a luncheon meeting of the Indonesian British Business Association that he was unable to detect a single glitch on Indonesia's economic horizon. Even as the Thai crisis broke, not only Indonesians, but foreigners as well continued to laud Indonesia's perceived rock solid fundamentals. As late as mid-October, de Tray was again praising Indonesia's sound macroeconomics, albeit, this time, with a sting in the tail. He was quoted as saying: "Given Indonesia's sound macroeconomic fundamentals, we see the Government's dedication to a strong programme of economic and financial reform, with support from the IMF, the World Bank and the Asian Development Bank, as a crucial step." Things were in good shape. They just needed a bit of tidying up.

    • In its 1997 country report the World Bank had praised

Indonesia's fiscal policies and congratulated it on its prudent foreign borrowings and even debt management. However, in line with new thinking within the Bank, as much as being a reflection of blemishes on Indonesia's record, the Bank had talked about bad business practices, poor business structures and slow Government action to bring about improvements. As the crisis unfolded, it seemed to the Bank that markets had lost confidence in Indonesia, because of these problems, as much as anything else. "The challenge it (Indonesia) now faces is to restore domestic and international investor confidence," de Tray was quoted as saying. 'Confidence' was identified as the issue - not the fundamentals! It was almost as if 'confidence' was disembodied from the 'fundamentals' - an inexplicable perceptual block which influenced the thinking of many in the Indonesian Government until they were at last forced to recognise that the country's fundamentals were not so sound after all.

There was nothing new in all the praise heaped on Indonesia. For years, virtually since the inception of the New Order Government, Indonesia had been accustomed to having its economic policies lauded. The very bedrock of the raison d'etre and success of the New Order Government has always been its painstaking economic and financial planning and its strongly prudent and conservative approach. Year after year, five-year-plan after five-year-plan, the Government received plaudits for its work from all of those who mattered in international financial realms. Its annual pats on the back from organisations such as the World Bank had begun to seem routine.

And its accomplishments were by no means made alone. At the beginning, economic strategies were drawn up and applied by US trained economic experts, the so-called Berkeley Mafia. Over the years, policies were applied hand-in-glove with American organisations such as the World Bank and many others besides - all of international repute and standing, including the IMF. Jakarta's corporations were awash with expatriate advisers, particularly Americans who made up one of the biggest groups particularly in banking, as well as in oil, gas and minerals. When the oil price collapse of the mid-1980s demanded a restructuring of the economy it was experts from Harvard and Berkeley who helped out behind the scenes. And, when Bank Duta got itself into US$400 million worth of forex difficulties in

1991, it did so despite the presenfce of very senior American experts in its downtown skyscraper.

Such was the Government of Indonesia's fear of getting its sums wrong that the state budget was always balanced with any actual deficit being made good from foreign loans and public overseas debt was held at levels the Government felt sustainable. Every effort was made never to default on foreign debt and, if possible to make repayments ahead of schedule. Successive deregulation packages made it ever easier for foreign direct investment in Indonesia and totals edged up to record levels as foreigners took advantage of what had come to be described as one of the best investment destinations in Asia. Despite ups and downs, non-MIGAS (oil and gas) exports had increased gratifyingly and Indonesia enjoyed an overall trade surplus. Growth in non-MIGAS exports had slowed in recent months and certainly there were concerns that one reason might be Indonesia's increasingly high cost economy. Thinking had begun about ways to try to bring some of the costs down, especially the so-called unofficial costs. However, with 'high cost' now enshrined as part of Indonesia's business culture at virtually all levels, the possibility of moving beyond mere thinking remained slight in the extreme.

From time to time, after the Government of Indonesia gave the private sector its head to spearhead economic growth in the early 1990s, there were 'crises' - but not about poor facilities or poor management. The crises were caused by overheating - apparently by being too successful. At such times, the Government became adept at using the interest rate mechanism to slow the economy and restore a more sustainable equilibrium. From time-to-time there were also fears about the level of overseas debt and, to be sure that it remained manageable, the Government began a general monitoring of overseas borrowings. Throughout these periods of mini crises, the rupiah remained stable, reflecting the global market's overall confidence in Indonesia's managers.

Generally speaking, unleashing Indonesia's private sector had worked wonders. After 1988, there had been an explosion of banking facilities, mobilising capital as never before, not only in the big cities of Java but throughout Indonesia's thousands of settled islands. As the private sector threw its weight behind the Government's own development efforts, growth accelerated rapidly from six percent through eight percent a-year. A frenzy of development gripped Indonesia, evidence of which was visible not only throughout urban areas but, to varying degrees, deep in the villages and even in what had hitherto been regarded as remote locations. Absolute poverty was coming down; per capita income was going up, eventuaslly to reach more than US$1,000 per annum.

At the start of the decade, banking had been deregulated in a blaze of international praise. Free from most controls, banks would now contribute to Indonesia's development as never before. Michael Vatikiotis notes in his book: 'Indonesian Politics Under Suharto:' "Just two years after the October, 1988 reforms, over forty new private banks had been granted licences. Savings on deposit doubled from a little over US$10 billion in 1987 to US$30 billion by the end of 1989." He went on: " With credit freely available through the banks and equity easily multiplied by issuing shares in the revived bourse, private sector growth was extraordinary."

As capital was mobilised on an unprecedented scale, the private sector was told that from then on it, and not the Government would be the engine of economic growth. More applause from the international audience. But aside from controls on Government borrowing there were none on private overseas borrowing and regulation of the number and quality of banks as well as of their operation was frighteningly thin. As we have seen, reflecting an aspect of Indonesia's traditional culture, bank loans were loosely given and even more loosely monitored so that the possibility of bad debt was formidable. Vatikiotis notes: " ...many of them (the banks) were expanding so rapidly that foreign banks extending them generous credit lines began to worry about the soundness of their asset base."

In his book, 'Black September' Ranjit Gill wrote: " Bank officials at the Central Bank privately acknowledged that the deregulation package (of 1988) was flawed. It led to the establish-ment of too many banks, poorly capitalised and linked to con-glomerates who were principal borrowers - and also not prompt in meeting their interest obligations."

Still, international fears about the banking system, while present, remained muted so long as the good times rolled. And, indeed, had the good times continued to roll, it is possible that there would have been no problem. As the rupiah crisis deepened to catastrophic proportions and the prospect of corporate bankruptcy loomed, not only was the stability of the banking system loudly questioned but also the political system which had allowed it to develop.

At the start of the 1997/98 financial year, as far as anyone could see, despite a certain opaqueness and institutional shakiness, which foreigners had long complained about, the whole, magical, high-growth, merry-go-round seemed based on the very firmest of fundamentals, monitored by the ever watchful and always prudent central Government.

After the Thai collapse in July, 1997, increasingly, the market showed that it disagreed with the relentlessly rosy pictures painted of Indonesia. It was becoming a strong case of suspicion mounting of all that glitters not being gold - like Busang.

Among Singapore-based forex dealers, there had been long-standing cynicism about Indonesia, especially about its corruption and prospects for long-term political stability. As a major regional financial centre, including being a hub for all types of international funds, as the monetary crisis deepened, Singapore-based traders were repeatedly singled out in the Indonesian press for their activities in off-loading rupiah and buying dollars, forcing the rupiah down and the dollar up. Of course, Singapore was not alone. The rupiah was now traded widely in global markets and dealers in far away London and other financial centres were also dumping Asian currencies.

What was happening? Basically, the forex dealers and fund managers had taken a look at Indonesia's widening current account deficit and soaring private debt and concluded that the country's fundamentals were far from sound. Although no comprehensive data was available, a substantial portion of private sector loans were thought to be short-term and, worse still, unhedged. the Government's long standing policy of a 5 percent annual devaluation of the rupiah against the US dollar had not suggested that hedging was any kind of priority. If Indonesia turned out not only to be a nation of debtors, but of bad debtors, tghe rupiah was massively overvalued. The sheer absence of information fuelled doubts and deepened suspicions.

Just how little the Government knew about the private sector debt was highlighted by a comment of Bank Indonesia

Governor, Soedradjad on October 2, when he said: "Hopefully, not too many companies are looking for the American dollar." He may have been right about the number of companies but the dollar volume which would soon be sought was huge!

Even in July and August forex market players and analysts had begun to detect the beginning of a process of large dollar purchases by Indonesian companies. The demand for US dollars was by no means limited to Indonesia but had its counterpart in Thailand, Malaysia and South Korea. In Indonesia, the money-men scratched their heads, started digging, added up the numbers and slumped back in their chairs in shock. The level of private debt, repayable in 18 months or less and subsequently estimated by one banker as requiring 8 years to repay, seemed enormous. Looking at turnover, profits, and even assets, there was no way that the bills would be paid! Forex dealers and hedge fund managers throughout the region began to beat a retreat. They were widely accused of speculation and there were even allegations of a plot to deliberately destabilise southeast Asia's currencies and economies. "There seems to be a baton passing among the emerging currencies. It is evident that they are under rotational selling pressure from offshore funds," commented one Singapore dealer.

Reflecting region-wide resentment at the activities of 'speculators', Thai Finance Minister, Thanong Bidaya said that, although Bangkok realised that market forces had to be respected, ways should be found to curb the kind of rampant speculation which he obviously felt had been so harmful to Thailand. In Malaysia, the term 'speculators' took on a strongly perjorative connotation and practitioners were singled out for tough criticism. In his book, 'Black September' Ranjit Gill quotes Sudomo, Head of Indonesia's Supreme Advisory Council as saying: "I deem the activities of the speculators at the money market as subversive." He called on the Government to investigate the market, identify the speculators and "take tough action against them." In Hong Kong, in early September, Malaysia's Prime Minister, Mahathir Mohamad told the Group of 24 Ministers, which represents developing countries in negotiations on international monetary affairs: "I (-) suggest that currency trading be stopped, made illegal, because it is unnecessary, unproductive and immoral." The free markets were shocked. Torrents of criticism poured down on the Malaysian leader.

Dr. Mahathir was not dissuaded. Later in the month, ahead of the annual meeting of the IMF and the World Bank, Dr. Mahathir again urged the IMF to rein in the speculators. Commenting on the absence of regulations to control hedge funds and investment houses he said: "A market without supervision will fall prey to financial gunslingers." Each time he issued such statements, inferring or threatening market intervention, the Malaysian Ringgit dived, presumably prey to the very speculators he was attacking.

Much later, in February, 1998, World Bank chief, James Wolfensohn, was quoted by the 'Jakarta Post' as saying that the Bank was looking at ways to slow down global currency flows which others had said could be akin to war ravagement if flows became negative. Ironically, he said he would be seeking ideas from Prime Minister Mahathir, the man the West loved to hate.

In early September, even before Dr Mahathir's intervention, but following earlier examples set by Malaysia and Singapore, Bank Indonesia moved to curb speculative forward selling against the US dollar. Forward selling by domestic banks to foreign customers, banks, corporations and individuals, was limited to US$5 million per customer. The plan worked and the rupiah strengthened somewhat, if only briefly.

As July wore into August, global investment funds had also become alarmed. Bad debt meant bad investments for their clients. By early August the world's mutual funds were thought to have dumped up to US$15 billion in southeast Asian currencies - about the same amount as local Governments had spent defending the Ringgit, Baht, Peso, rupiah and, finally, the Singapore dollar. The US alone has more than 2,300 hedge funds with assets worth more than US$100 billion.

In Indonesia, according to SocGen Crosby Securities, most foreign investors were said to have fled the market after rupiah losses, with little sign that they would be in any hurry to return. What had been begun by forex dealers and currency speculators had now been taken on board by investors. Investment fund managers were acting only to protect their shareholders' and clients' investments. The central concern was solvency - of indebted corporates and of the entire regional banking systems. At the same time, as regional Governments resorted to a battery of monetary instruments to try to halt the slide in the value of their currencies, speculators played the field in a big way, buying and selling for short-term gain.

An atmosphere of unease had settled over the region in August, as currencies headed downwards in line with the perceived mismatch between currency values and economic fundamentals. Nervous markets watched more and more economic damage being inflicted by falling currencies throughout the region, damage which brought beleaguered currencies under new rounds of pressure from selling. The pressure on the rupiah became remorseless but was still described as a crisis of 'sentiment'. The reasons why overseas forex speculators and fund managers didn't like what they saw in Indonesia seemed incomprehensible and inexplicable to most Indonesians, told so often and by such reputablme people that their fundamentals were strong. Each time the rupiah dived, market confidence dived with it. The more bearish and negative the dealers became, the higher Bank Indonesia felt obliged to hike interest rates until, at the end of August, private banks were charging borrowers 40 percent and more.

Earlier in the month, the still bemused Government was prompted to protect its reserves by first widening its support band for the rupiah to 12 percent and then, in mid-August, with the rupiah at Rps 2.755 to the US dollar, to abandon the band completely and, for the first time in Indonesia's history (since 1945), simply float the rupiah. Demand for US dollars was too remorseless to counteract. To a free marketeer like Bank Indonesia's Governor, Soedradjad, in any case deeply engrossed in the implications of the globalisation of financial markets and free trade within the Association of Southeast Asian Nations (ASEAN) early next century, freeing the currency must have possessed a hard-to-resist logic.

In any case, a modest and bearable de-facto devaluation of the rupiah from Rps 2,400 to one US dollar to Rps 3,500 to one US dollar, promised to assist Indonesia's flagging non-MIGAS exports against worsening international competition. It should also help to depress imports and lower the current account deficit - all highly desirable objectives. At this stage, Governor Soedradjad did not have accurate figures describing the amount and term of private sector offshore borrowings and could not guess at how low the rupiah might sink if dollar demand turned from the steady to the torrential in a very short space of time.

The Government had watched Thailand, Malaysia and the Philippines throw away billions of US dollars of their reserves in a Hain attempt to halt the slide of their respective currencies and, after already seeing US billions disappear down the drain, had no intention of repeating the same 'mistake.' The float took the pressure off the Government's reserves but it left the currency fully exposed to the frosty, negative, sentiments still blasting it. As dollar buying pressure mounted and the rupiah sank steadily, to protect the currency, the Central Bank resorted to the tried and trusted instrument of again raising interest rates. In the circumstances, it is hard to see what else could have been done. the Government had to at least try to protect the value of the rupiah by raising interest rates and, if that failed, it would score no points by throwing good money down the drain in a useless rearguard action aimed at creating adequate rupiah scarcity.

Also for the first time in Indonesia's history, a floating rupiah gave the world an opportunity to register what it truly thought of the country by its attitude to the currency. And what it thought was evidently mostly bad. A factor not well understood in Indonesia was the massive negative view of the country in the influential Western press - a view which definitely influenced 'sentiment'.

This view was that President Soeharto and his family were draining the country of funds for their private use and had no desire to eradicate corruption on a scale said to be ruining the economy. Whenever there seemed to be a chance to make big money, the Soehartos were alleged to favour themselves and their friends. It was said that it was this access to the national cookie jar that compelled President Soeharto to cling to power into his late 70s with the prospect of his continuing in power until he reached the age of 81 - making him one of the world's longest ruling leaders. Despite all the talk of the constitutionality surrounding his succession, foreigners feared that, without the grooming of a successor, chaos could break out and instability ensue. Indonesia's apparent inability to put out some of the world's worst forest fires also created a very bad impression. To these current issues

Aceh and Irian Jaya and alleged rights abuses by a Government consistently characterised as a military dictatorship.

The economic downturn in much of southeast Asia as a whole gave the Western media a unique chance to pour out all its pent-up doubts and criticisms of such concepts as 'Asian values' and even of the so-called Asian 'economic miracle'. Asian values, they said, had not produced an Asian economic miracle but an Asian economic nightmare. Asian values included breath-taking levels of self interest, greed and corruption, with a major casualty being, not only the economy, but also the environment. Everywhere in Asia plants and animals were on the run before the insensitive but tireless steel blades of bulldozers, making way for more shopping malls, shop houses, homes, apartments, offices, factories, hotels, golf courses and resorts., many of which it turned out weren't needed and even more certainly wouldn't have been if regional population growth had been kept in better check. Never mind that it was hard to believe that many of Asia's cities had even been exposed to a whisper of planning, that in many, traffic congestion was so severe that it was faster to walk, and air and water pollution was way above tolerable, if not absolutely safe, limits.

Asian values, the critics went on to say, amounted in many cases to docile and, anywhere beneath the top strata, poorly educated and informed populations, on low pay, being materially or ideologically persuaded to unquestioningly support their local Governments. Many Western observers thought that regional populations only stayed quiescent so long as they were seeing at least some improvements to their living standards. Once there was nothing left to 'trickle down' it was feared that they might not remain quiet for much longer. Instability seemed to loom.

While foreigners certainly couldn't be said to know all there was to know about Indonesia, its economy looked weighed down by debt and the regulatory and legal environment in which the debt would, or would not, be repaid seemed far short of standard international practice. Indonesia had now earned the reputation of being the most corrupt country in Asia, placing a large and heavy question mark over its reliability, the environment was becoming seriously ravaged, threatening domestic health and even the global climate. If spasmodic riots were anything to go by, the people were becoming potentially dangerously rest-

go by, the people were becoming potentially dangerously restless. Even sections of the upper class were talking about the normally unmentionable - a looming political crisis accruing to the Government's apparent inability to solve Indonesia's worst crisis in three decades.

Against this background, following the float, the rupiah fell to another record low but Bank Indonesia Governor, Soedradjad, assured that this was to be expected and "temporary." In fact, among those who knew that Indonesia wasn't as bad as critics painted it, there was a widespread feeling, even among some foreign observers, that the currency had basically 'overshot.' Within a week, there was indeed some small cause for congratulation because the tumbling rupiah appeared to recover somewhat, rising by over 11 percent. There was even dollar selling and short-term rupiah buying on the basis of jacked-up interest rates. The 'Jakarta Post' quoted one local dealer as saying: "I salute the Government's success in stabilising the rupiah. It proves that our economic fundamentals are really good." The long-beleagured stock market gained ground.

However, by the end of August, constantly rising interest rates and a constantly devaluing currency were inflicting great damage on the economy and revealing critical weaknesses in the way most business was done in Indonesia. To the suspected inability of Indonesia's private sector to repay its offshore loans, swingeing interest rates now threatened a tide of domestic bad debt, bank insolvency and even large scale bankruptcies.

The property sector was one of the first and worst hit. As interest rates rose, less and less property could be sold. As less property was sold, so more and more developers faced difficulties servicing and repaying the short-term loans they had made to develop properties. The crisis was now reinventing itself. Throughout the last quarter of 1997 property sales plummeted, chronic oversupply set in and developers faced bankruptcy. Ironically, while Indonesia had always been a cement importer, by the end of the year its largest producers, PT Indocement Tunggal Prakarsa, PT Semen Gresik, PT Semen Cibinong and PT Semen Kupang were scrambling for export markets, hoping to sell nearly five million tons overseas in 1998. Before the crisis, Jakarta's large and lucrative property market was in relatively good shape. According to Procon Indah, Jones Lang Wootton, office occupancy was at almost 90 percent, retail occupancy at over 90 percent, rental apartments at over 70 percent, strata-title apartments at over 80 percent and industrial occupancy at over 80 percent.

A combination of rupiah devaluation and high interest rates was bringing business to its knees. Some new business initiatives were being postponed by individuals and companies who felt they could earn more just by leaving their cash on deposit.

Around the region, by the end of August, market attention was now shifting to the havoc being brought about by high interest rates, themselves brought about as a response to the market's deliberate testing of regional currencies. The market was now running from the consequences of its own actions, in Indonesia, resulting in further downward pressure on the rupiah and further upward pressure on interest rates. Share prices continued to tumble as the markets saw companies getting into deeper and deeper difficulties as a result of the very high interest rates being used to protect the currency.

As the currency crisis had developed, the Government of Indonesia had been in constant contact with the IMF and other international agencies. At the end of August, the IMF now turned a microscope on Indonesia, searching out the underlying problems. As usual there was plenty of praise. Thirty years of strong economic growth on the basis of prudent direction and management, high investment and savings rates and successive rounds of deregulation had raised incomes, slashed poverty and improved the social lot of the people. "Indonesia's progress in these areas has generally been faster than any other ASEAN member," said the IMF. Like the Indonesian Government itself, the IMF focused its attention on the ramifications of the nose-diving rupiah. There was still an assumption that Indonesia's 'fundamentals' were firm. Its recommendations can be summarised as: keep costs and prices low and seek to maximise state revenues.

The Fund's executives chose to take the view that negative market sentiment stemmed principally from such economic distortions as monopolies and subsidies - characteristics of Indonesia's economy that domestic critics of the Indonesian Government and laissez-faire America had long cherished overturning. The Government was urged to promote economic efficiency by further and consistent deregulation andparticularly by scrapping monopolies, which, it was claimed, had the effect of keeping prices artificially high. Such measures would enhance the country's weakening competitiveness. The Government of Indonesia was urged to proceed with eliminating business restrictions which led to rent seeking and abuse and to do more to apply transparent regulations evenly, especially those relating to the collection of tax - a source of revenue more important than ever as the currency devaluation diminished the contents of the Government's coffers. In this way costs would be kept down and revenues and efficiency boosted. Implicitly, reform of the banking system was also said to be urgent.

The IMF had targetted three monopolies. One was the state Logistics Agency, BULOG. As Indonesia had floated its rupiah back in August, a World Bank report had slammed the country's monopolies, which, it said, raised costs and hit low income consumers particularly hard. As the devaluation of the rupiah forced domestic prices upwards, there were mounting fears that the monopolistic activities of BULOG could only worsen the situation. If social unrest was to be headed-off the prices of basic necessities must be kept as low as possible, at all costs. This, in fact, was the very role of BULOG, to keep prices low and supplies normal. There was an element of propaganda in the World Bank's position because Indonesia's senior economist, Sumitro Djodjohadikusumo, though he favoured the complete abolition of monopolies, had already pointed out that, once prices were free, some would fall and some would rise, in line with world market prices. Twenty-five years ago BULOG had been assigned to maintain stable prices for strategic food commodities including rice, wheat and wheat flour, refined sugar, soybeans, garlic and onions. It bought from suppliers at fixed rates and sold when prices were high, ostensibly to maintain an acceptable equilibrium. The newly floated rupiah posed an instant problem for BULOG because, from then on, it would be extremely difficult to set and maintain prices as hitherto.

On August 20, announcing that BULOG's monopoly would be scrapped, the Coordinating Minister for Economics and Finance, Saleh Afiff, denied that BULOG's prices were high. But, clearly, there was a fear that that was indeed the case and that its higher than market prices would be less and less affordable as the rupiah devalued. Opinion was divided among ministers with some arguing for its retention, because of the good job it appeared to have done in stabilising prices in the past, and others arguing in favour of the free market. Vested interests were also at play. The wrangle over BULOG was so protracted that little had happened four months later.

From the point of view of the Government of Indonesia, despite their shortcomings, monopolies and subsidies had not driven down the rupiah during the past 30 years. One of the most visible of the monopolies, the Clove Marketing and Buffer Stock Agency, owned and operated by one of the President's sons, Hutomo "Tommy" Mandala Putra, had generally been a fiasco and was to prove troublesome in its dismantling, but the monopoly of certain basic items by BULOG, the state Logistics Agency, had maintained an even supply and kept prices low. Even the plywood monopoly had had very respectable beginnings. In 1980, the President had encouraged Mohammad "Bob" Hasan to impose tight export controls on a sector plagued by overproduction and low prices. A decade later, Hasan had raised Indonesia's share of the world plywood market to 80 percent. Certain monopolies could be argued to have been helpful to Indonesia. While outsiders could argue that some of the monopolies had been harmful or had enriched certain people unfairly, some subsidies, at least, had been much appreciated by a poor people and had done much to maintain social and therefore political stability. Later, the prospect of the removal of the subsidies at IMF insistence would be the subject of public concern and student demonstrations.

The IMF's so-called bailout strategy had contained another component which, while it did not sew the seed, certainly fanned the flames of doubts even some Indonesians now had about their entire political system. War on corruption, which was blamed for a host of economic, social and moral problems in Asia, had been adopted as the IMF and World Bank's theme in 1996 so it was perhaps not surprising that these concerns should have been at the top of their list in Indonesia. The IMF had placed great emphasis on transparent, fair and good governance being crucial to Indonesia's ability to recover from the severe lack of confidence among investors. When none of the IMF's medicine was seen to work, more and more voices in Indonesia and overseas began to say that the real hub of the crisis was the New Order Government itself, especially President Soeharto, both of them said to have been in power too long.

If there were long-standing grievances with Indonesia overseas, principally over alleged human rights abuses; domestically, the pot of frustration had been bubbling for years. Some people felt that the Government was preventing them from playing the fullest possible role as citizens; others, especially the new generation, looked forward to change because they were simply fed up with seemingly not ever having any. There was a deep sense that the same Government had been in power for the whole of some people's lives and that change should at least be tried. There were also people at all levels who complained that the President's family, while always defending their business activities as a legitimate contribution to national development, in fact, achieved much of their success by taking unfair advantage of their links to the head of state.

The IMF was directing its recommendations at the culture of Government which characterised the New Order, almost at the culture of business in modern Indonesia. In Hong Kong, backing the IMF, Dresdner Kleinwort Benson's, William Keeling said: "If resolving the current crisis (in Indonesia) requires a break in the mutually self-serving relationship of Government and business, then a new style of Government must emerge to take Indonesia forward." He added perspicaciously: "This could be politically problematical."

From the Indonesian Government's standpoint, none of the kind of general jabs the IMF had made at Indonesia's culture of Government and business amounted to much more than ideological huff and puff and its response could be expected to be equally woolly.

Two very large and potentially serious problems loomed as a result of the policy of high interest rates, as Standard & Poor's, E.H. Chan, had so astutely forecast: the first was obviously business insolvency and the second bank insolvency. As if to stress the danger, Standard & Poor now downgraded some of the country's largest banks, a type of warning which was to become more and more frequent and more and more destabilising in the weeks and months ahead. The Government naturally wanted to try to restore confidence; the ratings agencies persistently torpedoed it. The downgraded banks included Bank

Negara Indonesia, Bank Danamon (subsequently earmarked to be taken over by Bank Central Asia) and Bank Umum Nasional. Bank Niaga had been put on "credit watch."

At the same time, the constantly falling rupiah was making it more difficult for corporations to service their overseas, foreign-currency-denominated debt, around US$15 billion of which was expected to fall due for repayment in the three months from the beginning of November and a further US$5 billion within three months more - a total of US$20 billion. Though it tirelessly reiterated that there would be no default, the collapsing rupiah was also making it more difficult for public debt to be repaid. Every drop of Rps 100 against the US dollar increased the Government's debt service burden by Rps 500 million.

As in Thailand, Indonesia's private sector had indeed run up huge debts, much larger than those of the state, and, much less prudently. Worse still they had borrowed short-term, often against highly speculative returns from real estate development and large scale consumer projects such as 'mega malls'. In normal times loans could be rolled-over or new loans obtained to pay off the old ones. In these times fewer and fewer banks were willing to roll-over or to lend anew. And, as was to be revealed in January, nobody in Government had the faintest idea about any of it - how much had been borrowed and on what terms. The data needed to ring official alarm bells didn't exist.

There had been plenty of foreign funds available to be borrowed. An ocean of foreign public and private investment funds had swept through the southeast Asian regional banking system throughout the decade of the 1990s, attracted by and fuelling southeast Asia's "economic miracle." Foreign companies were falling over themselves in the rush to get into Indonesia and seemingly prepared to overlook almost anything in pursuit of new business. Record levels of direct investment more than amply reflected this. According to the World Bank, in 1996, private foreign investment in developing countries reached US$255 billion. Official flows were estimated at one fifth, or US$51 billion. Ninety five percent of these funds went to China, Mexico and Brazil and, of the remainder, Indonesia was included in the top twelve recipient countries.

Much of these funds were lent under circumstances of extreme laxity, with lenders being willing to extend loans up to

40 times the annual profits of borrowers. Taxi company, Steady Safe was able to borrow US$270 million on a profit base of only US$9 million. When the company defaulted, lender, Peregrine Brokerage of Hong Kong, went bust.

On January 22, in the Singapore 'Straits Times', Senior Minister, Lee Kuan Yew was to say of this sort of process: "Private sector companies were the main borrowers. But Governments were to blame for failing to check excessive borrowing. Indeed, they abetted the process by adopting policies which created a euphoric environment."

As some corporations snapped up dollars for offshore debt repayment, while others held onto theirs rather than change them into rupiah, dollars became scarce with their value rising at a rate commensurate with the fall of the rupiah. While before it had been only the crisis of 'sentiment' pushing down the rupiah, now large-scale dollar buying had to be added into the mix of reasons for its precipitous decline. At the same time, domestic prices began to creep up, especially of imported goods, threatening to push inflation up dramatically.

Far from seeing a country with firm fundamentals, what the market now felt it saw was an economy with a dangerously widening current account deficit - equal to almost one third of national reserves, a currency so fiercely under attack that the rest of Indonesia's reserves risked being quickly drawn down, a growing inability to service or settle offshore loans, a rising tide of domestic bad debt and the spectre of corporate and bank failures - plus all the other factors foreigners identified as promoting lack of confidence. Suddenly, rock solid Indonesia began to look like a country increasingly unable to pay its way. And its Government either didn't seem to know what to do or acted only in a half-hearted manner. It was feared that one reason for its being half-hearted might be that corporations with the largest offshore debts might be politically well connected disposing the Government to indulge them rather than confront the problems. Little did many know that the real reason was that, at this stage, the Government still had very little idea of who owed what!

In Indonesia, the crisis was still being described as a 'currency' crisis or as a crisis of 'sentiment'. Still, there seemed few other priorities more urgent than simply stabilising the rupiah. Everyone was puzzled. Why did it continue to fall? Why wouldn't it stabilise? What was going on? Day after day throughout the second half of August, the media reported that the market was waiting for this to happen or for that to happen, for the outcome of a meeting here or there, but whatever they said and whatever happened, the rupiah edged lower while dollar demand escalated unstoppably upwards.

CHAPTER TWO

A Blip
And A
Glitch

In September, Singapore Prime Minister, Goh Chok Tong, still felt able to describe what was now recognised as a regional crisis as a blip on ASEAN's radar screen. And US President, Bill Clinton, said that southeast Asia had struck a glitch which he implied would soon disappear. Even World Bank President, James Wolfenshon, described events in the region's financial sectors as a "hiccup." Hong Kong's new leader, Tung Chee-Hwa, joined the chorus by announcing that, despite everything, "the fundamentals in Malaysia and the rest of Asia are good. We should look forward with confidence." But the blip and the glitch and the hiccup not only did not disappear but grew bigger and bigger. Investor confidence continued to dip dramatically.

Nervous investors and traders now began to see their worst nightmares translated into reality. Indonesia's banking system was badly run and now it had to cope with a rising tide of bad debt of historic proportions. At the same time, the rupiah's now chronically worsening exchange rate against the US dollar was making it horrendously difficult for private borrowers to service, let alone repay, their offshore loans. Indeed, a question mark began to hang over whether Indonesia Inc., as a whole could continue to service its foreign loans. Finance Minister, Mar'ie Muhammad, remained adamant that it could and would. On September 9, he added that with more funds needed to service the debt there might have to be some budget belt-tightening, especially if revenue from taxation fell in the wake of an economic slowdown. The Minister continued to deny that Indonesia was facing any kind of economic crisis.

On September 3, the Government decided on actions which it hoped would look bold and dramatic to the market and which might give some immediate relief to the rupiah and also to the besieged Jakarta Stock Exchange. To help the stock market, restrictions on foreign share ownership were removed (previously a maximum of 49 percent), exucept for banking and securities, arguably two sectors which would benefit most from foreign access. To help boost confidence that the Government, at least, was not over-borrowing or over spending, it was announced that public sector projects would be reviewed with a view to postponement - especially those with a high import content. To help boost Government revenues as well as further slash imports, increases in luxury sales tax were announced. Even though excessive Government spending had played no part in the crisis so far, based on its experience elsewhere, one can detect IMF advice here for the Government to be sure to pull in its horns. An appeal was made to the private sector to follow suit and avoid any immediate borrowing that could be postponed until later. Unspecified assistance would be given to banks which faced liquidity problems. Bank mergers would be encouraged and insolvent banks liquidated. There was a promise to try to reduce interest rates as market conditions permitted.

The next day the rupiah remained stable and stock prices strengthened. But, there was no rush. The watchword in the market was very much: "Let's wait and see what happens." The IMF issued a statement saying that it was "very impressed with the steps announced by the Government of Indonesia." First Deputy Managing Director of the IMF, Stanley Fischer, was quoted as saying: " The IMF has been very impressed by the fact that Indonesia has moved decisively in the foreign exchange market, on the budget and on structural measures in the economy." He added that the measures were the reason why "Indonesia is seen so positively in international capital markets."

In the light of prior and very rapidly unfolding subsequent events it's hard to understand how the IMF deputy MD gleaned this impression! The fact of the matter was that most of the Government's 'measures' were not measures at all but fell into that category of wishful thinking and persuasion which

Governor Soedradjad had already found to be so hopeless. The markets, at least, were not fooled. Fischer went on to praise Indonesia for its prompt action. He was quoted as saying: "The length of the (currency) crisis (in Asia) depends on how rapidly Governments take the actions that need to be taken. But, in the case of Indonesia, your Government has made decisions very rapidly indeed. I don't expect that this crisis will last very long provided that other Governments in the region act as your Government has." The Government of Indonesia didn't think that the crisis would last long either - at least not in Indonesia. Indeed, that was the biggest explanation for the timidity of its corrective 'measures.'

On September 8, Bank Indonesia Director, Paul Soetopo, told a conference of southeast Asian forex dealers in Bali that dealers' perception that the rupiah had been overvalued had been corrected. "Indonesia retains some of the strongest economic fundamentals in the region and, from a domestic economic viewpoint, the rupiah need not be depreciated further." He added that it seemed to the Bank that foreign investors, fund managers and forex dealers had tarred the region with the same brush of skepticism about fundamentals, even though each country was different. "These misperceptions will persist until the market sees fit to analyse and weigh the strengths and weaknesses of each individual economy, and not make imprecise generalisations. Until then fluctuations brought on by speculation will possibly persist." The fluctuations did persist - but all downwards as far as the rupiah was concerned.

Two weeks later, seeming to maintain the momentum, which had so impressed Mr. Fischer, the Government announced the postponement or review of 15 major development projects worth more than US$34 billion as well as the clipping of more than US$1 billion from current expenditures to be sure that there was no deficit at year's end. Most of the projects were in the sectors of mining, energy, transport and public works and even included certain 'glamour' projects beloved of members of the President's family, such as the plan to link Malaysia and Sumatra with the world's longest bridge.

The new measures were aimed at a number of targets - in the short-term, to reduce private and public overseas borrowings and enhance Indonesia's solvency, to try to bring

41

more foreign funds into the country and to counteract the impact of the fall in the rupiah on the Government's budget by cutting back public projects. There was recognition that persistently high interest rates were strangling business but no guarantee of any relaxation. It was also a major attempt to squash the negative sentiment said to be driving the bear market by highlighting Indonesia's macroeconomic prudence - a quality for which it had been praised for 30 years.

While welcoming all the Government's moves, in line with relatively long standing IMF observations and warnings, Fischer had also said of the regional crisis: "Making sure that the financial sector pursues sound lending practices, making sure that banks have strong and adequate capital and that lending is based on economic criteria and not political or other criteria - this is the key to resolving the crisis in Asian markets." All well and good for the long-term. But the immediate crisis of unpaid debts still breathed fiercely down Indonesia's neck.

The IMF approach was certainly implicit in the Government's announcement. But, as the days ticked past, there was no well publicised sign of any major initiatives from the Government of Indonesia. Meanwhile, corporate and bank solvency remained threatened as never before. With hindsight, perhaps the IMF's qualified praise of Indonesia, though almost traditional, had been given too soon and made too lavishly. After all, what really had changed?

Restrictions on foreign access to the stock market had been removed at a time when foreigners had abandoned the market anyway, advice, with little hope of being effective, had been given to the private sector to curb its offshore borrowings and the Government had signalled a willingness to trim its own sails by postponing projects, many of which had not even begun and some of which were later quietly resurrected. A promise had been made to assist and straighten out the banking system but as far as anyone could see nothing much had changed. There were even fears that things could get worse if insolvent banks were bailed out by the Government. When the promised straightening out and tidying up of the banking system didn't seem to be happening, when major project postponements came to be perceived as hollow after some of them were rejuvenated, the market felt that Indonesia meant to carry on as if it was business as usual, complete with what was seen by foreigners to be wasteful spending and a mountain of bad debt. Indeed, in the very same newspaper that carried Fischer's optimistic comments on its front page, lower down on the same page ran the ominous headline "Stocks plunge, rupiah falls." This was the reality!

A month later, economic analyst, Laksamana Sukardi, was to be quoted as saying: "Government officials had displayed no real awareness of the crisis. Before the crisis occurred, for instance, they tolerated the widening current account deficit, swelling foreign debt and worsening banking problems. When the crisis struck, it turned out that the Government (Central Bank) was in the dark about how much the private sector owed to private creditors and about the maturity dates of their debts." From the beginning, these were the very problems which were spooking the market. Nearly four months after the crisis broke, they were still problems and still unresolved.

By the third week of September, despite the IMF's optimism about Indonesia, other experts were beginning to give voice to the hitherto unmentionable. Perhaps the 'currency' crisis was an economic crisis after all. Or perhaps the currency crisis had triggered an economic crisis. Indonesian economist, Mari Pangestu, of the Centre for Strategic and International Studies, warned of falling GDP growth on the back of continuing high interest rates and declining corporate and consumer spending, accompanied by rising inflation caused by the impact of the long dry spell and by rising fuel prices. The possibility of rising exports was the only bright spot on the horizon, she said.

As if to add an even blacker pall to the choking haze covering much of southeast Asia from forest fires in Indonesia, the growing impact on health of a severe drought, Britain's Princess Diana was killed in a Paris car crash. Shortly after, Mother Teresa died. The world as it had been known seemed to be ending! From the highest to the lowest people were dying. Large chunks of the planet's rain forests were on fire. Here and there people were running out of food and water. A Hong Kong risk agency warned that in Indonesia fires, famine and shakey financial fundamentals now risked riots and social turmoil.

As October opened, the rupiah plunged down toward Rps 4,000 to one US dollar and analysts described traders as in a "panic selling mode." The issue for the market now was very squarely that of Indonesia's solvency. Could corporations pay what they owed, at home and abroad? Could domestic banks meet their obligations? Could and would the Government find some way of bailing out the debtors? Was there still hope for the economy? The market doubted it and the rupiah continued to fall.

Day after day, as the rupiah plunged, there was a floundering around for possible reasons. And then a floundering around for scapegoats. Among foreign observers, particularly in the West, the President and his family and his alleged way of doing business and governing Indonesia were sitting targets. Observers and commentators in Australasia, North America and Europe blamed the crisis on President Soeharto and his style and substance of Government. And, of course, on his children. In the market, on the other hand, there had never been any suggestion that the crisis was about more than worries about corporate and even sovereign solvency. While the President's family may have been on the list of offshore borrowers they would have been just some among many - all caught out by the unexpected collapse of the rupiah. Underlying anxiety about the stability of Indonesia's political system was there but it had been there for years and life and business had gone on.

With no sign of any halt to the rupiah's slide and talk of "panic" in the air, the general feeling in Indonesia was that perhaps the Government had little alternative but to turn to the IMF for heavy-duty help - although few seemed very clear what help was being sought. Few understood why they needed any help! If only the rupiah would stabilise it would be business as usual. In any case, the IMF had already been consulted. Measures had been taken which the Fund had praised. Why hadn't the market responded positively? What else could be wrong? What else could be done?

Becoming seriously worried about corporate forex exposure and interest rates, the Chairman of the Indonesian Chamber of Commerce and Industry, Aburizal Bakrie, for the first time, called for the establishment of a Government/private sector task force to monitor the impact of the deepening crisis. Later the Bakrie Group would be among those having to try to renegotiate their offshore loans.

While people wanted a solution to the problem of the tumbling rupiah, there was a fear that, in exchange for any so-called IMF 'bailout', Indonesia might be forced to take steps it would rather not take, such as the removal of subsidies, increased electricity tariffs and cuts in budgetary spending - all highly sensitive in a country still with millions of very poor people. Since its successful armed struggle for independence in 1945, Indonesia has been sensitive about any hint that foreigners were seeking to tell it what to do or, worse still, to dominate it in any way. This sensitivity lay behind the reluctance to approach the IMF.

The Government was well aware that IMF demands in exchange for assistance could include the Timor car and the programme to manufacture aircraft - matters which it deemed to be internal and absolutely beyond intervention by outsiders. It was also aware that the subject of disbanding monopolies and the withdrawal of subsidies might be raised and, these too, were regarded by many in the Government as essential for social stability and welfare and not, as the IMF asserted, undermining economic efficiency. With these threats hanging over its head, the Government of Indonesia seems also to have been uncertain what it wanted from the IMF. Most of all it wanted magic. It wanted the very name of the IMF to re-instill confidence, as it had seemed to do in Thailand and South Korea.

On October 8, the Government decided to☐œ emulate Thailand and South Korea and turn to the IMF for technical assistance. At the same time, it sounded out multilateral agencies, including the IMF, about the prospect of support funds for Indonesia's reserves. President Soeharto stressed that, at this stage, proud Indonesia was not asking the IMF for money, only technical assistance. He was quoted as saying: "We've already set up our own reform programmes and we've asked the IMF to look at them because of their experience." Minister/State Secretary, Moerdiono, echoed a view held by sections of the bureaucracy and even the intelligentsia that, even if the IMF gave money as well as advice, Indonesia need not be afraid of any conditions they might request because the economy had been managed well. "So far we've done our homework well and if we do our homework well there should be no conditions attached," the Minister was quoted as saying. "Just like a company that wants to borrow money from a bank, if the company has done well, the bank will not request too many conditions."

Though finite, foreign currency reserves remained

high, at more than US$20 billion - down from US$28 billion a frighteningly short time ago in June. In the face of this rapid draining of reserves, it was thought that a little 'topping up' could do no harm in the current, highly volatile, atmosphere and might yet be necessary if corporations maintained their pressure to buy dollars. If dollars became scarce, this would certainly further push down the value of the rupiah. If they did not become scarce, there was the possibility that any additional funds might not need to be touched. Finance Minister, Mar'ie Muhammad confirmed that the Government was sounding out the availability of such "stand-by" funds. Reserves had already been deployed to support the rupiah after bouts of massive dollar buying, a step the Government felt bound to take to prevent "panic spreading among the people." Simultaneously, the Minister met with 20 major fund managers to explain what steps he was taking to restore confidence in Indonesia's fundamentals - now widely accepted by the market, at least, as meaning its public and private ability to pay its bills.

While the IMF examined and ruminated, the Government asked corporations with dollar debts to try not to enter the market simultaneously, a hope steeped in optimism since it depended on one company knowing what another was doing and then being willing to postpone its market activities in the national interest - assuming this was possible. The inspiration for this approach came from President Soeharto, who, knowing better than anybody how things work in Indonesia, doubtless anticipated that the Central Bank would introduce an instrument or at least a well defined mechanism to make this possible. In fact, nothing systematic was done, and the market was left to its own devices. Commercial banks were allowed to reduce their foreign exchange reserves from 5 percent to 3 percent in another effort to increase dollar availability. An attempt was made to further increase the supply of US dollars by opening up swap facilities to exporters. As the rupiah sank, this facility possessed as much attraction to exporters as holding rupiah did for the rest of the population and there is little indication that it was successful. In any case, relatively few companies were said to enjoy such facilities.

In the face of the ongoing rupiah volatility, new stress was placed on the need to maintain not only price stability but even the supply of vital goods. On October 9, Widjojo Nitisastro

46

was appointed as a special economic adviser to the Government to coordinate these policies aimed at restoring health to Indonesia's ailing economy.

On the same day, in far off Sydney, Australia, The National Institute of Industry and Economic Research warned that Asia was facing negative economic growth and a regional economic meltdown from which it would take years to recover. Bad debts were firmly identified as the culprit. Few other international commentaries were as gloomy or, possibly, so accurate. Standard & Poor seemed to agree because by the end of the week, on October 11, they had downgraded their rating of Indonesia's currency, triggering fresh downward pressure on the rupiah and providing yet another example of the way in which the crisis fed on itself. Every time one of the ratings services downgraded a currency or a company, the crisis promptly got worse.

In the days that followed the announcement of the turn to the IMF, markets seemed to be optimistic and, by October 10, the rupiah rose to around Rps 3.400 to one US dollar and stocks gained. Even though it slipped slightly the following week, there was nevertheless said to be hope and optimism in the market. To those whose dominant fear was insolvency, the word 'bailout' associated with the IMF truly had the ring of magic. In a leader on October 7, the 'Jakarta Post' said: "To be fair, the Government has done almost everything in its power in dealing with the crisis. Many of its responses this past one-and-a-half months have won praise from international lending agencies: from the decision to float the rupiah, and the shelving of huge and costly Government projects, to the new economic deregulation package announced in early September." It was hard to imagine the extent to which the newspaper would change its tune a few months later.

As October spun out, the currency crisis no longer dominated the news. Instead there was Indonesia's big win at the South East Asian Games, the "all-out battle" to identify who might become the next president of the Republic, how to put out the still-raging forest fires, talk of the desirability of restricting alcohol sales to preserve a healthy life-style and dozens of features and articles mesmerised with the glitzy, luxury lifestyle of the newly-rich and, sometimes, famous. The atmosphere was very much one of "business as usual."

On October 8, Governor Soedradjad had still referred to the rupiah's 33 percent devaluation as a "market correction", adding that Indonesia's 'economic fundamentals' were still strong and that the market had 'overshot.' The message was that, in reality, the rupiah was worth a lot more but, for some inexplicable reason, the market just couldn't see it that way. And there was still a feeling that once the troublesome private debts were paid - or not paid, as they case might be - the rupiah's roller-coaster ride would end. There was frustration in the corridors of power that the private sector was being so apparently slow in paying its bills. At this stage no one really knew why. The debtors were under no obligation to let the Government into their financial secrets. In fact, that would be about the last thing most of them would want.

Even the World Bank's, Dennis de Tray, was puzzled. On October 10, he was quoted as saying: "The rupiah's free fall over the past few weeks was triggered by factors that we do not fully understand." If the World Bank was in the dark how could Indonesia be expected not to be puzzled, too.!

The reprieve to the rupiah, following the Government's request for IMF assistance, was short lived. What the market most wanted to see - a solution to Indonesia's debt problem - wasn't forthcoming. Indeed, the Government had expressly said that it wasn't asking the IMF for money and ruled out any role for itself in settling the private sector's overseas bills. The market maintained its stubborn downward course. It seemed that the only thing that would satisfy it was money! And money handled by a solvent banking system with all its leaky holes firmly plugged!

On October 27, Malaysian Deputy Prime Minister and Finance Minister, Anwar Ibrahim arrived in Jakarta promising US$1 billion as a supplement to any IMF package. There were the usual familiar accolades for Indonesia. The Minister was quoted as saying: "We believe in Indonesia's economic fundamentals and support efforts to restore confidence. We've also said that we are ready to provide funds to help restore confidence." The next day Australia's Prime Minister, John Howard flew in - although this time there was no promise of money. Actually, Singapore had been first off the mark a week earlier, on October 21, when Prime Minister, Goh Chok Tong, had flown to Jakarta to offer Indonesian US$10 billion, to strengthen the country's foreign exchange reserves - as part of an expected IMF package. Japanese Prime Minister, Ryutaro Hashimoto, telephoned President Soeharto to pledge his support and offered a further US$5 billion, also on condition Indonesia accepted whatever advice the IMF might give. Subsequently, Brunei weighed in with US$1.2 billion and the US with US$3 billion.

Although Indonesia had only asked the IMF for technical assistance, Western diplomats in Jakarta lobbied the Government to accept whatever cash aid was needed for a 'bailout' and to be prepared to accept the IMF's 'medicine'. But market reaction to the offers of cash in the international finance centre of Singapore was swift - and cruel. "This is not very good because it suggests that they (Indonesia) cannot stomach the IMF's conditions," a "regional economist" was quoted as saying. This was the first time that Indonesia's alleged reluctance to swallow IMF 'medicine' had been mentioned. Later, it would balloon into a major issue. Indonesian economic analyst, Laksamana Sukardi, commented: "A financial solution alone would not work. Even if we get US$50 billion in new loan commitments, the market would still react negatively. (US$43 billion was finally offered and the market did!) "Any financial aid should be supplemented with a bold reform package to restore confidence in the economy and in the Government's capability to manage the economy." After the promises of financial aid, the press reported that the rupiah was "stable" at about Rps 3.700 to one US dollar - but only as a result of days of Central Bank intervention.

Despite all that had been said and done the market took the view that more had been said than done. The market was only interested in real fundamentals, not what seemed to be a lot of hot air about 'reforms.' To outsiders, the Government of Indonesia still seemed to be hoping that the crisis would solve itself. Indonesia was not alone in this. Simon Ogus, the Chief Asian Economist at SBC Warburg's branch in Sydney, Australia, commented: "These guys (the southeast Asian regional Governments affected by the crisis) just don't get it. I rather suspect we need to see these guys go into a full-blown recession and a full-blown banking crisis before they come to terms with the situation." The British 'Financial Times' added: ....leading businessmen behaved as if they thought themselves affected by a temporary liquidity problem manufactured by foreigners."

Discussions between the Government of Indonesia, the IMF, the World Bank, the Asian Development Bank and bilateral sovereign lenders took place throughout October and on October 31 the IMF announced a US$23 billion aid package for Indonesia to be accompanied by a package of reforms aimed at restoring international confidence. The cash was to be provided by the IMF (US$10 billion), the World Bank (US$4.5 billion), the Asian Development Bank (US$3.5 billion) with US$ 5 billion from "Indonesia's own foreign assets." There would be an additional US$20 billion funding from bilateral donors including: Japan (US$ 5 billion), Malaysia (US$ 1 billion), Brunei (US$ 1.2 billion), Singapore (US$ 10 billion) and the United States, (US$ 3 billion).

The multilateral and bilateral aid package was to be used largely for very specific purposes, such as trade finance or banking reform. Psychologically, it was thought likely to overcome any fears the market may have had about possible national insolvency - although there was never any suggestion that the funds would be used to augment reserves which might be fed into the market to improve dollar liquidity. The notion that the package was any kind of bailout was a misnomer from the beginning.

The Vice-President of Hong Kong-based, Morgan Stanley Asia Ltd., Timothy Condon, was quoted as saying in Jakarta on November 4, that the IMF funds promised that Indonesia would be the first to escape the monetary hurricane sweeping the region. "What is needed in Indonesia is confidence that the rupiah will not go into free fall as the short-term debt overhang is unwound. The IMF is precisely what will deliver this confidence." A month earlier, Dennis de Tray had said much the same thing: "What we need to do is to put together a package that is so good that we can say to the world, financing will not be a problem."

Unlike the September package, some of the October 31 reforms looked as if they might have teeth, although by no means all seemed relevant to the country's ongoing and deepening problem of debt. Since the October package was basically a continuation of what had been begun in September, once again, Government promised to trim its spending but now it also promised to dismantle certain trade and price distorting monopolies, to do away with the local content programme for automobiles, to push ahead with trade deregulation generally, to abide by any decision of the World Trade Organisation regarding the Timor car and to introduce measures to boost exports and to restore health to Indonesia's entire financial sector, including the capital market, insurance and pension funds, financial institutions and banks. Many of these measures looked like the result of the West's crusade to bring about global free trade on level, Western-marked-out, playing fields. They didn't pay any debts. Whether their funding really weighed in creditors' minds or not, the opportunity had also been taken to target the funding by the Government of allegedly unviable projects, such as the manufacture of aircraft and cars. To strengthen and help clean up the banking system the IMF had specifically allocated US$8 billion.Experts from the US Federal Reserve Bank and the Federal Deposit Insurance Corporation were to assist Indonesia with the needed reforms.

There had been heated debate over the direction of Government spending, with the Government of Indonesia happy to balance its books and avoid a deficit and the IMF pressing for a surplus equal to one percent of GDP. The difference between the two positions was broadly that the Government's position seemed to guarantee some growth while that of the IMF seemed to risk recession, a condition the Government naturally wanted to avoid and, in any case, thought unnecessary. The market was cautious about all this. A recession would obviously make the debt problem close to insoluble.

Certainly, if long-term devaluation reduced Government revenues, projects would have to be postponed or cancelled, otherwise the Government really would end up with a huge which it was already clear, foreign funding sources had no wish to pay. But the IMF's harping on the need to cut Government expenditures at this time seemed more to reflect its experience in other parts of the world than Indonesia's. The crisis aside, it wasn't Government spending and debt which had triggered the confidence crisis in Indonesia but that of the private sector - an issue untouched either by the Government's reform package or by the IMF.

The October Agreement with the IMF also contained a seeming contradiction. Indonesia's private sector was already screaming from the hurt inflicted by persistently high interest rates and while the Government wanted to be seen to be aware of this and to be promising to reduce rates, at the same time, the IMF and its supporters were adamant that it must commit to keeping interest rates high and at a level likely to maintain the stability of the rupiah. By trying to keep interest rates down, the Government wanted to head-off a recession it feared might develop while the IMF insisted that only its 'medicine' of high rates would save the economy.

By October, the problem of liquidity had become acute. Interest rates had been raised astronomically. Back in August, Bank Indonesia's benchmark interest rate had shot up as high as 30% prompting one Singapore-based analysts to comment: "It (the policy of high interest rates) can only go on for a matter of weeks, or maybe or month or so but beyond that we are in for a real liquidity crunch. Some of the smaller banks can't take these kinds of interest rates for too long." In September, under pressure from the business community, the Government took advantage of an apparently strengthening rupiah to reduce interest rates by one or two percent. Nevertheless, as far as business was concerned, they remained critically high. Even by mid-October, when there were new hopes that the rupiah had stabilised at ab´out Rps 3.500 to one US dollar, benchmark rates were still up at close to 23 percent resulting in commercial bank lending rates being maintained at 40 percent and above.

From the market point of view, the October reforms, enacted on international advice, amounted to little more than an effort to achieve good housekeeping under circumstances of increasingly free trade. Banking reforms, though included, would inevitably be very long-term. On the day the package was announced the stock market again fell and the rupiah was described as "dithering' at Rps 3.625 to the US dollar. Economist, Nyoman Moena, summed up the mood in the marketplace. He was quoted as saying acidly and succinctly: "the Government needs to move beyond that (the October reforms) to satisfy the market."

To restore banking sector solvency and to impress markets and investors, the IMF argued that what was needed was for bankrupt banks to be closed down. Rumour had it that the IMF wanted 50 banks shut down. Reliable Jakarta foreign banking sources put the number at 42. It was hard to see how this would reassure lenders or even the markets. To send this strong, allegedly positive signal to the market, immediately after the October 31 deal with the IMF, 16 of those banks which were deemed to be the most flagrant violators of best banking practice were closed down and 9,000 employees laid off with three months severance pay, commencing December. Finance Minister, Mar'ie Muhammad, confirmed that bad debts meant that all the banks had more liabilities than assets. Because of continuing losses they resorted to the interbank market for emergency funding, always short-term and high interest - occasionally as high as 75 percent or more.

The terminated banks were Harapan Sentosa, Andromeda, Pacific, Astria Raya, Guna Internasional, Dwipa Semesta, Kosagraha Semesta, Industri, Jakarta, Citrahasta D, South East Asia, Mataram Dhanata, Pinaesaan, Anrico, Umum Majapahit and Sejahtera Bank Umum.

Whether due process had been followed or not was disputed by several of the closed banks, but Government stuck to its guns that all the banks had been warned to improve their performance but with limited response.

Several of the closed banks were run by politically connected business figures, one with the 25 percent involvement of the President's third son, Bambang Trihatmodjo, and another was owned by his half brother, Probosutedjo. Cynical traders and analysts said that these were the kind of banks that perhaps Governor Soedradjad had shrunk from taking to task when, by objective banking standards, he should have done. And they wondered how many more there were whose powerful and influential owners, directors and clients were forestalling legitimate reforms, including liquidation. Without IMF prodding it was felt that the 16 banks would probably have still been in business.

Depositors with less than Rps 20 million in any of the banks could be reimbursed from one of three state banks, Bank Rakyat Indonesia, Bank Dagang Negara and Bank Negara Indonesia. Sums of this scale accounted for 93.7 percent of all deposits at the banks, or some 600,000 accounts. Reimbursements were slated to begin on November 13, to prevent anxiety among depositors. Other depositors could hope to recover some or all of their money from what remained from the sale of bank assets after tax. Owners and shareholders would also be held responsible for any losses to clients.

First reactions, even from Government critics, were generally positive. But as time passed, instead of sending the strong, positive signal to the market presumably anticipated by the IMF, the closure of the 16 banks, at least two of which argued that they were not insolvent or badly run, led to growing panic about the stability of the entire banking system. Large private banks were suddenly cautious about having foreign currency transactions with smaller ones; some joint venture banks severed their ties with such banks, the public began moving money en masse from private to Government banks, which it hoped would be more stable. To try to retain clients, private banks were obliged to push up their interest rates far above those of the state banks. Despite this, some people began withdrawing their money from the banking system altogether. To head-off panic and possible bank runs, the Government said that no other banks would be closed. Such a promise flew directly in the face of the IMF but the Government had decided that, if possible, no 'medicine' was better than bad 'medicine'. The abrupt closure of the 16 banks was all the more shocking because it came totally without warning from Bank Indonesia, ostensibly the watch dog of the banking sector. While he must surely have been aware of them, Governor Soedradjad had publicly never hinted at the existence of such serious problems and yet, suddenly, the problems were so severe that banks had to be shut down in order to try to restore confidence in the system as a whole. In the all-to-often absence of information which characterises life in Indonesia, the rumour mills worked overtime. Some said 19 banks were insolvent, another 23, others that over 40 of the country's more than 200 commercial banks were involved. Later, about this number would be taken under the wing of an agency specially created to take care of ailing banks. Although the Government had guaranteed that all small depositors at the closed banks would get their money back there was still an element of public clamour until everything became clear. In the event, it was not until February 20, 1998, that all depositors finally received a Government guarantee of reimbursement in the interest of "justice".

Virtually since the start of banking deregulation in 1988, the Government had been monitoring the performance of private banks. In some cases they had recommended changing bank commissioners or directors, requesting shareholders to increase their capital, improving the quality of earning assets and seeking new investors. They had also encouraged mergers and acquisitions although, it has to be said, without much success. In some cases Bank Indonesia had injected its own funds into an ailing bank and installed its own supervisors in the bank. This nursing of ailing banks had been criticised for many years, especially if public money was committed and especially when it was widely known that some bank owners used deposits simply to fund their own private businesses.

State banks and not private banks were traditionally accused of having the largest amount of bad debt. The long-term plan for the state banks remained privatisation, as much as anything else to raise fresh funds. The state banks now suddenly benefited from a windfall. In the wake of the bank closures there was a veritable stampede of clients away from what now seemed to be highly risky private banks and into the state banking system, perceived as likely to be propped up by the Government at all costs and therefore essentially no risk.

The stampede from the private banks meant that the commercial banks felt they had to maintain high interest rates to attract the attention of depositors - from September, as high as 70 percent or more. Their lending rates were correspondingly steep. Although the interest charged by state banks had been allowed to decline, many companies had loans from the private sector and continued to suffer from punishing interest rates. Of course, new borrowers couldn't dream of asking for loans from private banks, thus contributing to the drying up of credit. Also, every depositor now wanted to be quite sure that his or her money was safe and the spotlight was now firmly turned on the problems of lack of transparency and lack of adequate disclosure. Who in their right mind would be prepared to risk their money at a bank which refused to fully disclose its asset and trading position. On the other hand, if the private banks opened their books for public inspection, confidence should return and interest rates fall - assuming, of course, that the books would bear public scrutiny! If not, full disclosure at this time could only lead to another round of panic.

There can be no doubt that the Government agonised long and hard over the decision to close insolvent banks. If they did nothing about the banking system, market sentiment would remain negative. If they did too much or the wrong things, panic might spread, threatening the entire system. Worse still, whether banks were closed or not seemed not to be the issue. The nub of the crisis was the repayment of debt. How would bank closures facilitate this?

US Federal Reserve Chairman, Alan Greenspan said in New York on December 3 that growth would return to Asia once its banking systems were put on a firm foundation. Greenspan described banking systems in emerging markets as the "weaker links" in global financial markets. He was quoted as saying: "Lax lending has created a high incidence of non-performing loans, supported by inadequate capital, leaving banks vulnerable to declines in collateral values and non-performance by borrowers." How very true! But it was done now. The question was not how to avoid a new crisis but how to solve the old one.

On December 5, a little over a month since Indonesia's October 31 Agreement with the IMF, the World Bank announced that a loan of US$20 million of its US$4.5 billion contribution was ready for Indonesia to pay for reforms to the banking system. As if to emphasise how bad things were in the banking sector, on Monday, December 8, the top four floors of one of Bank Indonesia's new office towers under construction off Jalan Thamrin were gutted by fire and 15 people killed. The rupiah promptly sank to a new record low. In a statement, the World Bank said that Indonesia needed to improve the efficiency and soundness of its banks, improve the Central Bank's supervision capacity and establish regulations and laws commensurate with best modern banking practices. The reform package was expected to take two years to implement. Naturally, this was not music to the market's ears. Two years would be needed to reform the banking system? And between now and then, what? While it would be nice to have a secure and well-run banking system, would putting it in order now pay the bills? Of course, the answer was 'no.'

The Government had clearly felt that its new measures would be enough to satisfy the market and not only were the public reassured that there would be no further bank closures but there were also no overt signs of the more drastic reforms demanded by the IMF - an attack on monopolies across the board - including but not merely BULOG, the removal of subsidies and the withdrawal of funds and favours from unviable enterprises such as IPTN, the state aircraft manufacturer and PT Timor. Funds for PT Timor were a special drain on the banking system with little hope of any rapid repayment to lending banks.

To take these further steps seemed to many to be

tantamount to bringing about a sea change in the culture and way of life, not only of the New Order Government, but of virtually the whole society which had grown up with it and around it. There was widespread skepticism about whether such things would ever happen. Vested interests in the status quo were legion and extended throughout the business community.

The IMF's First Deputy Managing Director, Stanley Fischer, had let it be known on the signing of the October 31 deal that, all countries in receipt of IMF aid must also implement the Fund's "guidelines on good and clean governance." This was likely to be a tall order in a country where civil servant's salaries were dramatically low and 'unofficial' earnings almost a necessity. High level corruption and collusion fell into a different category and although there were few among the public who felt this was a 'necessity,' the 'sickness' had been present in Indonesia for a long time. Although denied by Government, some analysts said that up to a third of the Government's annual budget and, worse still, a third of World Bank loans to Indonesia, were lost to corruption - the former by Professor Sumitro Djojohadikusumo and the latter by Associate Professor, Jeffrey Winters, at the NorthWestern University of Illinois. Even worse, if that was possible, back in September, the 'Jakarta Post' had quoted the Development and Finance Comptroller, Chairman Soedarjono, as telling the House Budgetary Commission that "Government officials were very slow in acting on malfeasance practices." Though it was true, as Fischer said, that more and more voices were being raised in Indonesia against corruption and collusion and in favour of clean Government and administration, nevertheless such concerns looked very nebulous to traders. As always it was loans and repayments in which they were interested. Anyway, if the IMF wanted to crusade for clean Government it had its work cut out not only in most parts of Asia but in south America and Africa as well. It would be a very long crusade.

Immediately after the closure of the 16 banks, the President's relations threatened or started legal actions against the Government to have their banks reinstated. His son, Bambang, promptly bought the license of another bank, Bank Alfa which it was said would acquire all the assets and liabilities of the closed Bank Andromeda. Bank Alfa had earlier been taken over by Bank Risjad Salim International, a member of the giant Salim Group.

In Indonesian Government circles, with uncertainty about what was causing the monetary crisis and IMF-fanned optimism that it would be short lived, the public thought it detected wavering as to whether all the doomed banks would really have to close. During his November visit to Jakarta the IMF's, Michel Camdessus, had said breezily: "I believe the stabilisation of the rupiah and financial stabilisation itself shouldn't take a long time." The feeling that the crisis was one of 'sentiment' affecting 'currency' was persistent and widespread; belief in Indonesia's 'strong fundamentals' was enduring. Against this background, it was hard for many of the players in Government and in business to be able to understand either the gravity or the longevity of what was happening around them.

On November 7, the Government announced that some of the 15 postponed capital projects would be allowed to proceed after all, several of them linked to the President's family. The Presidential decree giving the projects the go-ahead was actually signed on November 1, the same day as the announcement of the IMF package - so certain was the Government that the problems Indonesia faced were no too deep going and that the IMF's 'magic' would work rapidly. Eight power projects, four toll roads, an airport, a construction project and an equipment provision project would be allowed to proceed after all. Two of the power projects involved President Soeharto's daughter, Siti Hediati Prabowo and his long-time friend, "Bob" Hasan, the timber king. A second daughter, Siti Hardiyanti Rukmana, also known as M'bak Tutut, was involved in the airport project, to replace Medan's Polonia Airport, near which a Garuda Airbus had crashed recently in heavy smog from the forest fires. The airport project seemed demonstrably needed, whoever undertook it. Other resumed projects were said to be too beneficial to postpone, rupiah financed or more than 50 percent under way. Later, US-based CalEnergy was given permission to proceed with several thermal energy plants on which millions of US dollars had already been spent and substantial work commenced.

For whatever reasons the projects were resumed, the green light clearly indicated that the Government thought the IMF package would be accepted by the market as a final solution enabling life (and projects) to resume more or less normally. Of course, it was a risk. Clearly it would take time for the market to digest recent events and time for its response to be registered in the exchange rate for the rupiah - of utmost importance to any element of foreign funding in the projects and also to the Government's revenue position. Until the exchange rate stabilised how did it really know these projects could be afforded?

While the Government of Indonesia stopped and started, IMF Managing Director, Michel Camdessus bolstered the Government's confidence that the IMF package would be enough to soon solve the immediate problems and restore confidence. He said in Paris: " I am very satisfied with by market reaction to a multi-billion dollar aid package for Indonesia. The rupiah has consolidated and confidence has begun to return." US Assistant Secretary for International Affairs, Timothy Geithner, commented: "The markets have reacted quite favourably to the programme so far, which is a testament to the clarity and force with which the authorities have acted and the credibility of the authorities' commitment to a strong programme." World Bank President, James Wolfensohn, was quoted in the Jakarta Post' as saying: "I think the Indonesians are very, very committed to try to get this (programme) done and, under Mar'ie Muhammad, the Finance Minister, my guess is that you will see a lot being done." Later on, it was easy to say that the Government of Indonesia had been over confident but with this sort of backing who could blame them for thinking that they were on the right track and everything was turning out all right after all. In Kuala Lumpur, on November 5, for the G-15 Summit, President Soeharto seemed to shrug off the crisis with the thought: "The Indonesian crisis is actually now a crisis of confidence in the rupiah and this is what we are trying to revive."

For a while, some things actually did look better - the rupiah-US dollar exchange rate for example. But the stock market kept its nose pointing downwards amid regional gloom and uncertainty. SocGen Crosby Securities', Goei Siauw Hong, slated the IMF for taking a "long-term approach." Another analyst was quoted by the 'Jakarta Post' as saying: " The response from the local stock market to the bailout package is not as good as expected due to the absence of foreign investors." Yet another said that he thought that foreign investors might steer clear of Indonesia's stock market until after the March session of the People's General Assembly, which would elect a new president and vice-president, approve the state guidelines for a new five-year plan and give assent to the budget for fiscal 1998-99.

There were plenty of reports throughout the local press to suggest that 1997 had been a year that foreign investors would prefer to forget. Their mood was one of extreme caution until market volatilities subsided.

On November 11, with little sign of any improvement to the value of the rupiah, IMF boss, Camdessus flew in to Jakarta in what was described by the press as a "show of confidence." Hopefully, a visit like this would make the longed-for IMF 'magic' effective at last. At Soekarno-Hatta International Airport, Camdessus rose to the occasion and, smiling and confident, told the assembled media just that - he was confident. Next day, after a meeting with President Soeharto, he repeated his message, adding that he had found the President's personal commitment to the reform programme extremely encouraging. At the airport he had gone out of his way to stress that the reforms to be implemented were not the IMF's but Indonesia's - supported by the IMF. "With this programme I trust that Indonesia will be in better shape and better equipped for long-lasting growth after the time of difficulty. I'm certain that the crisis will be a blessing in disguise and that Indonesia will leave it stronger than it was before." Confirming stock analysts' fears, Camdessus said that he thought that Indonesia's recovery would take about three years!

What the "time of difficulty" was likely to be like was described by economist Kwik Kian Gie - "We may witness the bankruptcy of many companies, the laying off of workers, the abandoning of building activities, the decline of sales and low occupancy rates at hotels,. Many traders will leave their outlets at shopping malls because they cannot afford to pay their dollar denominated rents, unemployment will increase and economic growth will slow down." - enough difficulties to be going on with....

CHAPTER THREE

Pay The Bills -
Or Else..........

Continuing to see the crisis firmly before them and witnessing the Government's apparent shilly-shallying, observers asked themselves whether the Government of Indonesia had really understood the seriousness and magnitude of the crisis and of the problems it faced in restoring confidence? Would it really go ahead with the proposed budget cuts, needed more than ever as rupiah devaluation slashed state revenue? And did the closure of the 16 banks point to determination to clean up the whole system or was it just token. By now, behind the scenes, the Government was working closely with US advisers on necessary reforms but from the market point of view nothing seemed to have changed - a familiar feeling by now.

Cleaning up the whole system would be by no means easy, and everyone appreciated this. Even some of the Government's more forthright critics admitted that perhaps now wasn't the best time to begin a major overhaul. While there was agreement that the closure of the 16 banks was necessary and a good start, some observers felt that the timing and impact of the closures had been wrong, conveying yet more negative signals. Only two weeks later, as the rupiah dived to new lows, Luis Luis, Director Of Emerging Markets Research at Scudder Stevens and Clark said that, while it was fine for the Government to weed out insolvent banks, what the market had really needed was liquidity. He went on to describe the bank closures as a 'debacle".

By the third week of November, the steps taken apparently somewhat half-heartedly to date were now said by most commentators to have signalled that Indonesia was not serious about doing what the market was said felt had to be done - cleaning up the whole banking system, indicating a solution to the ever more pressing problem of ballooning short-term, private, overseas debt and attacking monopolies and subsidies. As the rupiah plunged it was increasingly feared that the overseas debt may have risen way beyond anyone's ability to repay. Naturally, the persistent devaluation made the dark clouds over the banking sector look even blacker.

As if by cue, on November 18, Finance Minister, Mar'ie Muhammad, suddenly stressed the importance of curbing private sector borrowings. He blamed the precipitous fall of the rupiah on panic among private sector companies, all scrambling in the market at the same time to buy dollars to pay off their debts. Obviously some of them were even trying to make payments ahead of time in case the rupiah slumped even further. He revealed that Indonesia's total offshore debt stood at US$117 billion in September, 1997 with a fall in the public portion to US$52.3 billion but a rise in private borrowings to US$65 billion. The debt service ratio was expected to rise to 34.5 percent or about 3 percent above Government estimates. Approximately 43.3 percent of the foreign loans were denominated in US dollars, 39.5 percent in Japanese yen and 17.2 percent in other currencies. According to the Bank of International Settlements, 59 percent of Indonesia's private offshore debt was short-term. The Finance Minister was quoted as saying: "To reduce the burden on our balance of payments, we need to curb private sector borrowing." What Mar'ie did not say, but the Bank of International Settlements did, was that, of the private sector's US$65 billion debt, US$34.2 billion was short-term, meaning repayable in 18 months from the date of securement. The Bank estimated that US$20 billion would fall due between November, 1997 and May, 1998. The fact that later other assessments of this debt would crop up and that foreign news media were able to spook the markets even more by quoting unsubstantiated and perhaps inaccurate figures points up graphically the problem created by the absence of any effective monitoring and recording system by Bank Indonesia. This debt mountain was the time bomb ticking away beneath Indonesia's economy. This was largely the reason for the huge dollar demand and the continuing fall of the rupiah.

Of course, while they may not have possessed fine detail about how much was owed and when it was repayable, the

Government certainly realised that debt repayment was now a large part of the reason for Indonesia's currency problems. Indeed, as dollar demand increased, the topping up of state reserves suddenly looked more important than had perhaps first been thought. The fact that the sums promised to Indonesia by international financial institutions and bilateral donors exceeded the country's short- term debt was calming to observers but seemed to have little impact on players in the marketplace. Presumably, those who knew the IMF also knew that its funds would not be used to directly pay down debt. As always, it was a case of seeing being believing. Until the debts were paid the market refused to relax.

The news for the market on November 20 was not good. Newspaper headlines in Jakarta screamed "No bailout for private debtors." The only good element was that the Government promised to help debtors negotiate roll-overs with foreign creditors. They had already been lobbying in Japan, where the Government had declined to intervene, saying, quite reasonably, that it was a matter purely between debtors and creditors. A debt roll-over was very much in everyone's interest, especially from the point of view of the rupiah as it would alleviate the buying pressure for dollars. However, there was no indication of how this was to be done or of the systematic approach to the problem that seemed more desirable than ever. Of course, no Government in the world could easily agree to pay private sector debts; that was understood and went without saying.

Next day, the Jakarta Stock Exchange dived to a four-year low and the rupiah sank to Rps 3.625 to one US dollar. Whether, by strict definition, it was or wasn't a crash, Paribas Asia Equity chief, Robert Allison, was quoted as saying: "It's a crash." In the absence of accurate data and of positive statements from the debtors, it is not clear whether this pessimism was justified or not. However, the market was in no mood to take chances.

Sofyan Wanandi, Chairman of the Gemala Group, and a man whose comments were often taken as reflecting the views of Indonesia's ethnic Chinese-run conglomerates, now said that the Government's harping on the private sector debt "damages foreign creditors' trust in Indonesian private companies." He stressed that most borrowers still had money to pay their debts and added: "We will never ask the Government to pay our foreign debts. We only need moral support from the Government."

In the early days of the crisis, the Government had either not realised the impact on the market of the private, offshore, debt or had chosen to ignore it. Now, when it had at last recognised the importance of the debt and thereby provided the markets with some hope of resolving the problem, the private sector asked the Government to keep quiet so as not to undermine lender confidence. Perhaps some of them were hoping for roll-overs; perhaps some hoped for new loans. If the Government remained silent on the debt issue the markets were spooked; if the Government spoke out lenders and borrowers were spooked.

Unfortunately for Indonesia, just as the contagion which had spread from Thailand had exposed weaknesses in Indonesia's economy, now fears of a crash in South Korea deepened market belief that Asia's currencies as a whole were doomed to not only remain weak but to weaken further. The death of proposals for an Asian fund to help support weak currencies signalled that even the Asian countries themselves shared this gloomy view of the immediate future.

As in Thailand, excessive short-term foreign borrow-ings were identified as the main cause of South Korea's problems and as that country's reserves edged toward zero there was speculation about a need for a US$100 billion bailout. South Korea's offshore debt stood at US$120 billion with short-term loans accounting for over half at US$66 billion. Nine banks had to be suspended. Later, another five would be put out of business. To make matters worse, across in Japan, where the economy had been stumbling for years, there was talk of writing off US$12 billion in bad bank debt. As the fall of the Thai Baht had brought down regional currencies, now the South Korean Won added its own negative pressure. To investors, the pattern all looked very similar: too much development too fast, too much money borrowed short-term in speculative anticipation of fast returns, especially from real estate, too little prudence in the operation of banks. Most of all - a mountain of debt. In Jakarta and around the region dealers were describing stock market conditions as "hopeless"and "dead." One broker in Jakarta was quoted as saying: "To tell you frankly, it's a hopeless market for the whole region. People are doing nothing ......"

To help revive Indonesia's stock market, President

Soeharto ordered state companies to use up to one percent of their profits to buy shares, a gesture well meant but unlikely to enhance the balance sheets of the purchasers in a falling market. In 1996 state company profits were said to be US$1.7 billion. To assist ailing large and medium size companies, KADIN Chairman, Aburizal Bakrie was quoted as saying that President Soeharto had told him in South Africa that he would authorise the disbursement, through the state banks, of a US$5 billion stand-by loan from Singapore. Earlier the President had approved the release of about US$1.5 from the state insurances company Jamsostek at 14 percent interest. State banks would then lend this money to private companies at 17 percent. The Singapore funds were to be made available to large and small enterprises also at the very favourable rate of 17 percent. Jamsostek's funds were earmarked for smaller, mainly export oriented companies and for the developers of low-cost housing. The disbursements were described as a "rescue bid" aimed at heading off bankruptcies and boosting exports.

Assistance for some segments of the construction industry had become urgent. Out of a total of 1,600 members of the Association of Real Estate Developers, nearly half were said to be no longer active and hundreds of medium to small scale housing developers were said to be on the brink of collapse.

On November 19, the Indonesian Chamber of Commerce and Industry, (KADIN), made an urgent appeal to reduce interest rates. The 'Jakarta Post' quoted Chairman, Aburizal Bakrie, as saying: "The economy's liquidity is not enough now and we'll keep on asking the Government to provide more liquidity until the monetary policy is relaxed". Bank Lippo Chairman, Mochtar Riyadi, was quoted as saying on the same day that persistently high interest rates were "devastating the already weak business sector." Continuing high interest rates were deepening still further the inability of domestic borrowers to service or honour their debts.

At the end of the third week of November, Finance Minister, Mar'ie Muhammad, denied money policy was too tight. He provided figures to show an increase in the broad money supply and asked rhetorically: "Is it true that we pursue a tight money policy? In the beginning of the crisis, maybe yes, but not now. The figures speak for themselves." Of course, money supply was not the same thing as interest rates.

The Government was in a difficult position. If it lowered interest rates the rupiah would be less attractive and might fall further. If it maintained them, business activities were said to risk being 'crippled'. But what to do? Pressure on the rupiah remained intense. The demand for US dollars remained stubbornly high. Not only in Jakarta, but in markets around the region, there was talk of a loss of "rationality", of "confusion" and of "frenzy". While major investors and traders may have known what was going on, those caught up in the slipstream of the tussle between lenders wanting to rescue their money and borrowers increasingly looking unable to pay, seemed to have little idea.

As was to become apparent immediately the new year opened, there were, in fact, two reasons for pressure on the local currencies: one was the doubts dealers had about corporate, banking and even national solvency; the other was the demand by borrowers to repay their offshore debts in US dollars. For both reasons, while there may have been peaks and troughs, the demand for dollars increased remorselessly. In Indonesia, it seemed that whatever steps were taken, the rupiah was doomed to fall and the US dollar destined to rise.

There was instant confusion over the supply and use of Singapore's US$5 billion, so great that Singapore Prime Minister, Goh Chok Tong, had to telephone President Soeharto to confirm that the bilateral agreement would be implemented in the way intended. Later, Singapore Finance Minister, Richard Hu attributed the confusion to "rumours in the market." Singapore's offer was of a total of US$10 billion, half to be used as part of the IMF package and half to be used to support the rupiah through market intervention. Already the Monetary Authority of Singapore and the Bank of Japan had made joint interventions. Governor Soedradjad now explained that he was negotiating with Singapore, to see if the proceeds from these interventions and not funds directly borrowed from Singapore could be used to support companies in the export sector only. Non-MIGAS exporters were to be helped with dollar loans, especially those in the high performing textile industry. The loans were being arranged by Bank Indonesia, the Finance Ministry and the Ministry of Industry and Trade. Welcoming the news, Bakrie issued a statement saying that he had never intended to suggest that such funds could be used to bail out private companies. On December 2, joint operations to prop up the rupiah ended anyway and the issue became academic. Predictably, the rupiah immediately sank toward the Rps 4,000 to one US dollar level.

Aburizal Bakrie had also been quoted as saying that the President had told him in South Africa that there was no need to worry too much about the crisis because Indonesia always enjoyed strong economic growth and the current problem was likely to be short-term only. A few days later, the President urged people not to give up hope because the Government had not yet found the right solution to the problems confronting the country and he pointed out that it was not only Indonesia that was suffering but the region as a whole.

The President did not form his views in a vacuum. Almost simultaneously the head of one of the international institutions advising Indonesia and assisting with funding, said the same thing. Asian Development Bank President, Mitsuo Sata, said in New Delhi that the currency crisis sweeping many parts of Asia was temporary - the very word much favoured by officials of the Indonesian Government. He went on to say: "The currency crisis does not mean the end of the Asian economic miracle. Fundamentals in east and southeast Asia are very, very strong" - again echoing to the letter thinking about Indonesia by foreigners and Indonesians alike. While acknowledging that the current crisis was resulting in economic slowdown and even negative capital flows, the ADB boss said that, in the future, the economic downturn would be reversed and foreign investment would not only resume its traditional interest in the region but could be expected to increase. Australian economist, Ross McLeod, writing in the 'Bulletin of Indonesia Economic Studies,' was quoted as saying: "The dramatic fall of the rupiah has been driven largely by panic, rather than careful analyses of Indonesia's economic fundamentals."

Even as President Soeharto urged calm, Bank Indonesia Governor Soedradjad revealed that at least US$9.6 billion of Indonesia's private sector debt was due to be repaid before the end of the current financial year, providing little hint or chance of a respite for the battered rupiah. The Governor said that the information had been obtained from a recent survey of custodian banks, reports from commercial banks, from corporate borrowers and, incredibly, from publications! In the markets and the media, there was speculation about how much money might have been borrowed by companies in the largely unregulated short-term debt market, especially promissory notes.

Whereas, at the beginning of the month, the appeal to the IMF had been described as being for technical help Soedradjad now said that the approach to the IMF was, in fact, to try to convince the world that Indonesia had the money to pay its bills. Practically to a man, foreign experts and observers had thought this all along. It was confirmed. Much had been said and done, tried and failed and despite his official optimism, at the close of the stormy month of November, with the rupiah having tipped the 3.700 mark to one US dollar, President Soeharto went to Mecca to pray.

There is no doubt that, as December opened, the President was feeling frustrated. He was besieged by an enemy he could not see and against whom he could launch no 'strike.' Around him, even the experts were saying that no "quick fix" was in sight. Echoing similar but more acid comments by Mahathir Mohamad, President Soeharto lamented: "The hard work and sacrifices over several decades that have been exerted for social and economic development are being wiped out overnight."

While the Government sought solutions to the crisis President Soeharto appealed to the nation to unite and for all sections of society to help each other weather the storm. At the same time, human rights campaigner, Marzuki Darusman, was quoted as saying that even those Indonesian people suffering most were unlikely to join social unrest so long as they were confident that the Government was doing its best, that all sections of society were treated fairly and that the supply and price of basic food items was maintained. Of course, if it should happen, jobless, penniless or starving people would not be likely to stay quiet for long.

This was a message the Government didn't have to be given. Measures were being taken to guarantee the supply of rice and other basic goods and even the prices of certain items. Nine items were regarded as particularly essential: salt, sugar, cooking oil, kerosene, rice, salted fish, detergent, textiles and unbleached textiles.

Increasingly, President Soeharto seemed to feel that

the currency crisis showed very clearly that Indonesia was perhaps not yet ready to enter the global marketplace. He was quoted as saying in Jakarta: " Let us take a lesson from this bitter (experience) to enable us to continue our national development process. Let us boost our national efficiency because only with such strength are we able to open a more free and open world economy."

At the end of November, Finance Minister, Mar'ie Muhammad, had visited Japan to urge a roll-over of some of Indonesia's private sector debt. Given the scale of Japan's own banking sector problems, this initiative had seemed doomed from the outset, if not to outright failure, at least to limited success. Japanese banks were said to have lent Indonesian companies about US$20 billion, with South Korean banks accounting for a further US$12 billion. No visits were made to South Korea, itself, now one of the major targets of the regional crisis.   Now, in December, the Finance Minister decided to go to the US, this time taking with him representatives from leading private companies, a suggestion emanating from KADIN. At an estimated US$4.5 billion in bank loans, US exposure to Indonesia was relatively slight, four times less than the amount owed to European banks. The mission to the US had two objectives: 1) to try to get some of the private debt rolled over and 2) to boost confidence in Indonesia's commitment to reform. The business leaders included: Mochtar and James Riady from Lippo, Ciputra, Sofyan Wanandi, Sukmawati Widjaja of the Sinar Mas Group and Aburizal Bakrie, representing KADIN. In all probability the Americans were in no mood to agree to roll-overs. What most wanted was to get their money back and get out . Later, nervousness among international bankers about Indonesia's dwindling ability to pay its debts would result in even Indonesia's export trade being severely impeded after foreign banks refused to recognise Indonesian letters of credit.

When the crisis first began mid-year, it had been perceived very much as Thailand's. Next, the devaluation of the rupiah had been blamed on speculators. By October it was unquestionable that, while it may be being prolonged by an ever mounting combination of factors, one leading to another and all feeding off each other, the primary problem was, without question, the demand for dollars caused by excessive short-term private debt.

Australia's Ross McLeod, had a novel solution. With the rupiah floated, he said, Indonesia should no longer use its reserves to try to influence its level. Much of the reserves could therefore be released, flooding the market with dollars, allowing debtors to repay their loans. Even Indonesian exporters would probably release their dollar hoardings once the market was flooded with greenbacks. And, of course, the rupiah should strengthen. Presumably the risks inherent in all this simply looked too great to the Central Bank and to the Government of Indonesia and there was no public discussion of McLeod's suggestion.

The so-called IMF bailout might have provided a solution had the money been delivered immediately and had it been fed into the market to maintain the dollar supply. This did not happen and, even if it had, it would have greatly increased Indonesia's public debt, something the Government naturally wanted to avoid. Foreign crisis-related aid was very much regarded as stand-by, unless project specific and as many other ways as possible were sought and tried to influence the market, short of injecting borrowed dollars, and without burning up dwindling reserves. The issue wasn't even whether the private sector could pay or not. There was simply too much debt to be repaid in too short a time. The answer had to be a debt roll-over and the Government wanted this as eagerly as some of the companies now having trouble servicing or repaying what they owed. On the eve of the trip to the US, Aburizal Bakrie was quoted as saying: "the Government and the private sector are now of the same opinion that we should share the responsibility for (dealing with) the current crisis."

Confirming the huge sum of private overseas debt, the Country Manager of the ABN-AMRO Bank, Cees de Koning, suggested for the first time in mid-December, that a special body should be created to mediate between Indonesia's foreign debtors and creditors. He said that most, if not all, the offshore lenders were foreign banks and therefore possible to identify without too much difficulty. Borrowers, he said, should be dealt with on a case by case basis as some could pay and some not and some could pay sooner while others only later. He estimated that portion of the debt to be repaid in 1998 as US$43 billion, fortuitously exactly the total eventually agreed with the IMF and other donors.

'Bisnis Indonesia' called for the setting up of a one-stop facility for the monitoring and controlling of future offshore debt. One of the President's sons, Bambang Trihatmodjo called for the establishment of a special team of professionals drawn from Government and private sector to help handle a crisis which was obviously now thought to be way beyond the ability of the Executive to cope with alone.

As the crisis deepened there was a persistent hum of background comment from analysts. Some of the comments still contained that element of underlying bewilderment which had for so long characterised thinking in Indonesia. For example, the ADB's Chief Economist, Vishvanath Desai, was still saying in mid-December that regional currencies had overshot because "until six months ago, in conventional terms, all the fundamentals were right." He was by no means alone. According to Reuters, a spokesman for Fraser-AMMB commented: "Although the corporate picture is somewhat hazy, the macroeconomic fundamentals (in Indonesia) are relatively sound compared with (Indonesia's) Southeast Asian neighbours." Desai repeated the view that the overshoot was a product of lack of confidence and identified flaws in the banking and financial system as the true culprit - something the IMF had been saying about Indonesia since July and a factor which, despite bank closures and verbiage still inspired very little confidence. By this stage there was nothing new in any of this but one of Vishvanath's remarks pointed up loudly and clearly the feeling that at least Indonesia and Malaysia shared, namely that the market had wronged them by ignoring the real strength of their 'fundamentals'. Even at the end of the third week of December, Finance Minister Mar'ie Muhammad, was quoted as saying: " I don't think that something abnormal can last forever. The rupiah (exchange) rate no longer reflects the true condition of our economy." Virtually as the Minister spoke, the US's Standard & Poor downgraded Indonesia's sovereign debt and Moody's Investors Service downgraded Indonesia's foreign currency ceiling for bonds. Moody's also put on review the financial strength ratings of five state and one private bank - Bank Danamon. Moody's was quoted as saying that the downgrade reflected: " the deterioration in the country's financial position as a result of a more than 50 percent drop in the valuation of the rupiah and a drop in investor confidence."

71

Theoretically, the promise of a bailout from the IMF should have fended off such downgrades. That was part of the Indonesian Government's very large hopes from the IMF. But it did not. And not only in Indonesia but in other troubled countries in the region where ratings agencies also downgraded bond quality. Quoting "fund managers", the 'Jakarta Post' said on December 24: "The US$100 billion plus IMF-led rescue package did not lead the market to believe that the three countries (Thailand, South Korea and Indonesia) would return soon to fiscal health. The Asian countries are facing a long, hard road to recovery." One fund manager was further quoted as saying that he was worried about "slow growth under the IMF austerity plan(s)."

As 1997 drew to a close there were dire warnings that Asia's weaker currencies could be expected to take a further battering in thin holiday markets and even steep declines early in the New Year once market players had had time to assess trends and to adopt aggressive new positions.

CHAPTER FOUR

Wanted: Inspiring, Decisive, Leadership

While the market was acutely concerned about the stability of Indonesia's banking system and the solvency of its corporations there was also that underlying chronic fear that the country lacked political stability until President Soeharto appointed a capable and convincing successor. The President is aged 76 (life expectancy in Indonesia is around 64) and had recently undergone a round of tiring transcontinental travel to South Africa, Namibia, Saudi Arabia and Canada. Instead of resting during the long flights it was President Soeharto's custom to spend the time working. While the President's doctors were adamant that he was healthy, nevertheless, upon his return to Jakarta on November 28, a trip to the Summit of the Organisation of Islamic Conference (OIC) in Tehran scheduled for December 9 - 11 was cancelled. Earlier, it had been announced that President Soeharto would attend an informal summit of ASEAN in Kuala Lumpur on December 14 to discuss the regional crisis and possible further neighbourly responses. The day before the summit was due to open, the trip was called off. Even a family outing to pay homage at the tomb of Madame Tien was cancelled.

Already jittery markets began to fear the worst. When the trip to the ASEAN summit in Kuala Lumpur was called of, people feared that the President might actually die. Rumours spread like wildfire that he was in hospital or already dead - not only in Indonesia but in Singapore, Hong Kong and Japan. Defence Minister, Edi Sudradjat, even found it necessary to deny that the military were planning to maintain stability by mounting a "coup."The rupiah slumped to Rps 4,600 against the US dollar - the largest single-day drop in recent history. To assuage fears, it was necessary for friends and family to speak out and for the President to be seen in the media as being still very much alive. Unfortunately, one photograph showed him in the garden of his home, dressed informally in a sarong, watching and listening to a pet parrot - hardly the right image for a man the markets hoped was in firm command of one of the world's larger economies with a population of 202 million.

Doubts about the President's health grew faster than the speed of light, not only to rumours about what might happen if he died, but to a new dimension for Indonesia's economic crisis. A problem that had begun on the basis of "negative sentiment," that had snowballed into a "currency crisis," that had developed into a crisis of "confidence" in the economy as a whole, that had ballooned into a full-scale "economic turndown" was now said to have become a "political crisis." Hashim Djojohadikusumo, Chairman of the Tirtamas Group and a shareholder in one of the 16 banks closed on IMF advice, was quoted as saying: "The rupiah's depreciation is really crazy. This has become a political problem and we need a political solution to the problem."

At the University of Indonesia, a seminar on good governance was held, with respected Muslim intellectual Nurcholish Madjid telling delegates that Indonesia's economy could only recover if there was transparency in the implementation of all policies as well as accountability to the people. Echoing the IMF, he said that the nation and its leadership must be willing to engage in a radical programme of economic and political reform. In a leader on December 18, the 'Jakarta Post' said: "It is certainly no coincidence that the growing public calls for political reform should be gaining in strength during these times of monetary turmoil. As the current crisis proceeds with no hope or sign of abating any time soon, it is becoming more and more clear to many Indonesians that economic and monetary decisions are not taken in a political void. For the average Indonesian, who stands to lose the most, it is becoming increasingly frustrating to observe that, being outside of the decision-making process, there is nothing whatsoever that he and she can do to influence the course of developments. If anything good has come out of the current crisis, it may be the growing comprehension that the need for accountability and transparency in Government is no longer a choice, but a reality - that is, if we are aspiring to become a modern nation capable of standing on par with other members of the global community."

As far as the cause of the plunge of the rupiah was concerned, President Soeharto was no closer to enlightenment than anyone else. This was the day on which, like everybody else, he had admitted that he was "puzzled."

From the outset, the IMF had placed heavy emphasis on good and transparent Government as being as much a likely solution to Indonesia's currency and economic crisis as the macro and micro-economic measures it proposed. And although there were many Indonesians who might have agreed, until mid-December, there were few who were prepared to speak out boldly in its favour. This public clamour to link the demonstrable failure to find a solution to the economic crisis with a failure of political leadership would rise to a crescendo in the New Year.

Sofjan Wanandi said on December 18 that worries about the presidential succession, the choice of vice-president and about economic distortions and favouritism, such as evidenced by monopolies and the so-called national car policy, were growing concerns among foreign business people. Though he may have been right, this was an overstatement because these concerns had been present long before the onset of the Thai-triggered crisis and had always been overridden by the potential for profit in Indonesia's booming market, with its recent near 8 percent-a-year GDP growth. Almost certainly referring to the confusion surrounding the closure of the 16 banks and the on-again, off again capital projects, Wanandi said that the market was now thirsty for consistency, clear signals and especially for transparency. Linking his comments to business confidence as a whole, Wanandi said that confidence among foreign creditors was so low that some of them were recalling their loans before the due date for fear they would not be paid. He was quoted as saying: "If the Government cannot restore public confidence in the coming year (1998), I am afraid that most major Indonesian companies will collapse."

Of course, confidence in the ability to repay loans was one thing. Confidence in the economic and political system as a whole was another. At this point the two had become intertwined, the one short-term, the other long, the one likely to soothe businessmen increasingly worried about huge potential losses, the other a long-term guarantee that such losses would not occur again.

Wanandi had spoken out frequently about the damage being inflicted by high interest rates. Although state banks had pushed their lending rates down, they remained relatively high with those at private banks still higher. This combination of high interest rates and a sharply devaluing rupiah was proving deadly to companies large and small. Layoffs were already taking place and projects and production being scaled back. Aware of the social problems that could ensue if thousands or even millions of workers lost their means of livelihood in the run up to and during the Christmas, New Year and Islamic festive seasons, President Soeharto ordered funds to be set aside for emergency job creation programmes - dredging rivers, renovating dikes and repairing water pipe lines. It was estimated that a million people had lost their jobs in the last quarter of 1997, in Jakarta alone. These programmes guaranteed that, at the very minimum, jobless workers could afford a meal.

The World Bank also promised US$1 billion for such programmes, to be drawn up by the National Development Planning Agency (BAPPENAS). Work gangs were soon seen in Jakarta and Surabaya cleaning up waterways and repairing streets and sidewalks. In the capital city alone the city Government pledged funds to employ 5,000 people-a-month for three months, until the end of March.

A day earlier, former Finance Minister, Ali Wardhana, now an economic adviser to the Government, had said that safety nets should be put in place to protect society's more vulnerable elements while reforms were instituted. The solution to the crisis, he stressed, lay in: " ...pressing ahead with policy reforms that level the playing field, are transparent, and are applied fairly and justly." Wardhana was a technocrat from the New Order's early days and reflected closely economic thinking regarded as orthodox - by the IMF.

Whether or not long-term reform was even relevant to Indonesia's short-term problems, foreign and domestic attention had now become riveted on their alleged need, apparently, whatever the cost in terms of unemployment and social hardship. Even among Indonesia's friends, there were many in the foreign community who believed that, despite its promises of widespread and deep going reform, in fact, the Government of Indonesia had done very little. This perception may have owed as much to lack of information as to the reality. The Government had apparently still not accepted that, if it was doing things, it needed to shout about them from the roof tops. The World Bank's, Dennis de Tray, told a seminar that the Government needed to issue a strong and quick sign of its implementation of reform measures. He was quoted in the media as calling on Indonesia to implement globally recognised rules in its "culture system, legal system and infrastructure" as well as in the banking and financial services industries. The 'Jakarta Post' thundered in an editorial: "Money, stability and confidence will not return until the Government consistently takes painful steps to fix the structural problems of the economy and improves the transparency and accountability of its transactions, including those by state-owned enterprises. Foreign confidence in the business sector will return only if companies improve the integrity of their financial reports."

Ironically, given that the Government of Indonesia was perpetually in the dock over its foot-dragging in respect of implementing reforms and introducing transparency, on December 12, in New York, Mar'ie Muhammad was saying much the same thing. He was quoted as telling the Asia Society that the key to Indonesia's economic recovery was "transparency in the markets." Speaking generically he was quoted as saying that that the operations of "Governments" should become "more transparent and less distorting." He voiced the hope that the role of "Government" would continue to decrease as a result of deregulation and liberalisation.

Like so many others, including the IMF, Mar'ie spoke of the need to rebuild "confidence" in Indonesia's economy by rigorous implementation of the reform programme agreed with the IMF. He did not mention, as so many others were already doing, that the IMF package had not worked and had not halted the precipitous and disastrous collapse of the rupiah. The core problem facing the currency, he confirmed, was Indonesia's "huge private foreign borrowing and the fragility of the banking sector", the two inextricably intertwined.

In Singapore, Merrill Lynch's Fixed Income Strategist, Vincent Low, said that at the end of any year there was always a heightened demand for dollars. But, he added, in 1997 it was much larger than normal throughout the region and contributing significantly to pulling down local currencies. As currencies fell, stock prices declined and economies faltered, market players were becoming increasingly nervous and trading in currencies and stocks ever thinner. One result? Even in a wafer thin market currency traders could inflict mega-damage on the Baht, Peso, rupiah or Won.

As the rupiah dived below Rps 5,000 to one US dollar, and the stock market plunged to a four-year low, a public chorus broke out claiming that the month-old IMF package had failed and that Indonesia's economy was sicker than ever. Kwik Kinan Gie was quoted as saying: " .... people do not believe in the rupiah's stability. They believe that the rupiah will continue falling and they are hastily buying dollars." Speculators were busy in most markets, especially Singapore and London, exchanging rupiahs for dollars. This was a new development, at least in semantics. Until now the rupiah had been said to be being forced down by the demand for dollars to meet debt payments. Now it was said that people generally had lost confidence in the national currency.

Inflation had increased to the highest monthly levels in 10 years, prices of even basic goods weflre rocketing upwards to socially dangerous levels, bankruptcies were rising, whole industry sectors were paralysed, the number of newly unemployed was beginning to run into millions, even the supply of a very popular food was threatened by the fact that 80 percent of poultry farmers couldn't afford imported feed for their chickens. This was important, but it still took the Government two more months to make provision for domestic feed supplies. An outsider might be forgiven for wondering why Indonesia needed to rely on imported feed. What had happened before imports were available? Was it really impossible to feed chickens from domestic resources? If it wasn't, the luxury of importing feed should surely be foregone in the long-term, even after the crisis was over and done.

The President could see that the IMF medicine was not working, the people felt that the Government was doing too little too slowly and, but for the upcoming Christmas, Chinese New Year and Muslim holidays, a potentially explosive social situation was building up. Those who dared to raise prices or were foolish enough to hoard were increasingly subject to summary mob retribution. While foreigners were feared to have lost confidence in the economy, among the people of Indonesia, a new and potentially far more serious crisis of confidence was brewing - in the Government itself. On the eve of Christmas 1997, it was not only clear that the market wanted to see Indonesia's debts repaid and that the nation was beginning to ask for an account of how the country's finances had been allowed to fall into such a state.

Political Analyst, J. Kristiadi, was quoted as saying: " Despite the international rescue package, people have started to lose confidence because the Government has not carried out its economic reforms from the heart." He described the Government's reform measures as lacking boldness and transparency and, worse still, its stop-start approach as signalling only inconsistency to watching markets. In Kuala Lumpur, at the ASEAN Summit President Soeharto had missed, delegates were criticising the IMF. Malaysian Foreign Minister, Abdullah Ahmad Badawi, was quoted as saying: " No one is making any suggestion that the IMF must leave, but they are taking note of the fact that IMF action has not brought improvement in the currencies."

Virtually from its first rescue steps in Thailand, the advice given to Asia's troubled 'Tigers' by the IMF had been the subject of controversy. The bottom line in this controversy was whether the IMF really had the requisite experience to go around the world telling, not Governments, but countries in financial crisis what to do, as if it really knew. A broad band of criticism was centred on the very different symptoms displayed by the Asian economies compared with those previously bailed out by the Fund. Low domestic savings, high public foreign debt and profligate Government spending were not the issues in southeast Asia. Yet, all IMF advice assumed that they were, and recommended harsh belt-tightening and high public and private saving encouraged by high interest rates. In the case of Thailand and Indonesia, later the IMF had to modify its harsh and inappropriate 'medicine' to better fit the economic facts. Aware of the social and political consequences to which belt-tightening and high interest rates would lead, in the form of bankruptcies and unemployment, Indonesia tried to wriggle off the hook, only to find itself sternly reproved by the IMF.

In southeast Asia, the IMF positioned itself as the champion of Western-style business, legalistic, anonymous, objective, impartial - the very antithesis of Asia's culture of business through connections, special favours and concessions. In Indonesia, at least, there was a distance the Government could go towards implementing IMF commands and a distance it felt it could not go. Thousands of years of business culture could not be jettisoned in a minute. The complex relational base of the New Order Government could not be unravelled in a minute, if atinge overnight.

While Indonesia squirmed under the Fund's ideological and Western-orthodox lash, the Director of Harvard's Institute for International Development, Jeffrey Sachs, weighed into the region-wide discussion in mid-December to give the opinion that: "IMF measures will do more harm than good, transforming a currency crisis into a rip-roaring economic downturn." This was what Indonesia feared most - and saw no reason to invite. In mid-December, Australian economist, Ross Mcleod, outlined an alternative to the IMF's advice. He called on the Government " to seek an expansion to its spending to drive domestic economic activities rather than belt-tightening measures which would be counterproductive to the economy." He was quoted as saying: "The cutback in Government spending seems quite unnecessary. To the extent that it is real, it will simply exacerbate the slowdown caused by reduced liquidity." McLeod was quoted as condemning the policy of high interest rates. He was quoted as saying that "...the liquidity squeeze had failed to defend the rupiah and instead, had brought many economic activities, especially those of the modern sector, to a standstill."

Later, Yilmaz Akyuz, Chief of Macroeconomic and Development Policies at the United Nations Conference on Trade and Development, would cite Malaysia's low interest rate policy as evidence that the Fund's approach in Thailand and Indonesia had not been sound. And he was also quoted as saying: "By the same token, strict adherence to the orthodox programme has not protected the Philippines against contagion." Akyuz added pointedly that in the crash of 1987, the US Federal Reserve Board had created "one of the deepest post-War recessions by applying a policy of tight money. By the early 90s the route out of the pit was found to lie in low interest rates and boom conditions reasonably quickly returned to the US.

The IMF and its supporters were everywhere in the

majority and everywhere speaking with the loudest voices. It was easy to miss the fact that other voices were offering other alternatives. These alternatives looked much more attractive to Indonesia than the advice of the IMF. In the first draft of its budget it is more than likely that, faced with the failure of the IMF's policies, the Government of Indonesia listened to these Keynesian voices.

While Indonesia felt that it was the IMF which had failed to find a solution to its economic crisis, many foreign and domestic observers felt that it was inconsistency and foot dragging on the part of the Indonesian Government which were to blame. Meanwhile, the rupiah continued its fall, reaching Rps 6,000 to one US dollar a few days before the Christmas holiday. With bad debts multiplying, not only did Standard & Poor put more Indonesian banks under review but, Indonesia's own agency, PT Pemeringkat Efrek Indonesia also downgraded three banks as well as their long-term bonds. As far as the public could see the Government continued to place most of its trust in the measures being taken to protect the rupiah and the banking system as a whole by Bank Indonesia.

Worryingly, there were few signs of dramatic developments being initiated by the Bank. Its daily market patrols and operations continued to try to protect the rupiah, while avoiding economic stagnation and, on December 18, Governor Soedradjad, speaking at a public conference, repeated his, now stale, assertion that the national bank was consistently pursuing policies to create a sound and secure banking system. The banks efforts were said to include, bank restructuring by encouraging mergers or acquisitions between commercial banks, promoting the use of proper risk management techniques, increasing professionalism and using appropriate information technology. It all sounded extremely vague and seemed to include nothing to solve the debt problem which, therefore, went on and on.... Commenting on the closure of the 16 banks insisted upon by the IMF more than a month earlier Soedradjad was quoted as saying that it had produced a "shock wave across the economy." He added: "The banking system is in distress beyond what we expected at the time when we formulated the restructuring programme."

What was the Government doing about it? As far as the markets were concerned, the fire at Bank Indonesia was one of the few public indications of anything happening at Bank

Indonesia. There were many complaints that the Bank was failing signally to keep the market informed. More often than not it was only reports to committees of the MPR which gave the public even a small insight into what was going on. Economist, Anwar Nasution, was quoted as saying: " Nothing is clear about our banking industry. Even Bank Indonesia's weekly reports never tell us about the condition of our banking industry."

Naturally, bankers were as worried as the Government about the stability of the banking system and as they waited for the outcome of the Government's IMF backed reform measures, Lippo Group Chairman, Mochtar Riady, somewhat impatiently told Bank Indonesia at a public seminar what he thought it should do - increase the statutory minimum capital to US$100 million and set the maximum individual or group ownership of a bank at 15 percent. At a stroke this would force the merger of scores of smaller banks and eradicate the distortions and inefficiencies arising from bank ownership by powerful and well connected people.

This bold statement of advice masked the fact that many of the bankers were their own worst enemies. Pressures to merge exerted by the Central Bank on private banks in order to strengthen their asset bases were ignored and few private banks could agree on who to merge with. There were several abortive courtships but few marriages. Even with the prospect of marriage, there were disputes about who should be the "big boss" of the new bank. Business rivalries, family rivalries, and disagreements among the conglomerates greatly weakened their willingness or ability to respond to Governor Soedradjad's friendly persuasion. Perhaps, as Mochtar Riady inferred, what was needed was no longer persuasion but force - for example a greatly hiked minimum capital requirement.

In the securities industry things were very much happening - 16 houses were suspended by the Capital Market Supervisory Agency (BAPEPAM) for failing to meet capital requirements. The minimum paid-up capital required is US$2.62 million. Like banks, owners of securities companies were accused of siphoning off capital into other businesses, leaving their securities companies dangerously under-financed.

In what began to look like the beginnings of a clean up, four of the seven directors of Bank Indonesia were "honourably dismissed." The directors were respectively responsible for private foreign exchange bank supervision, market operations, legal affairs and the supervision of private non-foreign exchange banks. Their replacements included one Syahril Sabarin, a Bank Indonesia director from 1988 to 1993, after which he was the Bank's representative to the World Bank in Washington, USA. As is so often the case in Indonesia, no explanation was given. Later, all four were summoned by the police in connection with "bank scams" at Bank Arta Prima, Bank Dwipa, Bank Asta and Bank Perniagaan. Three of the directors were later charged with corruption. Governor Soedradjad was quoted on Christmas Eve as saying that he hoped the new directors would inject fresh blood into the Central Bank. Somewhat alarmingly he was said to have added that that he hoped they would have some "new thoughts and ideas" to cope with the monetary crisis and the growing weakness of the banking system. Did this mean that he had run out of ideas of his own? The Secretary General of the Federation of Private Domestic Banks, Leonard Tanubrata, said that the banking community was now awaiting fresh tactical programmes from the new board of directors to tackle the crisis.

Now, for the first time, the Government called upon the private sector to help it solve the crisis. President Soeharto was quoted as saying: " I have ordered ministers to approach the private sector to work jointly to solve the ongoing monetary crisis with the Government, because it is not only the Government's responsibility but also the entrepreneurs."

Indeed it was! Indeed, one could argue that the private sector was entirely to blame. They had been too eager to accept short-term funding for long-term projects, they had borrowed too much, they had borrowed against inadequate equity capital. But for the devaluation of the rupiah they might have got away with it, as they had in the past. But with a devaluation so huge, corporate ability to service and repay loans quickly diminished. Earlier, the Government had offered to assist the private sector, especially in the negotiation of loan roll-overs. Now, it was clear that the private sector could not climb out of the hole it had dug itself and that, other than by paying off the private debts, the Government was virtually impotent to bring the crisis to an end. Many of the borrowers were suspected to have money stashed away overseas. Whether liquid caches existed or not, now, on the assumption that they did, many of the debtors were asked to repatriate enough of it to pay their bills. With conglomerates even as large as PT Astra International in the red and the giant Salim Group trying to reduce its debt by selling off an enterprise in the US, it hardly seemed likely that there really were huge sums parked abroad. Other conglomerates were already selling banks, businesses and real estate bought overseas during the golden days of Indonesia's boom. Still, fact can sometimes be stranger than fiction.

On December 22, at a meeting with nearly 70 leading businessmen in Jakarta - most of them offshore borrowers - the President announced the setting up of a special joint task force to examine the debt problem This task force was to be chaired by former Coordinating Minister for Economics and Finance, Radius Prawiro, and included Salim Group boss, Anthony Salim, The Nin King, Chairman of the Argo Manunggal Group, and Rachmat Gobel, Chairman of the Gobel Electronics Group. Long time Government critic, Kwik Kian Gie was quick to denounce the plan on the grounds that the rolling-over or even the forgiving of debt was strictly a matter between lenders and borrowers and should not be assisted by Government intervention. In any case, he wrote, it was vital to Indonesia that no debtor defaulted. They must simply find ways of paying what they owed. ABN-AMRO's, Cees de Koning, had earlier suggested that a suitable payment term to pay off the whole accumulated private debt might be eight years, with payments totalling US$3.6 billion per year.

Providing good information was vital for confidence-building yet week after week, month after month, the public and the markets were left guessing, often with ill-informed rumours pulling markets down unnecessarily. In the absence of a successor, market players were afraid what might happen if President Soeharto died; there were fears that the Government would seize private bank savings and convert them into bonds redeemable at a later date; there were fears of exchange controls; there were fears both of more bank closures and of continuing banking industry weakness if insolvent banks were allowed to stay open and, worse still, to be bailed out by the Government. There was now an indelible, perpetual, fear that the rupiah might become worthless, triggering a stampede into dollars. Columnist Kwik Gan Gie described most of these fears as "absurd." and most could have been calmed and eradicated by the provision of adequately repeated information. There were constant admonitions to the public, by the President and by his leading ministers, not to put faith or trust in rumours, but this was not the same thing as providing the concrete information the market required. Earlier, there had almost been a run on one of Indonesia's largest and most successful banks, Bank Central Asia, after it was rumoured that the owner, tycoon, Liem Sioe Liong, was dead. Like Soeharto, Liem had to appear widely in public and in the media before people would believe that he was still very much alive and the bank run was brought to a halt.

The ADB's, Vishvanath, had singled out the lack of adequate, correct and timely information throughout the region as being a major difficulty in resolving the crisis. So serious was the lack of information in Indonesia that national leaders and top level financial experts felt obliged to make the trip to Jakarta for face-to-face meetings whenever any serious needs arose. This lack of information was traditional as far as the New Order Government was concerned and perhaps for Indonesia as a whole. Unwillingness or inability to explain what was happening in the country had made Indonesia extremely difficult for observers of Indonesia to understand and led to the spread of largely negative views of the country around the world. Information, explanation, consistence, comprehensiveness and greater transparency - favourite words forever on the lips of foreigners - might have done Indonesia a lot of favours.

As public demand for certain information became increasingly shrill in the New Year, economist Sjahrir wrote in 'Warta Ekonomi' that, much though it was wanted and needed, obtaining more information in Indonesia was extremely difficult so long as the political culture remained 'closed' and, he might have added, top down. He might have gone on to say that just as Indonesia's top people had fostered a tradition of secrecy, the ethnic Chinese, who dominate big business, also deliberately adopt a low profile attitude. Everybody seems to think that the less known about them and what they are doing the better - of course, anathema to open markets. Significantly, KADIN Chairman and Bakrie Group Chairman, Aburizal Bakrie added his voice to the national clamour for transparency when he told a press conference in Jakarta on December 20 that there was now a clear need for corporate, economic and political transparency. He was quoted as saying: "There are many questions from foreign fund managers about political transparency and I believe that the Government can accommodate such concerns. I also believe that in the future, transparency at the economic and corporate level will improve because the current crisis will teach all of us about the importance of it." Economically, he said, transparency would help create healthier competition in the domestic market. Unfair practices like giving protection, using connections to gain business and collusion should be reduced and eliminated.

1997 went out as a year Indonesians would prefer had never happened and certainly wanted to forget. The country had been gripped by an inexplicable and stubbornly intractable crisis which the Indonesian Government and even foreign experts thought was undeserved. And because it was thought undeserved it was thought 'temporary' with the obvious attractions this view had for foot dragging on large scale reforms, especially political ones. While the IMF did not use the word 'temporary', Michel Camdessus was quoted by Britain's 'Financial Times,' as late as January 15, as saying that the fall of the rupiah had been "overdone in extraordinary proportions." - an echo of the many earlier comments that the currency had 'overshot' and an indicator that, in its heart, even the IMF felt that Indonesia's currency and economy was stronger than market perceptions.

Meanwhile, Indonesian Sociologist, Loekman Soetrisno, blasted Government officials for their response to the economic crisis. He was quoted as saying: "We had been claiming that the fundamentals of our economy were strong when in fact they were not. This habit of denial is demonstrated not just by officials but by us as a nation." Abdurrahman Wahid, leader of Indonesia's largest Muslim organisation, the 40 million strong, Nahdlatul Ulama, added that even though people were dying in famine stricken areas Government officials denied there were food shortages. He was quoted as saying: "When facing a crisis we behave like an ostrich...we pretend there's no problem...we bury our heads in the sand." Amien Rais, Chairman of the 28 million strong Islamic Muhammadiyah, spoke about a decline in the Government's "legitimacy". He was quoted as telling a seminar at Gadja Mada University, Yogyakarta, that social unrest, brawls among the unemployed and protests against certain

Government policies were indications that the Government was "losing its political and moral legitimacy."

As the year closed, the rupiah had lost almost 75 percent of its value, the Jakarta Stock Exchange had lost about 80 percent of its value (down from US$100 billion to US$23 billion), projects were being cancelled thick and fast, corporate and bank debt was rising, businesses were scaling back and winding down, millions were being thrown out of work and the severe drought was sparking fears of food and water shortages, in some worst-hit areas, fears that became reality.

On January 28, the President himself issued a warning against social unrest, a development he said, which, if it became ethnic or religious, could "destroy the nation's unity."

Franz Magnis-Suseno wrote in the 'Jakarta Post' on December 31: "While the year 1997 is coming to an end our economy is tumbling into an abyss. The rupiah's fall through the Rps 6,000 to the US dollar barrier is not only a psychological shock, it is simply economically unsustainable. It must be reversed, otherwise what we have built up during he last 30 years would be cut by a third and we would find ourselves where we were about 16 years ago. Millions of people would in the end lose their source of liveliholod and the danger of large-scale riots would become increasingly likely.

"Up till now our Government has taken the right steps and pointed in the right directions. But the fact is that all this is just not enough. And time is running out if we want to avoid total economic collapse with all its terrible consequences. The compulsive buying of dollars.......is a sign of a complete loss of trust in the rupiah. And this means nothing less than the loss of public trust in the Government's ability to safeguard people's livelihoods. People have lost faith in our Government. The question is not whether this lost of trust is justified or not - it is a fact. And this fact becomes more obvious as officials continue to act as if the situation was not so bad and that the public should not be alarmed. This is, in fact, the Indonesian way. Nothing other than decisive, inspiring leadership can save us now. Only decisive leadership by the Government can restore public confidence - without which there is no way out of the crisis.

"What would decisive leadership mean? First, a clear, unequivocal acknowledgement of the graveness of our

87

situation. Second, there needs to be a clear, credible sign that the Government, in taking steps necessary in the national interest, would override all personal interests - even for groups up to now deemed untouchable. This action should at the same time clearly show a commitment to national solidarity, meaning that while asking Indonesians to make sacrifices, the Government would show that it demanded real sacrifices from those in power."

CHAPTER FIVE

Panic And
Pessimism

As 1998 approached, with its March election of a new president and vice- president and the appointment of a new cabinet, there were ever increasing calls for "new blood" in the country 's leadership. The 'Jakarta Post' said in an editorial that "....problems and differences are tackled in the same old way as they were 20 to 30 years ago: by persuading people to conform, if possible, and clamping down on dissenters, if necessary. New blood is needed to revitalise our national energy."

As if to emphasise the 'bad old ways', on December 31, the very last day of the old year, news broke that the closure of Bank Jakarta, owned by the President's half brother, had been halted, pending final legal appeals against the shut down. Whether or not it was right for the law in Indonesia to be seen to be taking its proper course, the signal to the market was once again that Indonesia was not serious about reform.

As far as the state banks were concerned, the Government was apparently very serious. On December 30, the Finance Minister had announced the merger of Bank Bumi Daya, Bank Dagang Negara, Bank-Ekspor Impor Indonesia and Bank Pembangunan Indonesia into a single bank. To help guarantee transparency, shares in the new bank would be offered to reputable foreign investors. To help guarantee the strength of the new bank, all bad debt - estimated at about 5 percent - would be removed and placed in the hands of a soon-to-be-created company charged with the task of recovering the debts or otherwise reaching a settlement. It was further announced that Bank Tabungan Negara would become a subsidiary of publicly listed

Bank Negara Indonesia. News of the merger was welcomed as an important step toward restoring health to Indonesia's banking system as a whole. the Government almost certainly hoped that this merger would act as a lead for the private sector to follow and Central Bank Governor Soedradjad continued with his policy of persuasion.

As one year closed and another opened, the 'Jakarta Post' perhaps summed up the mood in a leader on December 31, which said: "More than in previous years Indonesians have reasons to ponder the year's events as the nation stands on the threshold of a New Year." In fact, the pondering was unusually loud and unusually clear, so clear that foreigners were surprised that the New Order Government even permitted some of the outpourings to appear in the media. At seminars and conferences and, especially in the print media, opinion after opinion slammed home the message that the principal reason for the country's unbelievable economic decline was the allegedly corrupt and opaque character of its management, including political management.

Just as the crisis had allowed and encouraged the foreign media to pour out its frustrations and criticisms of Indonesia, now, Indonesia's intellectuals and sections of the middle class poured out a torrent of dissatisfaction with the political system as a whole. And not only with the political system but also with many things those in power at any level were felt not to have done or to have done badly. The flood of frustration and criticism came to embrace the Government's failure to put out the forest fires, the mind numbing daily traffic jams in Jakarta, poor city planning, weak enforcement across the board and pollution, which in the capital, was often at health threatening levels. Suddenly, nothing was right with Indonesia.

Virtually from the close of the 1992-3, parliamentary and presidential elections there had been voices raised against corruption, collusion and nepotism in Indonesia. And there had been a rising tide of voices in favour of openness, a concept the President had cautiously endorsed provided, as always, it did not threaten political, social and economic stability. The heavy-handed closure of three magazines seemed to bring this flirtation to an abrupt end. Had there been no cataclysmic economic crisis, these voices may have amounted to little more than an 'acceptable' background 'noise.' But once the crisis bit in all its terrible, unforgiving and unrelenting savagery, corruption, malpractice, collusion and ineptitude were trumpeted as the causes. While it was realised that President Soeharto had not caused the problem, his style of Government and even his continued presence as President of the Republic, now appeared to some as a barrier to the changes the market was demanding and without which Indonesia seemed to risk sinking to its knees - or lower.

Political scientist, Soedjati Djiwandono, wrote: " We are waiting for a change in the political scene. The same political system has been in power for over three decades, a record surpassed only by Cuba's President, Fidel Castro. The political system is not functioning fully and properly. There is a growing tendency toward a growing concentration of power in the hands of the Government's executive branch and, by contrast, a continuous weakening of the representative bodies power - one of whose main functions is to exercise control over the executive branch. Indeed, one would wonder, especially in the light of what has always appeared to be the executive branch's dominant role in the People's Consultative Assembly steering committee, whether the President is really mandated by the MPR or the other way around. There are increasing demands for greater public participation, greater freedoms of expression and association, an effective mechanism of control, judicial review, an antitrust or anti monopoly law, and a presidential term limitation - in other words for greater democracy and justice."

A few days earlier at Depok, near Jakarta, Miriam Budiardjo, one of Indonesia's most senior political scientists and the first woman to receive an honorary doctorate from the University of Indonesia was quoted as saying: "Many things which we used to consider unacceptable we now see as proper and common practice. We should restore our political life as we are now endeavouring to do with our economic life.These steps are necessary to prevent the situation deteriorating further and getting out of control."

To increase the accountability of the Executive, Miriam Budiardjo suggested that the People's Consultative Assembly should meet annually with the President's state-of-the-nation address being followed by several days of discussion. She was also quoted as saying: "As a result of the House's low legislative productivity many problems which should be regulated by laws are not regulated at all, or handled through a variety of decisions by the Government apparatus." She was quoted as saying that "many questions that should be discussed in a general forum are decided by ministers, governors or other officials, thereby creating a lack of transparency in the Governmental process."

First, the call had been for transparency in business. Now, the call was for transparency in Government. From a crisis of sentiment, to a currency crisis to an economic crisis, by the end of 1997, Indonesia appeared to have arrived at a political crisis. Said the 'Jakarta Post: "Behind an economy that has made tremendous progress until recently, there has lurked the dark shadow of monopoly, favouritism, nepotism, public distrust of the rupiah, institutionalised inequality and a weakness of supervision. Politically, Indonesia lacks transparency, an uncertain succession scenario, increasingly weak legislative and judicial bodies, rampant corruption and a freedom of expression which has been turned into an art of whispers."

As we shall see later, President Soeharto was upset by this tide of criticism of his Government. Because of the visibility of the President's family in business and the popular suspicion that he himself has made billions of dollars out of his presidency, many foreigners thought of him as being in the same mould as the late President Marcos. Even some of Indonesia's so-called 'common people' thought so, with more disciples joining the viewpoint the longer President Soeharto remained in office and the longer the economic crisis continued. Even if the President had not made a cent out of his presidency, Indonesians generally believe that nobody does anything for nothing.

One thing we do know about the President, is that he is extremely hard working and extremely serious about his work as President and even about his image as president. One of the reasons doctors ordered him to rest was because he had worked throughout most of his transcontinental flights, instead of sleeping. It is common for him to give long briefings to the press while airborne, to hold meetings with cabinet colleagues, and to catch up with important paperwork. There can be no doubt that he has tried his utmost to create strong economic fundamentals in Indonesia as a result of which there could take place a reduction in poverty and a general increase in health, education and living standards. Until June 1997 he had received nothing but international praise for dedication and for its results.

Despite so much criticism from every side but feeling and believing as he does, at the end of 1997, President Soeharto saw his duty and his mission as once again to rally the nation behind him, at this stage to fortify its courage and deepen its resilience. He had several times asked people not to feel hopeless because the crisis was so long drawn out and a solution so elusive. And publicly and privately he had lamented how so much of what had been built in Indonesia could apparently be swept away so quickly. In his end-of-year speech President Soeharto called upon the nation to be strong and united in the face of the adversity inflicted upon it since mid-1997. He was quoted as saying: "We are now undergoing a severe trial in the monetary and economic sectors. "We are fighting with everything we have to get through this very difficult time. The Government has already prepared many programmes to deal with these upheavals and these already have the support of the International Monetary Fund and other countries. The Government is calling on all levels of the public, particularly the business community, to give their whole-hearted support in carrying out these programmes. Let us work hard and be orderly in our respective fields. Let's forge our unity and cohesion. Let's preserve national stability."

Most of these were familiar themes. President Soeharto's most deep-seated fears are that Indonesia may break up, or descend into social and political chaos, and, consequently, into economic chaos. More than anything else, he sees it as his job to keep the national ship afloat and on an even keel. While warning Indonesians that there were rough times ahead, he and his cabinet also took steps to create jobs and to guarantee the supply and prices of basic necessities. What eluded him - and everyone else for that matter - was a solution to the problem of the crashing rupiah. The fact that he did not seem to have a solution and that the Government did not appear to have a solution fanned public fears that perhaps the Government didn't know what it was doing and was leading the country nowhere while the crisis threatened to bankrupt, not just segments of the population, but the whole country. Loekman Soetrisno even went so far as to write in the 'Jakarta Post' on January 7: "The Government (should) apologise to the Indonesian people for making them poorer in this crisis."

Growing pessimism and panic, especially among the middle-class and intelligensia, led them to intensify their criticism every time the Government appeared to be foot-dragging or inconsistent in implementing reforms and solutions pressed on it by organisations like the IMF, which were thought to have all the answers. As a developing country, Indonesians have long looked up to the West, especially to the USA. For a long time there was a feeling among Indonesians that products made in Indonesia were inferior to foreign products. Even today, one can see clearly the ongoing and even burgeoning preference for foreign products, clothes, food and entertainment. Among the urban population, Indonesian culture per-se is dangerously threatened. Ironically, the destruction carries with it a heavy import bill which, of course, the country now cannot afford and, perhaps never should have tried to afford. If organisations like the World Bank or the International Monetary Fund gave advice, the assumption among the informed public generally was that they must be right - even if their recommendations seemed irrelevant and didn't work, a view held by the President and others in the cabinet, as the foreign prescriptions steadily failed to halt the slide in the rupiah.

As always, Indonesia's middle-class was segmented. There were those whose loyalty to the New Order Government was unquestioned. There were those who wanted to remain loyal but saw the need for change. There were those who thought that the New Order Government and its aging leader were incapable of change. Even among those who most felt the urgent need for change there was the fear that change might bring chaos. Especially during the worst crisis Indonesia had faced for 30 years, there were many who said that it was better for the leadership and the Government to continue in the old tried and true ways, at least until solutions were found. At election time, in March, there was no serious official opposition to President Soeharto and to the New Order Government.

Just as the President's statement had done little to reassure citizens or markets - particularly since his speech had omitted all the economic indicators which he traditionally included - the Finance Minister's close-of-year comments seemed far from reality. He was quoted as saying that the rupiah and local stock markets were "looking better." Meanwhile, in the markets, the Central Bank continued its struggle to support the ever falling currency, which had even breached the Rps 6,000 to the US dollar level, foreign securities investors kept their backs resolutely turned away, 1998's direct capital inflows seemed threatened by events in South Korea and Japan, and Standard & Poor cut Indonesia's long-term foreign currency rating. The Agency said that the downgrade reflected Indonesia's diminished fiscal and balance of payments flexibility.

On the first day of trading after the New Year Holiday, Asian currencies were said to have "taken a pounding" with the Thai Baht, Malaysian Ringgit, Philippine Peso and Indonesian rupiah all being sold down to new record lows. The only apparently good news was that the State Administrative High Court ordered the closure of Bank Jakarta to proceed. The owners instantly applied to Bank Indonesia for a new operating licence.

By January 6, the rupiah had slumped precariously close to Rps 7,000 to one US dollar and political as well as economic concerns in the market were now cited as the reason. The 'Jakarta Post' quoted "dealers" as saying that political concerns ahead of the convening of the People's Consultative Assembly in March to elect a president and vice president accelerated the fallout of the rupiah against the US dollar. "The political atmosphere approaching the General Assembly poses another important factor in the rupiah's decline," a dealer was quoted as saying.

The General Assembly was important for a reason other than the election of the new president and vice-president. It would also be the time when the state budget for the next fiscal year would be approved as well as the state guidelines leading up to a new five-year-plan - Repelita VII. A debate about the budget had begun in the media long before Christmas with December opinion veering firmly towards an austerity budget based on the losses the Government must sustain as a result of the devaluation of the rupiah and the decrease in tax revenues. For the Government to pay its bills, including meeting its foreign debt obligations, would be so much harder in fiscal 1998-99.

But the nearer the budget approached the more voices were heard - or at least read - saying that, above all else, the budget must promote growth. There began to emerge widespread concerns about the IMF's insistence on a contractionary one percent budget surplus of a kind which had also emerged in Thailand. More or less at the same time that the draft budget was being framed in Indonesia, in Thailand, the Government of Prime Minister, Chuan Leekpai, was saying that it might have to renegotiate aspects of its IMF package, especially the requirement for a 1 percent budget surplus. As in Indonesia, the Thai currency continued to plunge, despite the advice of the IMF.

As if to highlight the differences in approach, the January 4 edition of the 'Jakarta Post' carried a front page headline which read "Govt Must Make Hard Choices In New Budget" while on the very next page the heading was "Budget Must promote Growth: Business people". Aburizal Bakrie, the Chairman of KADIN, was quoted as saying: " We are relieved to hear that President Soeharto said that the next state budget would increase in size." Pontjo Sutowo, Chairman of the Hotel and Restaurant Association was quoted as saying: "The budget has to ensure that the development process continues." However, on balance, opinion was on the side of a 'care and maintenance' budget which would allow whatever development seemed possible. With revenues falling unthinkably, what other realistic approach could there be?

The draft budget was made at a difficult time, when no one dare predict what the rupiah's exchange rate against the US dollar would eventually be. But decisions had be made by the drafters and, convinced as they were, that Indonesia's fundamentals were really strong, that the currency had "overshot," and that the market, in effect, would soon come to its senses, the figure of Rps 4,000 to one US dollar was chosen. Given that, even as President Soeharto delivered his budget address to the House of Representatives, on January 6, the rupiah shot down alomost to Rps 8,000 to the dollar, the choice of Rps 4,000 to the dollar seemed high optimism. Immediately and unfortunately that was exactly how the market perceived it.

There was also a public relations downside to the budget. Thanks to the devaluation of the rupiah, it showed an increase of 32 percent in Government expenditures, chiefly for the purpose of servicing public debt and also to continue to subsidise fuel - a subsidy anathema to the IMF but essential to all the millions of poor throughout Indonesia whose incomes wouldn't tolerate even a small increase. Any rise in the price of fuel - priced in US dollars - affected everything from lighting and cooking to transportation and livelihoods, and was extremely sensitive. Back in November, all four factions in the House of Representatives had urged the Government not to do anything to raise fuel prices - a sure confirmation of the importance and sensitivity of this matter. Although the Government wanted to be seen to obey the IMF's advice to remove subsidies, to do so at such a time would have been to invite massive social unrest. It would also have fuelled inflation. Head of Indonesia's Central Bureau of Statistics, Sugito Suwito, was quoted as saying: " If there is a drastic cut in subsidies, then inflation will of course, shoot up quickly."

Once again, the Government was caught. It wanted to please the IMF but had also to look after its people and guard against inflation. The sum of money set aside to subsidise fuel prices was actually increased. Later, the Government revealed that to 'meet the IMF halfway, so to speak,' from April 1, while the poor would continue to be subsidised, there would be price increases for aviation turbine fuel, aviation gas, premium and industrial diesel and kerosene and automotive diesel for industrial and commercial use. The price of automotive diesel for public transport would also be kept low. Vital fertiliser subsidies were retained. Development spending was increased by a modest 5.6 percent, principally for poverty alleviation and equitable development programmes.

With state revenues falling, extra money had to be found from somewhere both to tread water and to meet the cost of even marginal growth. Increases in foreign aid and in revenues from oil and gas sales were identified as the principal means to achieve this. The price of oil was assumed to be US$17 per barrel. Public capital inflows would be used to cover a current account deficit expected to have fallen to US$5.39 billion from US$ 6.35 billion the preceding year. The budget made no mention of the 1 percent budget surplus being insisted upon by the IMF but the Finance Minister was quoted as saying that the Government still aimed to try to achieve it.

President Soeharto stressed that a number of development projects, including those specially targeted by international loan agencies because of his family's involvement, had been and would remain postponed and that there could be no increase in already low civil service salaries. His main point was that the New Order Government was committed to deepening the reforms suggested by international advisers and, by promoting economic efficiency, would do its best to smooth out the impact on less privileged groups. Calling once again for the nation to united behind the Government, the President was quoted as saying: "With this asset (national unity) we are convinced that the storm will pass. We shall reopen the sail of our national ship. We shall command it toward the shore of our destination." The President added that the Government was determined to press ahead with the reforms needed to restore market confidence. "It is extremely important to restore such confidence. It is precisely the lack of such confidence that has been behind the myriad of problems that have recently emerged." Sounding remarkably like some of those airing their views in the national media, the President was quoted as saying: "We must stop the erosion of confidence in the rupiah. We must reverse it, because if it continues, our national economic foundation will crumble, obviously with very serious consequences."

As President Soeharto spoke, it was reported that 1.4 million new job-seekers would be unsuccessful in their search for work in the New Year and that the number of officially unemployed stood at 4.4 million. Unemployment was forecast to reach nearly 6 million by the end of 1998. In fact, it was said to have reached nearly 10 million before the end of the first quarter. At this time, most of the newly unemployed were in the construction, textiles and garments industries. If underemployed people (those who work for less than one hour per day) where added to the unemployed, the figure rose to a staggering 44 million, expected to rise to close to 50 million in 1998.

Critics branded the budget as "too optimistic", particularly the assumptions about the rupiah/US dollar exchange rate and the price of oil, which, at US$16.13 per barrel on January 6, had slumped to a two-year low and was already below the budget forecast. The prospect of increased pumping from Iraq threatened to push down the price still further. When the Assembly met in March to ratify the budget, oil had slumped to US$13.00 per barrel. Most wondered how the 1 percent surplus required by the IMF would be achieved.

On the eve of the budget, the IMF had taken to the

war path to pressurise Indonesia into doing more to implement agreed reforms. The 'Washington Post' quoted an unnamed IMF official as saying: "We would like to see the senior leadership in Indonesia stand up and be counted on the reforms." The official was quoted as saying that if Indonesia did not implement the reforms in full, although it had received US$3 billion from the Fund in November, the country could very well not be given the next tranche of US$3 billion. This would be serious. All those who had pledged financial help to Indonesia, including for trade financing, had done so as part of the IMF package. If the package was stopped, their help would be stopped.

While insisting repeatedly that Indonesia was not implementing agreed reforms and while IMF was being criticised for not being good at telling its own story, the fact of the matter was that the IMF was also being very laggard in telling the world precisely what reforms Indonesia had not implemented. Clues escaped official lips from time to time but there was nothing resembling a report card which observers could then have used to fairly assess Indonesia's progress. The IMF's position seemed always very one-sided, the organisation with a reputation for secrecy, urging Indonesia to be open and transparent while itself providing only limited information.

Nevertheless, the public record for Indonesia did not look good. A merger of state banks, over which the Government had direct control, had been announced but progress seemed very slow. Private mergers were also moving slowly, on the basis of Governor Soedradjad's policy of persuasion. It would not be until mid-March that a one-stop centre would be established to assist banks with their merger plans. The closure of insolvent banks had been far below IMF expectations. The dismantling of monopolies had either not happened or appeared to outsiders to have been fudged.

Subsidies were still in place for the very good reason that to remove them at this time might be to risk a country wide conflagration as ordinary people with low incomes vented their anger on the easiest available targets - shops and Government offices.

On the other hand, liquidity was so tight that 80 percent of Indonesia's corporates listed on the stock exchange were said to be on the brink of bankruptcy. In early January, the

Government had appealed to the conglomerates to repatriate some of the large sums of money reputedly parked offshore and rumoured to be at least US$80 billion. If they exist, there is no indication that such funds were ever brought back.

From the point of view of Indonesia's corporates, the IMF-backed policy of high interest rates to defend the rupiah was beggaring the country. What the corporates and the banking sector needed most was more liquidity, not less. While the IMF and the Central Bank governor favoured the use of high interest rates the corporate sector was screaming that it was dying. President Soeharto agreed, but the Government was caught firmly in the middle. If interest rates were lowered and liquidity improved the IMF would say that its reforms were not being carried out. Carrying them out could mean the death of Indonesia's corporate sector. the Government tried to adopt a balancing p☐osition between the conflicting forces, promising that interest rates would be reduced as soon as circumstances permitted while maintaining them at high enough levels to satisfy the IMF. Had interest rates been lowered, there is no evidence to suggest that the rupiah would have fallen further because, thanks to its fall, people from company presidents to housewives were stampeding out of the national currency and into dollars.

While the IMF was castigating Indonesia for not carrying out reforms it supported, the President of the Federal Reserve Bank of Atlanta, Jack Guynn was blaming Asia's regional crisis on the alleged cold-shouldering of the free market and the pegging of local currencies at artificially high rates against the US dollar. He said that this encouraged foreign investors, just as low offshore interest rates encouraged Asian borrowers.

Writing in Washington, Holger Schmale was quoted in the 'Jakarta Post' on December 15 as saying: "The Asian model of state modified capitalism has obviously failed and IMF experts are there to help replace it with the US variation of unfettered interplay by free market forces. Quoting Jeffrey Garten, Dean of Yale University's Management Institute, she went on: " The is the triumph of Wall Street." Schmale went on: "The medicine currently prescribed by the IMF really is American. Large Government-controlled monopolies are broken up and the interdependency and cronyism created by the long established old boy networks that link bureaucrats, businessmen and trade unionists are smashed. Banks are forced to play a smaller role, as future capital is supposed to come from stock and bond markets." There was some inaccuracy and huge amounts of ignorance in all this, but it seemed that the American attack on 'fortress Asia' could not be denied.

CHAPTER SIX

An Uneasy Marriage

While Indonesia specifically and Asia generally was taking this ideological pounding, the persistent, region-wide, demand for US dollars was gathering new momentum. Across Asia there was talk of a "dollar drought." In a significant report on January 7, Reuters quoted dealers as saying: "It's a drying up of US dollars that is causing all the regional currencies to plummet to record lows." In January a 'Jakarta Post' report revealed that, since June, the US dollar had appreciated by a staggering 300 percent against the rupiah. Around the region the value of the US dollar was topping half-decade highs.

Here was another story completely. Indonesia had first been told that corruption and mismanagement had resulted in an historic loss of investor confidence. Then it had been told that, because its private sector looked unable to pay its bills, there was a mismatch between currency values and fundamentals. Now it was being told that what was really causing the currency crisis was a shortage of American dollars. It goes without saying that loss of confidence in regional currencies led to an unusually high demand for US dollars, not only from local people but from US fund managers selling out. But when one realises that this demand was taking place at a time when the greenback was at a six-and-a-half-year high, one can readily forecast the consequences and the problems. Interestingly, according to the Bank of International Settlements, the percentage of Asia's private debt, due to mature in 1998, was actually LESS than in 1997.

While US commentators were blaming Asia for bringing its woes upon itself, the fact of the matter was that the Clinton Administration was promising to deliver to the US the first budget surplus in 30 years - roughly the same amount of time that the New Order Government had been in power. According to APP the deficit for the 1997-98 fiscal year would be only US$22 billion, down from the almost US$ 360 billion forecast when the Democrats took office.

Much later, in March, speaking in Perth, Australia, and quoted by the 'Sunday Star', of Malaysia, Professor Augustine Tan of the National University of Singapore was to blame much of the crisis on the budgetary policies of President Clinton, the same man who had telephoned President Soeharto no less than five times to convey first his support and latterly his concern that Indonesia was not taking its IMF prescribed medicine - medicine which by then seemed totally inappropriate to cure ills on which the Indonesian Government may never in its heart have agreed - or perhaps partially agreed. The same man who had described Indonesia's crisis as a "glitch" that would soon pass.

Mr Tan was a hard man to ignore because in addition to being a full professor, he is a former Chairman of the National Productivity Board as well as political secretary to former prime minister, Lee Kuan Yew. He is a consultant to the Monetary Authority of Singapore, the World Bank and to a number of United Nations Agencies. Professor Tan said forthrightly that the IMF was treating Asia's liquidity crisis as if it was a crisis of insolvency - which it was not and never had been. Commenting on Asia's alleged defects in the way it does business Professor Tan observed acidly: "They have been there for a long time, so why has the crisis not happened earlier?" In a spirited defence of southeast Asia's economic policies he argued that it made total sense for regional corporates to borrow US dollars at around 5-6 percent interest when local rates were up at 20 percent or over. He said that many of the projects for which the borrowed funds were used were totally viable with returns of between 20 to 30 percent. No one expected currencies to plummet more or less overnight and it was this alone which had impaired borrowers' ability to repay on time. Cees de Koning commented that the fact that many Indonesian companies borrowed offshore showed that their needs had outgrown the Indonesian banking system, valued at a mere US$35 billion.

Professor Tan said speculators are always part of the market and he dismissed their role in bringing about the crisis.

So, what was left?

According to Professor Tan, the principal cause of the crisis was ever tightening liquidity in the US aimed at eliminating the budget deficit. When the US increased its money supply and ran a deficit, the Professor said it was good for Asia. But when the US reduced its money supply and reduced its deficit is was bad for Asia.

In Indonesia, in 1997-98, exports of key items fell an average of 24 percent and were projected to continue to decline in 1998-99. Affected categories included: rattan, feed, toys, sporting, music and educational goods, chemical goods (not raw chemicals), plastics, processed rubber, steel, machinery, automotive products, lead, copper, aluminium, marble and glass, handicrafts, footwear and leather goods. The Government cited lack of competitiveness as the reason. Professor Tan cited the devaluation of the Chinese Yuan by 35 percent in 1994 as one reason for Indonesia's loss of competitiveness and the 13 percent devaluation of the Japanese yen in 1995 as another important reason. Not only had the US fewer dollars to spare for imports but, Professor Tan pointed out that as it prepared for a single currency, the European Union was also in thrifty mode. And at the same time as major markets were being more conservative about imports, more and more countries, including the old Soviet Union, were joining the free market adding to competitive pressures. Of course, in Indonesia, there were other problems. Indonesian wages were no longer the lowest in Asia. And, levies and unofficial 'on-costs' made doing business more expensive than it need be by about 30 percent. Finally, there was the problem of the constantly appreciating US dollar, to which many Asian currencies were tied. As the dollar went up these currencies also rose, further undermining competitiveness by forcing up local prices and costs. Eventually, the gap between nominal and real currency values became too large and the great Asian currencies dump began.

As the currencies were dumped and values tumbled, a train of events was set in motion which had its counterpart in Thailand, Indonesia and South Korea and to some extent in Malaysia and Singapore. Debts suddenly magnified out of control and wherever there were weaknesses, such as in the banking system or in the ways in which businesses were run, these were exposed. In fact, on January 7, a Reuters report quoted one Singapore dealer as saying: "The Asian crisis is turning into a debt crisis." Increasingly, Asian business could not pay its bills - in the southeast anyway.

Professor Tan weighed-in heavily against the IMF who, he said, had prescribed 'medicine' for situations in which there were chronic Governments deficits and inflationary spending. In Indonesia there was no deficit and inflation was low - hallowed objectives of three decades of New Order management. Said Professor Tan: "What sort of prescription is it to say that all banks and financial institutions are bad and corrupt and that you must get rid of them and start all over again? And the deflation imposed by the IMF is causing more casualties (than recoveries)." He went on: "Look at the IMF record over the years. When they go in (to a country) they always say your growth will be zero percent for the next year, 1 percent for the following year and 2 percent in the third year. But the record shows it is minus 10 percent, minus 15 percent for two or three years. That is a colossal price to pay. You don't need to be an economist to know that you can squeeze any current account deficit out of any economy just to produce a recession."

Whether or not the crisis really was caused originally by a "dollar drought," just as Indonesia realised that its problem had now become that of the short-term private loans, Professor Tan agreed, and said that the IMF had completely failed to address the problem. He said that it was not equipped to do this and regretted that there was no such thing as a global bank of last resort whose lending could restore the liquidity so badly needed by regional markets. Throughout the crisis the IMF and the World Trade Organisation had pushed ahead with their respective crusades to create global financial and capital markets. Asian Governments had long had reservations about integrating and opening up systems within which there were still weaknesses and recent events had shown that the groundwork for such a development was nowhere near ready. The spread of unqualified freedom could only result in chaos.

Thai Prime Minister, Chuan Leekpai, was one of the first to say: "One of the lessons this crisis has taught us is that many of our structures and institutions were not ready for this new era." President Soeharto would eventually make very similar observations. The conservative 'Straits Times' of Singapore said in a leader on February 26, 1998: "Asian countries are discovering....that it is unwise to deregulate without regulating the deregulated, foolish to liberalise without binding the liberated to disciplined structures. If it is true that the current Asian crisis is rooted in bad private sector decisions, it is equally true that these bad decisions were made possible by poorly regulated banking systems and misguided exchange rate and monetary policies. Governments - or rather, the lack of them - created the conditions that led to the present debacle."

Thai Finance Minister, Tarrin Nimmanahaeminda, summed up the regional mood when he said that to avoid a repeat of the currency debacle "good Government is the only real protection." The 'Straits Times' leader continued: "....More, not less, Government? Clearly the emerging new consensus is a far cry from the Reagan-Thatcher creed of the 1980s which proclaimed that Governments need only get out of the way for the "invisible hand" of the market place to work its magic. The "invisible hand", it turns out now, is also an unsteady hand. In the absence of a coordinating brain - setting the rules, providing a framework, just saying "No" to foolishness, idiocy and outright malfeasance - hands, invisible or not, are apt to be not merely feckless, but recklesly feckless. This recognition (that good Government is the answer) does not by any means suggest that Governments in the region should pull back from liberalising their economies. That would be wrong. What it does mean is that liberalisation cannot get ahead of the development of strong domestic regulatory institutions. Recent events suggest that only those countries which combine strong governance with liberalisation can compete successfully in the global economy. Liberalised markets do not come ready-made with disciplined structures. Only Governments can ensure that liberalisation does not turn into a riot."

This is what many felt had happened in Indonesia in and after 1988 - the banking sector had been deregulated but, insufficient prudent guidelines and monitoring mechanisms had been installed. And, clearly, it was feared that market chaos might occur if the IMF and the WTO went ahead too quickly with their ambitious global plans under circumstances where no adequate guiding and regulatory structures were in place. Regionally, Indonesia threatened to be the biggest casualty in the emergence of this brave new global world, as Professor Tan put it, threatening to "blow up in flames" as the economy collapsed and desperate workers either rioted or fled as refugees to other countries in the region.

The announcement of the draft budget in early January was not only swiftly deemed to be wildly unrealistic but led to fears that Indonesia would have to renegotiate its agreement with the IMF - should the IMF be willing. In Hong Kong, Nikko Research Centre's Chief Strategist, Marshall Mays, was quoted as describing the IMF's Managing Director, Michel Camdessus as being a "strict disciplinarian" - just the kind of man least suited to working with Indonesians. Mays went on: " He won't flinch. He'll come back and say: 'This is it. No more money. Your next tranche sits in the bank.'"

Dire warnings of impending trouble!

Forty-eight hours after the announcement of the draft budget, Indonesia and its Government had troubles aplenty. The rupiah went into free fall, crashing through the Rps10,000 to one US dollar barrier. The stock market was said to have "collapsed." Fitch IBCA, the ratings agency, promptly downgraded Indonesia's long-term foreign currency rating. Standard & Poor followed suit. "The tabling of unrealistic budget proposals which publicly flout recently agreed targets with the IMF is a severe blow to confidence," Reuters quoted a company spokesperson as saying. On January 9, the 'Jakarta Post' quoted a dealer working for a Japanese bank as saying: "It's not just foreigners who have lost confidence in the region, but Indonesians have also lost confidence in their own currency. The whole picture is actually quite scary and stupid. The currency is just running on its own momentum."

As had been the case since before Christmas, due to lack of liquidity, trading was actually very thin and even low levels of transaction could drastically change the rupiah's value.

Fearing that the rupiah would spiral down further, in Indonesia's cities, there was a rush to stock up from shops and supermarkets, ironically by the more wealthy members of society, who could probably afford the higher prices anyway. Some outlets controlled purchases by rationing, or raised prices by as much as 50 percent to try to keep shop stocks at reasonable levels. In some areas, people thought that food supplies were threatened, not only because of the economic crisis, but also because of the year-long drought, which had scorched Indonesia throughout 1997, with the promise of a short, thin, rainy season at the beginning of 1998 and more crop destroying drought on the way. Security forces raided the premises of suspected commercial hoarders and released withheld supplies onto the market.

BULOG, assured the population that at least they need not worry about basic food because it could guarantee all basic necessities for a few months. Ships were photographed off-loading rice and other essentials brought from Thailand, Vietnam, China, India and Pakistan. BULOG announced that it planned to import 100,000 tons of unhusked rice. To keep the price of rice stable and to hold inflation in check, President Soeharto had ordered the Agency to sell from its huge stock of some 2.2 million tons. BULOG sold half of its total stock in 1997 but still expected to have 600,000 tons in stock by March, by which time substantial additional imports might be required to bring the stock up to a targeted 2.0 million tons.

Voices were now raised for the first time encouraging the spurning of imported goods in favour of Indonesian-sourced commodities and products, including food-stuffs. Crude palm oil exports were banned to maintain the vital supply of cooking oil, one of the people's basic necessities. The ban infuriated producers, the IMF and market analysts because a) it went against free market principles and, more to the point b) it was imposed at a time of rising market prices and profits. Palm oil was among Indonesia's top 10 largest export commodities. From the point of view of the Government of Indonesia, the judgment had to be: corporate profit or popular riots.

Muchsin Bafadal of the United Development Party called corporations to save precious US dollars by the selective repatriation of Indonesia's approximately 100,000 expatriates, mostly technical advisers and managers.

While all this was happening, Central Bank Governor, Soedradjad, had been out of the country having knee surgery. Upon his return, on January 9, the Governor was quoted as saying with great calm that the fall of the rupiah was only "temporary." Even when he added the clarification that the state budget target of Rps 4,000 to one US dollar was only an average, the market remained unimpressed. Once again he stressed that Indonesia's "fundamentals" were strong. With the rupiah shooting through the floor, only 22 of the 282 firms listed on the Jakarta Stock Exchange said to have sufficient assets to cover liabilities, shops under seize and the looming threat of social unrest, there was a near universal clamour for effective Government action. Governor Soedradjad merely said that the Central Bank planned to carry on as usual, making money market interventions where appropriate and collaborating with the IMF and other international agencies.

In Washington, US Deputy Treasury Secretary, Lawrence Summers, urged Indonesia to get on with cleaning up the banking and financial services sectors, adding that Indonesia was best advised to tighten monetary policy still further and cut back on Government spending. Former minister and economist, Mohamad Sadli, was quoted as saying: "Local and foreign markets have cast a vote of no confidence in Indonesia."

The draft budget was to blame. It was felt to be unrealistic, expansionary and to inflict no belt-tightening whatever either on Government programmes or the people that implemented them, the civil servants. The Government had defended not cutting civil servant's pay on the grounds that they earned little enough already. This is certainly true although cynics may have felt that the Government also wanted to minimise the risk of alienating its servants. The armed forces (ABRI), at least, felt they were in a position to help and postponed arms spending by US$20 billion, including jets and helicopters from Russia. ABRI said that the number of military attaches overseas would be cut by 70 percent and all optional functions and exercises not essential for military operations would be postponed. While inflicting little hurt on Indonesians, these measures promised to save substantial sums of money, especially dollars.

As the rupiah collapsed, the political dimension of the crisis intensified. Fitch IBCA were quoted as saying the political as well as economic stresses were rising in Indonesia since President Soeharto's Government had drawn much of its legitimacy from economic success. The 'Jakarta Post' quoted Mohamad Sadli as saying: "the Government must be replaced." It was not clear whether he meant changed immediately or changed at the People's Consultative Assembly in March. But his drift at least was clear. But, reflecting an ambivalence that has always characterised discussions about Indonesia's leadership, the Professor went on to warn that political reforms might not be enough to turn around Indonesia's critical economic situation. He was quoted as saying: "Thailand and South Korea have made political reforms but they are still in crisis." Economist, Rino Agung Affendi, was quoted in the same article in the 'Jakarta Post' as saying that the Government had lost all credibility as a result of the draft budget. "A complete economic reform package will not have any impact now if the Government does not have any credibility at all." Economist, Anggito Abimanyu, was quoted as saying: "What Indonesians, including myself, now need is the Government's genuine actions to seriously settle the crisis." He was quoted as going on to say that people needed the Government to provide a frank and open explanation about the cause of the crisis and the steps being taken by the Government to rehabilitate the economy. Another Gadja Mada University-based economist, Revrisond Baswir, was quoted as warning: "The Government should not ignore the political dimension of the crisis."

In its leader of January 8, the 'Jakarta Post' was as forthright as it is possible to be. The leader concluded: "The way it stands now reforms could happen in one or two ways: by orderly and peaceful means through the MPR, or outside the MPR, which could possibly be chaotic and, God forbid, violent. Those who call the shots must now decide what it is to be." President Soeharto was already planning to request additional powers.

Meanwhile, on January 10, there were numerous media reports of a 30-minute telephone conversation between President Clinton and President Soeharto in which the Indonesian leader had again promised to carry out reforms suggested by the IMF. Clinton said that Lawrence Summers would be sent to Jakarta to discuss the reforms. Significantly, against the backdrop of the expansionary draft budget with its hard-to-take seriously exchange rate and oil price, the IMF aid package was now described for the first time as "an austerity programme." From Washington the IMF was quoted as saying: "We'd like to accelerate the programme and strengthen it because a lot of people believe that the Indonesian Government wasn't really committed to the programme." The IMF chastisement of the Government contained the same seeds of political crisis as could be detected in comments from within Indonesia. Unlike the domestic comments, President Clinton was said to be confident that the reforms would be carried out under the leadership of President Soeharto. The rupiah received something of a respite while the markets waited to see what would happen next.

The 'marriage' between Indonesia and the IMF had been uneasy from the start, particularly fears that its demands would erode Indonesia's sovereign rights. To these fears had been added the certainty that far from bringing any 'magic' to bear on the situation, the IMF's 'medicine hadn't worked at all. The central issue was always the stabilisation of the rupiah exchange rate - and the rupiah was still sliding precipitously and, for all anyone knew, was nowhere near bottom.

One of the very significant words allegedly uttered by Bank Indonesia Governor, Soedradjad, on January 9 was that he thought that the IMF package was "relevant." This was, a priori, not a strong statement. He could have said that the IMF package was paramount, crucial, central etc but, instead, he chose to use the word relevant. The inference was that IMF aid was relevant but not central, relevant but marginal. After all, few could have been more aware than the Governor of just how little affect the policies of the IMF had had.

Into the picture now stepped Jeffrey Sachs of the Harvard Institute of International Development. Sachs was reported by Reuters as lambasting the IMF for failure to tailor aid packages specifically to the needs of the southeast Asian economies. "The IMF took its normal remedy off the shelf and started to apply it," he was quoted as saying in Madras, India. Sachs characterised the troubled economies as being open, with Government surpluses, high savings rates and low inflation and he argued that for no apparent reason investors had suddenly been scared off by the size of the region's short-term private debt (less than the preceding year). "It was an unjustified race for the exit," he was quoted as saying, continuing: "My sense is that the IMF added to the panic." He strongly criticised the IMF for insisting on bank closures which, he said, sent the wrong signals to the market. Later in the month, Sachs called the IMF's management of the crisis in Indonesia 'poor' and described that the closure of the 16 banks as "thoughtless" and responsible for melting down Indonesia's financial system and causing panic among the public. Sachs said that these truths were now recognised even by the IMF's own experts, who nevertheless, refrained from issuing any admissions of guilt or making any apologies. On the eve of the Islamic holiday of Lebaran he described the economic and financial situation in Indonesia as being 'completely out of control' and the temporary freeze on servicing foreign debt as 'an act of desperation.' It was a crisis which should never have happened, he said. "Perceptions of vulnerability created a self perpetuating crisis. A profound tragedy is happening that was wholly unnecessary."

Heady stuff!

In early January, few people were claiming to know the cause of the crisis. In fact, few were even in March. Rather than a cause, what could be seen, and, more to the point felt, were the effects of whatever was causing the crisis - the symptoms but not the sickness. The Government of Indonesia had done its best to wrestle with the symptoms but to no avail. Around it the economy descended into a pit of hopelessness and insolvency. Some foreign commentators painted a gloomy picture in which neither the President nor his ministers had the slightest idea what to do next. There may have been some truth in this, not because the President and his ministers were inept but because no one, including the IMF, really knew how to do the one thing which could be said to end the crisis - stabilise the rupiah.

Up untill now, through its recommendations and advice, the IMF seemed to be saying that corruption and bad Government were the root of the problem in Indonesia, side by side with such market distorting practices as monopolies, subsidies and the funding of projects like a national car or aeroplane which might be unviable if left to the market alone. As we have seen from Professor Tan's comments, it was hard, not only for many Indonesians, but for Asians generally, to subscribe to this view. As professor Tan had observed: "Everything had seemed OK, so why now?" And we have seen how he answered the question by describing the steep appreciation of the US dollar, coupled with the usual end of year scramble by Asia's corporates to use dollars to repay their short-term debt. As these developments forced down the value of the rupiah, Indonesians themselves began to lose confidence and panic, forcing down the rupiah further. From this point on, as Jeffrey Sachs, had pointed out, the crisis in Indonesia became self generating and perpetuating.

The weakened rupiah led to heavy question marks

being placed over the ability of private borrowers to repay their short-term debts; interest rates raised to defend the rupiah raised the level of debt among Indonesia's domestic banks and brought companies to the brink of bankruptcy. Suddenly, and in a very short time, Indonesia Inc., looked on the verge of complete collapse. Whatever was needed to solve the crisis it was not the ideology being so vigorously peddled by the IMF.

It is likely that the Central Bank and the IMF disagreed about interest rates from quite early in their association, but, true to its word, the Government successively lowered lending rates at the state banks. But these were only a handful and rates among the commercial banks remained high.

Later on, some foreign experts were to argue that raising interest rates under the circumstances prevailing in Indonesia during the last quarter of 1997 was bound to be ineffective given the high dollar demand and collapse of confidence in the currency. Nobel Prize winner, economist Merton Miller, was quoted as telling the Asia Society, in Hong Kong on January 19, that raising interest rates and tightening liquidity was a "mistake" because speculators stood to make such huge sums from their activities that even the highest interest rates were unlikely to deter them. The IMF policy of closing banks frightened the market to such an extent that private banks had no choice but to maintain very high interest rates just to survive, thereby contributing massively to the liquidity crisis and to the solvency problems being faced by Indonesian companies large, medium and small.

Other than its crusade for transparency and a level playing field, in addition to the closure of the banks, some of the IMF's other recommendations were plain wrong. the Government had not overspent, so why should it acquiesce in an austerity budget which would be very harmful to the public interest? Of course, once the value of the rupiah had slid precipitously, reducing state revenues, naturally Government realised that it would be wise to trim its sails. But this was a different matter. The cut-back would be to accommodate the crisis and not a response to alleged overspending. In addition, the Government had not borrowed excessively and, where it had, it had done so with great prudence to try to ensure low rates of interest and realistic paybacks. It had husbanded its reserves. True, there was a widening current account deficit but there was also a capital account surplus and, as the crisis lengthened, there appeared an increasingly large trade surplus, all combined, more than enough to cover the current account deficit. The last thing needed by the Government of Indonesia, it seemed was money in the form of an IMF bailout. But something was needed to halt the slide of the currency. The only way for Indonesia to solve the crisis appeared to be to try to peg the rupiah at a level affordable by the private sector - not more than Rps 6,000 - 7,000 to the US dollar. Later, in desperation, the Government would flirt with this very scheme.

Meanwhile, the Government was caught. The IMF's 'medicine' did not work and, domestically and internationally, many, if not most people, thought that the Government of Indonesia was itself to blame for this. The Government and its President faced a barrage of criticism and condemnation at home and abroad. Almost nobody, except Sachs, paused to think whether the IMF 'medicine' was appropriate, least of all the IMF, which daily seemed to aspire to new heights of arrogance, backed to the hilt by the leaders of developed countries among its 181 members. By March, the whole world seemed to be lined up behind the IMF against Indonesia. In addition to President Clinton, who promptly dispatched Lawrence Summers to confirm his message in person, President Soeharto received telephone calls from Japanese Prime Minister Hashimoto and German Chancellor, Helmut Kohl, with an overnight trip by Singapore Prime Minister, Goh Chok Tong - their joint objective to impress upon President Soeharto that his Government must take the IMF 'medicine'

In Washington, millionaire publisher and former US presidential candidate, Steve Forbes, was quoted as calling the IMF's policies in Asia "destructive." "Its austerity policies of devaluation and higher taxes are making the Asian economic crisis worse." Reuters rounded up a crescendo of anti-IMF comment from Hong Kong. The most important was that quoted from an article which had been published in the 'Far Eastern Economic Review'. In it, Martin Klor, Director of the International Policy Group of the Third World Network, wrote that the IMF lacked understanding of Asia. Quoting 'analysts' and 'economists' cited in Reuters' report, the 'Jakarta Post' went on in a news story: "Regardless of accusations of cronyism, Governments in this region can, on the whole, boast of balanced budgets, low public debt levels and high savings rates. Rather than the wrecked national economies typical of nation brought under IMF guidance elsewhere, Asia's problems lay in the private sector, with private business responsible for building up mountains of foreign denominated corporate debt. With currencies under attack this debt burden had become unmanageable - and this is the problem that must now be dealt with effectively and urgently." Finally, one economist was quoted as saying: " The IMF has failed."

On this note, on January 11, an IMF team arrived in Jakarta to 'help' Indonesia out of the economic quagmire it found sinking rapidly beneath and around it. Jeffrey Sachs arrived a day later. While the arguments raged between the parties cloistered in Jakarta, ratings agencies announced a slew of further downgrades.

CHAPTER SEVEN

In The Path Of The Battering Ram

In Jakarta, voices were now beginning to be raised against the IMF's 'medicine' and, to make a point, B.J. Habibie, the man soon to be nominated as the Republic's vice-president and a possible presidential successor, took deliberate aim at one of the IMF's sacred cows by insisting publicly that the country's project to design and build aircraft would continue. Although aircraft manufacture would from now on be at the mercy of foreign investors, Habibie was on relatively safe ground. Offshore investors had already poured in too much to IPTN to get out now. And to remove any political doubts, on January 14, the ruling party, GOLKAR, (Golongkan Karya) announced that it would nominate the incumbent president for another term at the March elections. "The nation wants Soeharto", GOLKAR Chairman, Harmoko was quoted as telling reporters. In a somewhat marginal bid to restore confidence in the plummeting currency, the Government backed a 'Love the rupiah' campaign, during which increasing numbers of public figures were seen to be changing their dollars into rupiah. One of the President's daughters, Siti Hardiyanti Rukmana appealed to Indonesians to maintain their faith in the rupiah. She was quoted as saying: "Let's stop the dollar buying spree. Whoever we are, we have to show our love for our own currency, including releasing our dollars." Public and market perceptions of this campaign were cynical.

Almost amusingly, given the IMF's insistence that cancelled projects should stay cancelled, on January 12, the US's CalEnergy protested to the Government of Indonesia about the further postponement of its power station project at Patuha, West

Java. This project was on the off-again on-again list which, on the eve of the arrival of the IMF team in Indonesia, the Government had announced was once again very firmly off, because the huge financing required could undermine the Government's efforts to deal with the crisis. Here was the Washington-based IMF twisting the Government's arm to postpone major projects while a major US corporate insisted they went ahead. The company's chief operating officer in Asia, Donald O'Shei, even threatened the Government with an insurance clause in their joint contract which protected the company against "violation of contract", backed, O'Shei added ominously, "by the US Government."

The IMF team had arrived in town determined to discuss their entire package, from ideology, through the state budget to the promised disbursements of money. The Government of Indonesia was under heavy pressure from the money markets and prominent leaders of free market economies. President Soeharto and his ministers promised the IMF that they would work harder to achieve the reforms already agreed and would review the controversial state budget. "There is no fundamental difference between us and the IMF in implementing the programme," Indonesia's Finance Minister was quoted as saying on January 14, as talks progressed. There was no mention of the IMF insistence on a 1 percent budget surplus.

The money markets seemed to be impressed and for a few days the rupiah hovered with some stability at Rps 10,000 to the US dollar. The 'Jakarta Post' quoted a dealer as saying: "Talks between the world leaders and President Soeharto have set most currencies in the region to strengthen against the American greenback." A sour note was the downgrading of Indonesia's sovereign risk by Thomson Bankwatch. The agency said that recent calls for President Soeharto to resign had greatly increased political uncertainty in Indonesia at a time of mounting economic crisis and even social unrest. In Hong Kong Peregrine Investments Holdings finally declared bankruptcy, accusing Indonesia's unprecedented and unexpected currency meltdown as the main culprit.

For a few days in January 1998, there was a mood of optimism abroad as world leaders and financial experts converged on Jakarta to work with Indonesia's Government to craft the definitive rescue package. More than 120 business 'tycoons' met with Governor Soedradjad to show their support for the Government during the IMF visit. Britain's 'Daily Telegraph' said in a report that: "The world rallied yesterday around President Soeharto of Indonesia..." - January 14, 1998. IMF Managing Director, Michel Camdessus, had arrived in Jakarta and one of this "stern disciplinarian's" first comments, as reported by the 'Jakarta Post,' on January 15, contained the warning: "This new letter of intent will certainly be structured in a way that will give a high incentive to early implementation."

The media reported that the IMF was focusing on three 'targets:' - structural reforms, revising the controversial budget and stabilising the currency. In fact, it is more likely that the Fund discussed all its recommendations to date with the problems created by the draft budget simply being added in. Reforms to the now critically damaged banking sector and an end to 'crony capitalism' were presumably at the top of the list. As to stabilising the currency this was an issue the Fund had never addressed, except with its proposals for long-term reforms.

While the deliberations went on, including a review of Indonesia's draft budget, the 'Jakarta Post' quoted Jeffrey Sachs as saying that criticism of the draft had been "unfairly harsh." Sachs said that the budget had increased 32 percent, but only in nominal terms, thanks both to the collapse of the currency and the hike in interest payments on debt. He argued that the world should help Indonesia to get the rupiah back to the Rps 4,000 to the dollar level before its banking system went into complete default. He also urged the reduction of interest rates.

When it came, on January 15, the announcement of the 50 point Letter of Intent between the Government of Indonesia and the IMF was welcomed by a near deafening chorus. It was hard to see why!

Government revenue was to be increased through the elimination of subsidies on fuel and electricity (fuel alone was ten trillion Rps), better tax enforcement and collection and increased incidence of VAT and the removal of exemptions. This was all positive but would not solve the crisis. It also held some dangers. The subsidisation of kerosene and benzene prices were critically important for the poor and on these President Soeharto refused concessions. Even the subsidy on other fuels he only agreed to remove gradually, in phases, to avoid too sharp an injection of higher prices and costs for electricity and transportation. Indonesia's Investment Fund and Reforestation Fund, (the latter already subject to a scandal of misspending), were to be included within the state budget to ensure accountability. Positive.

Next, restrictions on exports were to be removed - also very positive, along with many tariff restrictions on imports - not so positive. The insistence that Indonesia lift its ban on palm oil, which had only been made to safeguard local supplies, seemed calculated to court disaster. Even as the Agreement was being drawn up, large scale price riots were reported in a number of East Java towns.

All formal and informal restrictive marketing arrangements for cement, paper and plywood, were to be lifted and, while such cartels and arrangements might have kept prices artificially high and increased business costs, there was no evidence that such monopolies had played any role in the current crisis. As before, the IMF's advice seemed more ideological than problem oriented. (In connection with the plywood monopoly, the market was greatly angered when the plywood monopoly - the Indonesian Wood Panel Association or APKINDO - told exporters that they must still pay Rps 50,000 to Apkindo for every cubic metre of plywood exported. The new ruling was not rescinded until March, 1998.)

All agricultural products, including cloves, were to be allowed free internal movement and all district levies on export goods were to be abolished. The Clove Marketing and Bufferstock Agency had been operated by one of President Soeharto's sons, "Tommy," and was due for abolition by June 1998. Unfortunately, in February, the Government appeared to backtrack again - whether it did or not is irrelevant. The Minister of Cooperatives and Small Enterprises announced that farmers would sell their cloves to cooperatives as before, after which the cooperatives would sell the cloves to the Confederation of Primary Cooperative Associations which in turn would sell them to cigarette makers. "This way the clove trade regime will continue," he was quoted as saying in the 'Jakarta Post.' Even in April, the domestic press could still reveal that cigarette manufacturers remained under an "unofficial" obligation to buy cloves from a company allegedly controlled by "Tommy," PT Kembang Cengkeh Nasional (KCN). If not, they could not purchase excise stamps from the Directorate General of Customs and Excise. 'Kontan' quoted one cigarette manufacturer as saying: "The rules of the game are exactly the same. Only the name now is not BPPC (Clove Marketing and Bufferstock Agency) any more." The waters around "Tommy" Soeharto's clove marketing agency were not only murky but exceedingly deep. Was there a deliberate attempt to flout the IMF Agreement or were the new revelations merely part of the patchwork of normal Indonesian life. Cynical foreigners believed the former and it did not help that the Government repeatedly insisted that something had been abolished which even the local media claimed was still functioning or functioning in a modified form.

Some district Levies were abolished while others lingered on. Local officials were notorious for continuing practices which were supposed to have stopped or for identifying new ways of achieving the same objective.

BULOG's monopoly was confirmed as extending only to rice - accounting for an incredible 30 percent of the consumer price index - but the Agency said that it would continue functioning as long as stocks of other commodities lasted. Henceforth the market alone would set prices and the door had been flung wide open to investment and competition in most areas previously controlled by the Logistics Agency. How quickly private sector companies with general importer status could take advantage of this sudden opportunity remained to be seen. In the interim, BULOG carried on much as before, minus its monopoly status. As the crisis intensified in February, the Agency even began supplying basic commodities at below market prices.

In the case of BULOG, the impression of halfheartedness was strengthened when it was announced that a foundation of the agency's employees, backed by investors, would be set up as a new private trading company. Would-be entrants to BULOG's former markets were said to fear that this announcement made it look like business as usual!

As many state enterprises as possible were to be privatised with any remaining brought quickly to profitability. Privatisation, though welcome and positive, other than by ending any Government subventions, could provide no significant contribution to solving the current crisis and, once again, seemed mostly to reflect the IMF's mission to bring free market forces to the world.

The cessation of funds for the Timor car and for aircraft production by IPTN seemed almost gratuitous and to amount to interference in Indonesia's internal affairs. Admittedly these were controversial projects with which by no means everybody or even many in Indonesia agreed, especially the Timor car, but it was Indonesia's sovereign right to decide how to spend its own money.

The Agreement stipulated the full privatisation of banks, tighter bank supervision and the lifting of restrictions on the establishment of branches of foreign banks. This, too, was all very positive except that it omitted the vital stipulation that bank capitalisation should be increased - practically the bedrock of Indonesia's banking problems and an comission of huge proportions. It also omitted any specifics about mergers, presumably a related untackled problem and equally bedrock in the current crisis.

Finally, reflecting the spirit that anything which hinders investment should be removed, Indonesia's retail sector would be opened up for foreign participation, a move hailed by Indonesia's free marketeers but feared by millions of smaller businesses.

The free-falling rupiah appeared to have brought about a panic situation which culminated in what, for Indonesians was the humiliating spectacle of President Soeharto humbly signing the rescue package while Michel Camdessus looked on, with arms folded - like an angry schoolmaster chastising a naughty pupil, a gross insult to a Javanese, especially if this Javanese happens to be President of the world's fourth most populous country and the largest in south Asia. One wonders if Camdessus would have stood over President Clinton or President Chirac in the same way. As the IMF's 'medicine' was seen to fail it was an insult that rankled and festered in the minds of many an Indonesian nationalist. More importantly and significantly, the posture struck by Camdessus was exactly similar to the posture struck by supervisors at plantations, factories and offices during Dutch colonial days.

The signing and what it represented was another milestone in the lengthening list of the IMF's misunderstandings about Indonesia. Committing words to paper in Indonesia endows the words with extraordinary power. Committing words to a paper not only signed by the head of state but seen to be signed by the head of state endows the words and the letter with the status of near omnipotent power. In signing the Agreement himself, Indonesia's Javanese president was signalling that he attached the very highest importance to it and that this would be realised by all parties in its implementation. Traditionally, in Indonesia, even handling such a letter is equivalent to having direct contact with the writer; such a letter, in its handling, merits as much respect as if it were the writer himself. In March, when Stanley Fischer told an Indonesian state television reporter that signing an agreement was not important, he went directly against this aspect of Indonesian culture. A letter and its signing are heavily symbolic - like so much else in Indonesian culture.

The President also announced the setting up of a Council for Economic and Monetary Resilience with himself as head and senior economist, Widjojo Nitisastro, as secretary-general. The council would include all the members of the Monetary Council as well as representatives from the private sector.

Michel Camdessus was as confident as he had looked at the signing 'ceremoney.' He was quoted as telling reporters on the day of the signing: "This revitalised programme is bold and far reaching, addressing all the critical problem areas of the economy and deserving the full support of the international community. I am confident that, if this programme is implemented with the determination and commitment that I myself have seen over the past two days, Indonesia should be able to soon begin to overcome its economic crisis." World Bank President, James Wolfenshon was quoted as saying: "This is a huge step forward in restoring investor confidence." But was it?

The public generally wanted to believe that the IMF deal meant a new lease of life for the rupiah but the markets took a different view and, despite minor ups, stayed doggedly down in quiet trading. Standard & Poor again downgraded Indonesian banks. 'The Times' of London, quoted a Western banker as saying: "I am still pessimistic, especially about Indonesia's short-term prospects. I am not convinced that President Soeharto will implement everything he promised today, and even if he does it will be very painful for this country. If we don't see progress by the end of next week, I think the rupiah could well plunge to below 10,000 (to the US dollar) again. He will have to move extremely quickly this time. A stockbroker economist was quoted as saying: " Mr Soeharto does not have a good track record of reform so I don't think that market confidence will return until we see some concrete steps, particularly in the finance sector."

We must keep in mind that the fundamental cause of the crisis was the market perception that Indonesia could not pay its bills. The loss of confidence this provoked brought about an ever deepening crisis that was Indonesia's alone. And in Indonesia the economic crisis began to trigger social and political crises as well.

On January 17, quoting dealers, Reuters reported from Hong Kong: "People are getting a little jaded by Indonesia. I don't think anyone was paid in the last week from Indonesia and companies aren't even paying their rupiah debt. And what can people do. There is really no legal structure in Indonesia for people to get their money." Former Indonesian Mines and Energy minister, Subroto, wrote on January 19: "The reform package is OK but market players did not respond enthusiastically because they do not see that any of the massive reform measures will address the core problem that caused the monetary crisis - the private sector's huge debts." In world financial centres there was discussion about whether any Government might be prepared to guarantee the debts - reaching a universally negative conclusion. As the Indonesian Government had itself said much earlier, there could be no bailout of private debt. What then was the answer?

On January 15, Reuters had quoted Jake van der Kemp, Equity Strategist at ABN AMRO Hoare Govett Asia as saying: "There is only really one option for Indonesia - a roll-over and a huge write down by foreign banks. This, in the end, is a private sector problem and a lot of it comes down to foreign banks being too eager to lend money to foreign companies they didn't know enough about. It's their fault and they're going to have to take the loss."

Meanwhile, outside the markets, what increasingly seemed to many Indonesians and to a few foreigners like an IMF farce, went on in Jakarta, to the loud approbation of all those same world leaders who had earlier urged President Soeharto to do everything to comply with the IMF's rescue 'medicine.' The

123

strength of the IMF's 'magic' was irresistible, especially among those who really didn't understand the problem.

One who did understand the problem was much maligned Malaysian Prime Minister Mahathir Mohamad, who now arrived in Jakarta to see at first hand what was going on but also to offer a concrete way of dealing with the region's dollar drought. "Let's trade in local currencies only," he offered.

Behind the scenes, Indonesia's soul-searching about what had gone wrong, what had caused the country's near collapse, went on. Most focused on the need to eliminate corruption and nepotism, to promote political empowerment of the people's representatives and enhance accountability and transparency. Many blamed Government "backsliding" in implementing reforms recommended by the IMF as the reason for the deepening and now deeply distressing economic crisis - especially in respect of "Tommy's" clove monopoly and "Bob" Hasan's plywood marketing organisation. Indonesia had agreed to disband the monopolies yet new evidence continually emerged of their ongoing functioning, partially and in other forms.

The general tone of media comment now was: 'Reform or collapse.' Y.B. Mangunwijaya, described as a noted social worker, architect and novelist wrote: "Everybody knows that the best way to accomplish the common and desired goal would be the willingness of the responsible decision makers, or maker, of the past, to step down to make possible the abolition of corruption, collusion and nepotism and transform the whole economic, social and political structure into a better one." In the same journal, on the same day, Omar Halim, from the Centre for Strategic and International Studies wrote: "There are at least four kinds of reform: 1) immediate restructuring of the banking sector to enable it to rationally and efficiently channel financial resources into priority sectors; 2) elimination of monopolies, oligopolies and other restrictive business practices, which have up till now been used to provide privileges to select groups of people; 3) political reform which will enable potential leaders, especially among civilians, who truly reflect the choices of the people, to emerge and take over leadership in accordance with the constitutionally and legally prescribed procedures. The reform measures should also include creating an independent relationship between the executive and legislative bodies and reform of the judicial system by which the judiciary could perform its functions independently of political considerations."

Suddenly it was open season for reform. It no longer mattered whether the reforms were long or short-term, economic or political. A feeling was abroad that Indonesia's whole political and economic infrastructure was rotten and that the rottenness of the politician system had somehow led to the rottenness of the economy. The British 'Economist' was allowed into Indonesia with the front cover showing President Soeharto in a 5-Star army general's uniform and with the headline "Soeharto Step Down." Voicing his thoughts about the upcoming presidential in March 1998, Amien Rais stressed that the single most important goal was transparent, clean and just Government. Though the numbers of the apostles of change willing to speak out publicly was still small, they were growing, as the crisis made people increasingly desperate and forced them to look for some new scapegoat for their woes.

Majority of Indonesia's 'establishment' still held the view that President Soeharto was still Indonesia's "best son" and that to change leaders in the midst of the country's worst crisis in decades would be unwise in the extreme. Several ministers spoke out against the timing of political reform and in defence of President Soeharto. "Is there any guarantee that things will get better by Replacing Pak Harto," the State Minister of Youth Affairs and Sport, Hayono Isman, was quoted as asking rhetorically.

They seemed hardly likely to get much worse. The most unpalatable aspect of the new deal struck with the IMF was bowing to the Fund's insistence that there should be zero economic growth. Such a scenario posed very great risks and dangers in a country with an already huge underemployed and unemployed population, with over two million new job-seekers entering the market each year. Insistence on a budget surplus threatened to increase the risks. The removal of subsidies, especially fuel, was also danger-packed. The IMF's insistence that the inflation rate should be fixed at 20 percent was also frightening to Indonesians - although, actually, probably still too low, given the depth of the rupiah's devaluation. Some foreign experts were already predicting inflation of 60 to 90 percent. Price rises in Indonesia could easily trigger violent riots. The Fund's insistence on fixing the rupiah exchange rate at Rps 5,000 to the US dollar was about as low as it was thought safe to go if overseas debts were to have any chance of being repaid and corporate and bank solvency maintained.

On January 20, Government critic and IMF 'believer', Kwik Kian Gie, wrote in his front page column in the 'Jakarta Post': "I must admit that economist, Rizal Ramli, is right when he said that I was starting to doubt the merits of the IMF's intervention." In Jakarta, small groups of students began demonstrating against the IMF. One banner read: "Don't sell out the honour of the nation to the IMF." Kwik said that the markets lack of confidence in the IMF's recommendation had kept the rupiah down at Rps 9,000 to one US dollar, holding out the near-certain prospect of debt default, bankruptcies, bank failures and large scale unemployment. He said: "There has been no mention of how the rupiah might be shored up in the short-term."

The aid package assembled by the IMF now totalled US$43 billion but Kwik said there was no indication of what this money was actually for or whether it would be used to support the rupiah. He went on: "In some people's eyes the Letter of Intent signed, created an impression that the IMF merely wants to take over Indonesia's sovereignty while overcoming the economic crisis without distributing any money. This has been reinforced by the assigning of an IMF executive to the Economic and Monetary Resilience Council.....if there is no clear explanation about the planned utilisation of the aid, we suspect that the IMF might not have any plans to disburse the US$43 billion but merely wants Indonesia to achieve a current account surplus in 1999 at the cost of the extraordinary suffering of its people - which may also include social unrest. if such suspicions are true, the IMF's involvement will cause deep concern because it will be seen as being dictated to be a foreign party. Moreover, the ownership of good domestic companies may have to be transferred to foreign investors. Many people have told me that they were sad to see Camdessus standing with his arms folded as he witnessed the President sign the Agreement imposing hardships on Indonesians but offering no significant assistance from the IMF. That gave a distinct impression that the President had 'lost a battle."

Weeks later, on March 26, the 'Jakarta Post' published an article by Dr Mark Woodward and Dr Hermawan Sulistyo from Arizona State University and the Indonesian Institute of

Sciences respectively, in which they quoted a January issue of the domestic 'Suara Merdeka:' The publication compared the IMF and the Dutch East India Company. IMF officials were compared to agents of the Dutch company who imposed "political contracts" on 18th Century Javanese monarchs. These contracts were a form of indirect colonial rule which ultimately led to almost complete foreign domination of economic and political life."

Another prominent critic of the Government, Amien Rais, said in a similar front page column in the 'Jakarta Post' that if he was elected President of the Republic of Indonesia he would: "...restore the country's political and economic sovereignty." Speaking in support of greater democracy, 'clean' and transparent Government, more effective laws and, to achieve them, a complete change in the country's political leadership, Rais nevertheless wrote of the IMF agreement: "Although the package is within the reform spirit it has many weaknesses. It projects zero economic growth which means that the economy won't be able to absorb the estimated three million new job seekers this year. The high rate of company failures will also increase the unemployment rate nationwide. The economic contraction resulting from reduced Government spending, combined with an expected inflation rate of 20 percent, will substantially cut the people's purchasing power. I fear that people in the low income groups will vent their anger at the Government when inflation begins to bite and as soon as the Government goes ahead with its plan to increase fuel prices." (From April 1, 1998.)

While these thoughts were being penned in Jakarta, in 'The Times' of London, England, Janet Bush was writing: "The IMF knows very well that the American banking system was saved and nursed back to health after the 1987 stock market crash because the US Federal Reserve pumped masses of liquidity into the economy and kept interest rates low for a long time. It is no mistake that the very opposite is being imposed on Asia. At the same time as the IMF is ensuring a brutal shake-out of Asian financial institutions, it is demanding that Asian Governments open their financial markets to foreign investment at their point of maximum vulnerability and when assets are cheapest. Lest anyone dismiss this as a silly conspiracy theory, just remember the speech that Mickey Kantor, former US Commerce Secretary, made to the Confederation of British Industry this month." (December, 1997) he told his audience that the troubles of the 'tiger' economies should be seized as a golden opportunity for the West to reassert its commercial interests. When countries seek help from the IMF, he said, America and Europe should use the IMF as a battering ram to gain advantage. The pact that Asian Governments have made with the IMF is positively Faustian. They get billions of dollars in the short-term but lose control of their destinies. The 'tigers' will emerge from the current crisis declared and owned by the West."

In Malaysia, economist, Yen Yee Chong, was quoted as calling the IMF: "Uncle Sam's flunky, sent out to promote America's foreign policy" - financial, commercial and political. The 'International Herald Tribune,' in an edition of the paper available in Malaysia, wrote of: "The West, and its agent, the International Monetary Fund."

The world's largest economy, the US, is also the IMF's biggest shareholder providing 18 percent of the resources and holding 18 percent of the votes. From his comments, President Clinton seems to have genuinely believed that the crisis was only a "glitch." In his defence of more funding for the IMF, he spoke about the harm to US interests if Asian economies collapsed and were unable to purchase US exports. However, it is by no means so clear that the IMF took a similar apparently innocent point of view.

Could it be the case that the crisis which swept substantial parts of Asia beginning in mid-1997 seemed to offer the global money men a golden and unprecedented opportunity to smash down doors at which they and many others outside the region, including the United States, had been battering for decades, but with limited success? Was the clear ideological bias of the IMF's rescue packages an indication that this was in deed the case? And was the Agency prepared to be completely ruthless once Asia was on its knees at its feet, in the case of Indonesia, to the point of delivering hardship to millions and destabilising not only the country but the region?

Could there have been even more to it than simply grasping a heaven sent opportunity to turn some one else's economic tragedy into a triumph for the West and in particular the US? After all, as Peregrine Investments Holdings' Chairman, Philip Tose was quoted as saying in the January 28 edition of

'Newsweek', in a global world, wouldn't the US be the sole global player with others, such as the Europeans, filling in the niches? Sure enough, by January regional publications were describing Camdessus as "The man who is now Asia's most powerful banker."

In the case of Indonesia, could it have been true that once it had begun to be argued by the IMF that economic reform could not proceed without political reform, political figures in Washington began to see an opportunity to topple a regime that the Democrats especially saw as anti-democratic and repressive.

On January 22, the 'Far Eastern Economic Review' carried a story from Deborah Lutterbeck in Washington. The first paragraph said: "Less than 24 hours after US President Clinton phoned Indonesia's President Soeharto on January 9, Congressman, Patrick Kennedy, fired of a letter to the White House. I recognise the fears that Indonesia is headed toward both economic recession and political upheaval ....but .... this is a unique opportunity to affect political and human rights in Indonesia." On January 23, 'Asiaweek' quoted an analyst with Jardine Flemming as saying: "Bill Clinton has been waiting for a defining moment of his presidency, something that he'd be remembered for. Well, the Asian crisis can be that moment. rescue these debt-ridden countries in return for more open markets and complete deregulation. In the end, it will boost trade, expand US ties with Asia, create jobs there and also do the same back in America."

Did toppling the New Order Government, and especially President Soeharto, become the real name of the combined IMF, US and Western game in Indonesia, backed by loyal allies in Asia, whose eyes were perhaps more focused on money than on real politik? Or perhaps more on real politik than anything else, self-interest being a powerful motivator?In any case, in a crisis about which nobody knew the cause or the solution the IMF might have been right. Plus, there was always its 'magic' to be reckoned with. At this stage not a single sovereign voice disputed the might and right of the IMF.

Understanding US policy was by no means easy. Like everything in life it was developing and changing. There can be no doubt about the Treasury's agenda - in support of the IMF. The US was enjoying a budget surplus and an unprecedentedly healthy economy. Why, then, should the US Treasury be so steamed up about Asia? The answer? The US's huge trade deficit. The US trade deficit with Japan up to August, 1997, was US$ 35 billion and with China US$31 billion. By the end of the first quarter of 1998 the US's goods deficit with the world rose to a record high. Many of these suppliers, notably Japan, had refused to open up their markets to the satisfaction of the US. A persistently weak Japanese economy had shown little ability to absorb increased imports and earned constant needling from the US to revitalise growth. Did the Treasury now see an ideal moment to kick down some doors, thereby holding out the promise of a reduced deficit to match the federal Government's record in slashing the deficit?

There can be no doubt about the concerns of the US military that an ally might be on the brink of collapse and no longer able to make its normal contribution to regional security, including keeping open and free, the strategic Strait of Malacca, close to Singapore. Believing that it President Soeharto fell, the military would take over, the US cannily exploited a loophole to defy a US Congress ban on training Indonesian troops - exposed by the 'New York Times' on March 18, 1998.

The State Department feared that the Treasury and the IMF between them were beggaring Indonesia with the consequent threat of mass misery in Indonesia and lost orders and contracts for US business.

As head of the world's richest state, President Clinton seemed to take the view that, morally, Indonesia must be helped - perhaps the help his campaign finances were alleged to have received from Indonesia's Lippo Group helped tip the scale. As a Democrat he seemed to feel that such help should only be forthcoming if Indonesia took steps to put its house in order first, meaning an end to corruption and, by inference, in a more equitable and transparent overall environment, the beginning of better prospects for civil rights. In February his Government slammed Indonesia's human rights record, especially its "tight grip on the political process" which " denied citizens the ability to change their leader democratically." - 'Jakarta Post', February 2, 1998. Whichever way one looked at it, setting aside the concerns of the military, the thread of philanthropy was thin and US interest writ large. Indonesia, on the other hand, was hoping for simple, no-strings assistance. As the US and others knew well, 'strings' were always deeply resented by Indonesia and adding them could sometimes lead to cancelled contracts, such as for the F-16 fighter jets, cancelled projects and the expulsion of personnel.

On the money market, as if to give the lie to the IMF's claim that its 'medicine' would cure Indonesia, continuing high demand for dollars dragged down the rupiah still further, on January 20, reaching Rps10,500 to one US dollar. Neither in the Agreement nor anywhere else had the IMF done anything to tackle this central problem. The Head of ING Barings Regional Economic and Debt Research Unit, Chris Tinker, was quoted as saying at a Bank conference in Jakarta: "Restoring confidence (in the rupiah) requires clarification of what is going to be done with the private debts. Without this clarification the bear rally will continue."

It was not an easy problem to solve. Much if not most of the debt had been negotiated by Indonesian borrowers directly with foreign lenders as opposed to via or with the knowledge of the Central Bank. An array of lending instruments were used. Theoretically, this left the borrowers on their own to negotiate the best terms they could with their creditors. Horst Kohler, German Chancellor, Helmut Kohl's envoy to Jakarta, while backing the IMF's reform package, was quoted in the 'Jakarta Post' on January 21 as saying that a solution to Indonesia's private debt was vital to take pressure off the rupiah.

The debt problem would not be easy to solve from another point of view. As the rupiah went down the value of the debt went up. Quoting a report from G. K. Goh Research, Singapore's 'Straits Times' said: "A full repayment of the short-term debt could generate enough dollar demand to send the rupiah past the Rps 20,000 level and deplete Bank Indonesia's limited foreign exchange resources. At this juncture, a debt roll-over plan is essential."

ABN-AMRO's, Cees de Koning, was quoted by Britain's 'Financial Times' as saying: "If you demand all the money back you are talking about almost the full liquidation of Indonesian industry." He added that for lack of a bankruptcy law and proper procedures defaults were the only likely outcome. David Folkerts-Landau, Head of Emerging Markets Research at Deutsche Morgan Grenfell, was quoted by Reuters as saying in London that nothing short of an immediate write-down of Indonesia's offshore debts would suffice. He said that the write-down should be achieved with foreign creditors and the IMF. He also spoke hyperthetically about debt rescheduling and even exchange controls. (Folkerts-Landau estimated non-performing domestic loans at a staggering 40 percent.) He was quoted as describing Indonesia's problem at the end of January as: "more of a solvency than a liquidity problem." The World Bank's, Dennis de Tray, was quoted as saying on January 23 that Indonesia's economy was "close to paralyses" and that it no longer had a "functioning financial system." - Straits Times, January 23, 1998.

Again, the IMF appeared to offer no solutions. Yet, since November, foreign experts had been quietly busy in Jakarta working on bank reforms and "corporate debt". While the Government of Indonesia took a barrage of flak for its 'failure' to implement bank and financial sector reforms fast enough, the IMF and other involved international agencies appeared tight lipped about whatever it was they were doing. It might have helped the Government and Indonesia if they had issued regular interim reports. Eventually, a small bottom-of-the-page item appeared in the 'Jakarta Post' from Reuters saying that, according to CNN, Stanley Fischer had said on the programme 'Moneyline' that the IMF, the Government of Indonesia, the World Bank, the Asian Development Bank were putting together a package that "will reassure depositors and stabilise the banking system." Fischer was also quoted as saying: "Together with the Indonesians, we're thinking about next steps in dealing with the corporate debt problem in Indonesia." At this stage, what the package was or the measures were, remained a mystery! Until now (April, 1998) they are a mystery!

At long last, the Government of Indonesia took a more concrete initiative regarding the offshore private debt by appointing former minister, Radius Prawiro, to head a special team to assist the private sector resolve their problems. Mar'ie Muhammad was known to be frustrated with the private sector and pushing both for the debt issue to be resolved and also for mergers and acquisitions to rescue ailing companies. Announcing the establishment of the new team on January 21, the Finance Minister was quoted as stressing that the private debt was complex and difficult to manage as it has been negotiated directly with foreign lenders. This was true, but it was a pity that the Minister's statement seemed so lame and reluctant at a time when the market craved sight of a dynamic team working towards a rapid solution. PR has never been Indonesia's strong suit!

By the end of the third week of January, dollars were so scarce and/or expensive that Reuters reported from London that Indonesian banks had been repaying dollar debt in rupiah - further driving down the currency, which on the day of the report fell to Rps12,000 to one US dollar. Among London dealers, there was now said to be talk of the possibility of Indonesia being forced to impose a damaging debt moratorium - or else for the Government to take the step it had steadfastly said that it wouldn't, and guarantee some or all of the debt. Markets and dealers were thrashing around in the dark for solutions.

Meanwhile, Standard & Poor were quoted as saying that Indonesian banks were in such poor shape that they needed US$15 billion in fresh capital. The Agency forecast non-performing loans to rise to 20 percent with a corresponding erosion of the quality of bank assets. The previous week they had downgraded the ratings of 15 banks, some of them state banks, some private banks already locked in merger talks, some still struggling to survive alone. The Agency was quoted as saying: " Given the scarcity of private sector capital in Indonesia, recapitalisation funds must be sourced either from the Indonesian Government or from private investors." Needless to say, private investors were only interested in banks or any other type of company that seemed a) likely to survive and b) to have good growth prospects - difficult criteria to meet in Indonesia at this time. Of course, this did not mean that they would not be interested - ever. When the time was right and the conditions were right offshore investors were poised to return.

Plunged into increasingly desperate straits by the collapse of the rupiah, the pace of bank mergers was beginning to gain momentum - not because the Government had ordered it, or because the banks had suddenly decided to give into the Governor Soedradjad's persuasion, but because there was no alternative. There were now firm rumours that that the Government planned to force mergers by raising the minimum capital requirement and other measures. Among the ongoing difficulties, to owner vanity and conflicting market interests, could be added the problem of how to price each other's shares. Arguments were long and hard. Even by mid-March, according to the Chairman of

Indonesia's private banking association, only 35 private banks had actually succeeded in making merger plans.

The Bakrie Group announced the merger of its four banks, Bank Bukopin said it would join with Bank Duta, both the Tirtamas and Ramako groups planned to merge their several banks in to one each respectively, Bank Indonesia International began a merger process with Bank Dagang Nasional Indonesia, Bank Tiara Asia and two other smaller banks affiliated to Bank Dagang Nasional Indonesia. Bank Danamon, later to be fruitlessly courted by Bank Central Asia, also began a flirtation with Lippo Bank.

President Soeharto certainly realised that steps had to be taken quickly to halt the rupiah melt down. And he knew that he had to give the world some of if not all of the things the world said would alone solve the problem. Everyone agreed that an important key to solving the crisis was restoring international confidence. If markets lacked confidence in Indonesia they had to be shown that Indonesia and its President meant business. Against a backdrop of unprecedented criticism of himself and his regime from the people of Indonesia, President Soeharto also had to show his countrymen that he meant business. Only one week after the signing ceremony with IMF boss Camdessus, President Soeharto announced orders to implement an impressive list of reforms:

With 16 instruments he:
* Eliminated exemptions for import duty, VAT and luxury sales tax relating to the Timor car.
* Abolished the clove monopoly
* Liberalised the import of ships
* Exempted from luxury sales tax locally assembled automobiles with 60 percent local content
* Permitted the products of foreign industrial investors to be sold in the retail market.
* Allowed foreign trading companies to operate in the retail sector.
* Banned the state aircraft maker from obtaining state funds or state guaranteed loans.
* Revoked the local content rule on dairy products.
* Revoked the forced growing of sugar cane in certain areas of Java

* Freed foreign investment in oil palm plantations.
Other new measures:
* Granted autonomy to the Central Bank.
* Freed plywood producers and wood products manufactures to sell directly to foreign buyers.
* Banned the collection of levies on exports.
* Allowed the free movement of farm products within Indonesia.
* Restricted the activities of the state Logistics Agency, BULOG, to rice.

The majority of these IMF-inspired measures were ideological and aimed at promoting best free market practices. The removal of subsidies from goods being sold to people who hardly handled money plus opening up the entire retail sector to foreign penetration were outright harmful. NONE provided any kind of solution to the problem of the plunging rupiah!

Writing from London on January 26, William Keegan wrote: "One of the problems the Asian situation has highlighted is that the IMF does not know how to handle crisis in the private sector."

How true! But how come so many people seemed to think they did?

The markets agreed with Keegan. Next day the rupiah shot down to close to Rps 17,000 to the US dollar. Share prices fell by almost 5 percent. As usual, the problem was massive dollar buying. And the dollars were now in even shorter supply as offshore banks operating out of the financial centres of Singapore and Hong Kong choked off the supply for fear of a banking collapse in Indonesia. The 'Jakarta Post' reported dealers as urging, once again, that some solution be found to the problem of the offshore private debt.

Within Indonesia, dollars were in demand by off-shore debtors and the legions who had lost confidence in their own currency. Also, increasingly, by foreign banks and securities investors, eager to reduce their rupiah exposure. In fact, if the usually reliable Kwik Kian Gie is to be believed, Indonesia's domestic demand for dollars was mainly from foreigners and spooked non-corporates. On January 27, based on a study of market transactions, he reported that the total of dollar transactions had declined from US$1,5 billion in August 1997 to US$463 million during the first nine days of January. The usually cautious Kwik went on to sketch a scenario in which parties hostile to Indonesia could use quite small sums of money in thin trading to bring down the rupiah. He concluded: "Such an operation would be costly and the party responsible may have lost money by its operation even though its losses would not exceed its (notional) US$100 million capital. So, the question is, who could it be? I am sure no individual would be willing to take such actions. But for a political group in a foreign country, which has certain political goals, such an operation would be far less expensive than the old-style operations of the CIA, which used to send personnel to kill targets in other countries. The recent development of sophisticated technology has made it easier and cheaper to destabilise someone who is in power" - Jakarta Post', January 27, 1998.

Even before the rupiah shot down to Rps 17,000 to a-dollar, international dealers were firmly of the opinion that urgent steps absolutely must be taken to halt and reverse the fall of the rupiah. In London, 'The Sunday Times' published an analysis by Michael Sheridan and David Smith which quoted SocGen Crosby's Nilesh Jasani as saying: "We are at a point of dramatic action." A paper co-authored by Jasani and Manu Bhaskaran suggested Indonesia and other countries in the region might have to abandon floating currencies for pegs or capital controls.The paper went on to say: " At current levels the economic damage that could be caused by the market has reached proportions that cannot be tackled by simple liberalisation of foreign ownership rules or monetary/fiscal tightening. Governments, most particularly in Indonesia, and to an extent in Thailand and Malaysia, need to not only stem the fall but pull the currencies back up by at least 20 percent for economic survival."

Later in the month, it was easy to get the impression from the media that President Soeharto was the only man thinking about implementing a Currency Board, flying in the face of all 'expert' advice, but this was far from being the case. Many of those involved in the markets could see plainly that, unless the collapse of the rupiah could be stemmed, and stemmed quickly, Indonesia could collapse. President Soeharto and his Government were painfully aware of this. The IMF and its backers were apparently not, or perhaps they too had listened to or read the speech given by Mickey Kantor!

Four days after announcing the Agreement with the IMF, President Soeharto stressed that the deal did not mean the end either of Indonesia-built aircraft or of an Indonesian national car. From now on they would simply find funding from private sources. Sports and Youth Minister, Hayono Isman, was quoted as saying, after a meeting with the President that the Government had long wanted the ability to build a national car, instead of paying the very high price for foreign technology assembled in Indonesia. Indonesia-made small aircraft were also common sense in the world's largest archipelago.

Respected analyst and ABN-AMRO Bank Country Manager, Cees de Koning wrote on January 23 that after careful reading, he had concluded that the Agreement between Indonesia and the IMF was only half a programme. He said: "The IMF programme can be seen as half a programme since it does not directly address the fundamental question of how to keep Indonesian companies in positive foreign currency cash flow positions. The IMF programme for Indonesia addresses many structural reforms, including for the banking sector. But since it is designed to enhance the country's economic efficiency over time, how many companies will be left to take advantage of it? The IMF makes foreign currency loans available to the Government, but these funds are not meant to go to the private sector. The funds are meant to support the Government to raise confidence in the rupiah. Maybe it is not within the IMF's duties to maintain the financial health of the Indonesian private sector, but, in order to get the country back on its feet, the private sector's crisis should get at least equal priority, if not higher, than the structural reforms. A programme for both is needed. Over time, getting companies back on their feet leads to a much faster return to healthy economic growth rates, low inflation and a much stronger rupiah."

Below his article, in the 'Letters' column H.M.T. Oppusunggu wrote in an open letter to Michel Camdessus: "If one examines the (IMF) agreements 50 points more closely, however, one would be immediately struck by their lack of coherence. They are a far cry from being one integrated entity. Neither do they convey any picture of an economic or monetary policy in terms of a series of properly coordinated measures and instruments aimed at the pursuit of clearly defined aims. The agreement leads us nowhere with respect to the use of the US$43 billion loan and the envisaged reform of the financial system. The very few concrete actions in the industrial sector are like drops in the ocean. They do not represent elements in a scheme for the restructure of industries.

"For 1998, the agreement seems to provide certain items out of the blue: In quantitive terms a zero rate of growth for the economy to be accompanied by 20 percent inflation. An exchange rate of Rps 5,000 to the (US) dollar was also foreseen. No clues whatever were provided as to how these targets were to be arrived at. No quantitive estimates were given concerning business failures, and shutdowns which, in turn, would add to the ranks of the already huge army of the unemployed. The projected high rate of inflation would no doubt substantially reduce the income of the work force and civil servants who, for the last decade, have been paid an extremely low salary. Again, the cascading price increases would badly cut overall consumer demand and would create a fall in output. All these downturns would be happening, not due to faulty business practices or recessionary tendencies from abroad, but solely from the faulty exchange rate of the rupiah.

"The letter of intent is nothing but verbiage......All along our people have placed the IMF on a high pedestal since it is thought to have all the top experts in monetary and foreign exchange affairs. Our actual experience so far has shown that the IMF office in Jakarta has been acting as if it has its eyes closed......."

On Friday, January 23, the Finance Minister presented the 1998-99 draft budget to the House of Representatives, revised in line with IMF forecasts and requirements. Really, there were no surprises, not even in the response of the market which, said the 'Jakarta Post', quoting a dealer: "....remains cool ....as the market is largely concerned with the mounting private sector external debt." The fact that the IMF had quietly climbed down from its insistence on a 1 percent budget surplus seemed to get lost in the shuffle. Britain's 'Financial Times' quoted Stanley Fischer as saying: "It wouldn't make economic sense for it (the budget) to be in surplus under the circumstances. The IMF never insisted on the budget remaining independent of the state of the economy. I think it's reasonable to assume...the economy is not growing as rapidly in 1998 as we assumed two months ago." The new budget had no positive impact on the market and the rupiah stuck at around Rps15,000 to the US dollar.

The 'Jakarta Post' said in its editorial: "The Government has stubbornly resisted calls to bail out these debtors, which include some of the country's largest business groups. It is a Catch 22 situation. Bailing them out is politically unacceptable, but it is economically desirable - if not to save the companies, at least to save hundreds of thousands , and probably millions of jobs. The Government has only been willing to assist in renegotiating the debts, but not beyond that. Now, with its budget revised, perhaps there is another compelling reason for the Government to address the corporate debt one way or another, and to bring the exchange rate down to the targeted level. It is not only in the interest of the Government to have a stable currency. The volatile rupiah makes it difficult for any company to do business, let alone plan ahead. The Government is already going half way with economic reforms and budget revision. All these endeavours would come to nought if it fails to address the other half of the problem."

Actually, there had been few public and detectable calls upon the Government to pay the private sector's debts. Anyone knowing Indonesia can imagine a public outcry had that been the case. In turning its back on paying the debts the Government was doubtless correct - especially since in paying them the Government would have acquired the burden of the debt itself and under very disadvantageous repayment terms. But the desperation reflected in the leader can be well understood. Sure enough, soon afterwards, calls for a Government bailout began to appear in the media.

Earlier, de Koning had proposed, not that the debt be repaid by the Government, but that an Indonesian Credit Clearing Corporation be set up, in essence, to reschedule many of the loans, perhaps over a period as long as eight years. De Koning estimated that Indonesian corporates had raised so much offshore credit, repayable in such an impossibly short time frame that it was literally impossible to pay off on time, or anywhere near on time. It was such a pity that Mr. de Koning's audience could not embrace world leaders and media personnel who were telling President Soeharto that if only he implemented the IMF's "half-a-package" everything would soon be all right! In the world at large, the much better known George Soros suggested the establishment of an International Credit Insurance Corporation to act in concert with the IMF and, for a fee, guarantee international loans. A limit would be set to the guarantee available to each participating country, based on its fundamentals - i.e. how much it could reliably afford.

The IMF's iron man, Michel Camdessus, was quoted by Reuters as saying in Brussels, with far more complacency than anyone in Indonesia could ever have afforded: "I think that over time the Indonesian programme should lead to a strengthening of the rupiah as well as a strengthening of the economy in general." In Jakarta it couldn't have been more obvious that the programme was not working! And the more it failed, the more politicians and reporters blamed the Government and especially the President. The rupiah had collapsed, all US dollar lines of credit to local banks had been cut, very few Indonesian letters of credit were being honoured and foreign denominated loans were not being serviced. Insolvency, prices and unemployment were all rising.

CHAPTER EIGHT

Saving The Rupiah
And The Banks

At the end of January, alarmed lest Indonesia's export trade grind to a halt, President Soeharto appealed to the Government of Indonesia's largest trading partner, Japan, to help restore the confidence of Japanese banks in letters of credit issued in Indonesia. About half of Indonesia's exports include imports. 'Bisnis Indonesia' reported that not only Japanese banks but all foreign banks would only accept "sight LCs" from Indonesia. In other words, no cash, no goods. If Indonesia's export trade halted, a major still-viable source of foreign exchange would dry up, threatening not only the national economy but the solvency of exporters themselves. A response was more than a month in coming, after which, Japan said that it would indeed be prepared to implement a trade insurance scheme relating to Indonesian imports from Japan.

Singapore Prime Minister, Goh Chok Tong, had earlier suggested to President Soeharto that Singapore might join with others to help guarantee Indonesian LCs, aiming at creating a fund worth about US$20 billion. On February 12 Reuters reported from Singapore that the Republic's Government had pledged US$2.5 billion to underwrite an Indonesian trade finance guarantee, to be subtracted from the funds already offered to Indonesia as part of the IMF 'rescue' package. Later the amount of money for this purpose was pushed up to US$3 billion, to be used to guarantee Singapore export credits to Indonesia. A further US$2 billion would be made available to guarantee third party goods passing through Singapore to Indonesia. The scheme would be administered by the Singapore-based ECICS Credit

Insurance Ltd. Subsequently, Australia and the US promised credit guarantees and Germany and The Netherlands were expected to follow suit. However, other than follow-through from Singapore and the US, little else actually happened.

The US offer could only be used to import specific items from the US including, cotton, corn, wheat floor, meat, rice and soybeans and only if carried in US-flagged ships. Australia was upset because it felt that the US might be using the crisis to encroach on Australia's traditional markets in Indonesia. In March, 1998, the Chairman of the Indonesian Importers Association, Amirudin Saud was quoted as saying that few of the pledges made by developed countries to restore confidence in Indonesia's letters of credit had been honoured. The 'Jakarta Post' quoted him as saying somewhat bitterly: " They mustn't make promises that they can't keep." Analysts felt that the pledge givers were holding back, pending Indonesia's full implementation of the package agreed with the IMF.

As an alternative, Cees de Koning suggested identifying and designating up to 20 of Indonesia's banks as "Trade Finance Banks", granting pre-export and post import financing in US dollars or other convertible currencies. The Trade Finance Banks would be guaranteed by Bank Indonesia and ultimately by the Government.

On February 9, 1998, the Government guaranteed all letters of credit raised at Indonesian domestic banks. Bank Indonesia also agree to promote its long standing pre-shipment and post-shipment credit facilities to provide liquidity for exporters. Since exporters were also often importers, and a problem which had developed for importers in a very short space of time was the very high foreign exchange trading margin, forcing importers to buy dollars at very high levels while the exchange rate for exporters was set at low levels. Traders were losing out.

Within Indonesia there was a mounting tide of criticism of the management of the banking system and the role of the Central Bank. One critic described the Bank as a "lame duck." Outside Indonesia there was considerable doubt about the policy of mergers, the general tenor of the skepticism being that the merger of several unsound banks would only result in one unsound bank. In Hong Kong, Reuters quoted the President of BankWatch Asia, Philippe Dalhaise, as saying that the only steps which could restore Indonesia's banking system were foreign investment and Government protection of small depositors, while allowing insolvent banks to fail. Indonesians themselves wondered if merger alone could be effective without drastic improvements in bank regulation and supervision by Bank Indonesia.

Summing up the point the country had reached in terms of its banking system an editorial in the 'Jakarta Post' on January 27 said: "The situation is already quite critical. Domestic depositors have now shunned most private, national banks, preferring to put their savings in foreign bank branches or offshore banks. Another devastating condition is the tendency among many foreign banks to stop honouring letters of credit issued by most Indonesian banks. Letters of credit are the wheels of international trade and if these wheels stop rolling, the doors of international trade would eventually close to our companies precisely at a time when we are severely strapped for foreign exchange to get out of the current crisis. It is not an exaggeration to say that most of our banks are now living on borrowed time. Unless the Government acts firmly and quickly on the overall restructuring of the financial sector, as stipulate in the reinforced reform package agreed with the International Monetary Fund on Jan. 15, our economy is in for a deeper crisis from which it may take more than a decade to recover."

That day, the Government announced that for a period of two years, up to January 31, 2000, it would guarantee all deposits and obligations of Indonesia's banks, except foreign bank branches. The guarantee was announced by the Finance Minister and, after a meeting with President Soeharto, IMF Asia-Pacific Deputy Director, Bijan Aghevli, was quoted by the 'Jakarta Post' as saying: "With this guarantee in place, we expect that confidence in the banking system will begin to revive soon." Luis Luis, from Scudder Stevens and Clark was quoted by Reuters as commenting in New York: "The big error is that the Indonesian Government did not do it (guarantee deposits and obligations) sooner."

The hope was that the guarantee would restore public confidence in the banking system, head-off instability in the system, as well as assure foreign vendors and creditors that Indonesia's LCs would be honoured. Clearly, the guarantee had the blessing of the IMF, a crucial source of additional funds if the

143

guarantee drained the Government's coffers dry. Aghevli explained that the guarantee was expected to cost the Government about 10 to 12 percent of Gross Domestic Product. There was no indication of how this fitted into the recently announced revised budget. The guarantee of deposits was welcome. As Mar'ie Muhammad said: "This means that the public can now rest assured that their bank deposits are now completely safe and sound."

Well meant though it was, and targeted squarely at the menacing problem of the failure of foreign banks to recognise Indonesian letters of credit, market analysts were quick to spot a very serious weakness - the Government guarantee of liabilities. Reuters quoted a New York banking source as saying: " It's like signing a blank cheque. The claims and contingent claims could add up to some huge numbers." The source was quoted as saying that the new commitment smacked of "hollowness" unless there was a clear limitation of liabilities.

Three months later, the ECONIT Advisory group on Indonesia, was to call for the scrapping of the blanket guarantee which Director, Rizal Ramli, called a new "time bomb." ECONIT suggested the guarantee be replaced by a deposit protection scheme.

An Indonesian Bank Restructuring Agency was established, similar to Cees de Koning's clearing house for private debt, except that the new Agency would take over ailing banks, clean them up and sell whatever was left to private or foreign buyers. To assist this all restrictions were removed on foreign bank ownership in Indonesia. Of course, foreign investors would now be able to purchase equity in any and all banks of their choice. Further steps were promised to improve disclosure, contract enforcement, bankruptcy proceedings, obtaining and realising collateral and financial instruments.

Calls from the domestic and foreign business community, from the overseas banking and financial services industry and from media commentators, for the reform of the banking system had now reached deafening levels. The IMF had pointed out the weakness in Indonesia's banking system the previous June but seven months later precious little had happened save for some probably panic-driven mergers, more designed to rescue ailing banks than strengthen the system. Even now, the new measures did not represent reform. Worse still, a guarantee introduced with such patently good intentions seemed likely to exhaust the Government treasury by being completely open-ended with respect to bank liabilities.

To relieve pressure on the rupiah, Radius Prawiro's task force announced that it would seek a voluntary, temporary freeze on the servicing of the interest and principal of corporate offshore debt. A steering committee of creditors and a steering committee of debtors was being prepared to work together to try to resolve the problem. Committee members included: Anthony Salim of the Salim Group, The Nin King of the Argo Manunggal Group and Rachmat Gobel of the National Gobel Group.He revealed that his team had identified 228 companies experiencing difficulty servicing their debt. The Government stressed that this was not a debt moratorium and that companies which could meet their commitments would do so. Steering Committee spokesman, David Brougham, Group Executive Director of the Standard Chartered Bank, was quoted as saying in Singapore that he thought that it would take a year to sort out the debt. Other foreign banks thought to be assisting the committee were: ABN-AMRO, Citibank, Bank of America, Deutsche Bank, Societe Generale, Bank of Tokyo-Mitsubishi, Development Bank of Singapore and United Overseas Bank, also of Singapore. In Jakarta, the rupiah strengthened to Rps 11,000 to the US dollar, showing clearly the direction of market interests and concerns. The work of the steering committee, in effect, to try to renegotiate and roll-over a substantial portion of the private offshore debt was certainly feasible, if not immediate in its outcome.

With Indonesia's long Muslim holiday, Lebaran, beginning on January 30, in Indonesia, the Government and people alike hoped they had finally got things right and that the cataclysmic fall of the rupiah would finally be halted in its tracks. Markets would reopen on February 2 . Lebaran is the most important holiday in Indonesia, Traditionally, it lasted for two weeks, at least, and for many people it still does. During this period, the normally traffic-clogged, pollution-choked streets of major cities empty and quieten as millions of people stream home to celebrate the end of the month-long Muslim fasting month with their families. In the midst of the economic crisis, the quiet this year, especially in Jakarta, had an eerie feel to it. There was a suspicion that many homeward-bound workers would have no jobs to come back to in the cities and that major construction projects had closed down, not for one or two weeks, but for a very long time. There was an unmistakable sadness and dread in the air and a very poignant, almost pleading, by Indonesians, to be told what they had done to bring such a calamity down upon themselves. People spoke of 30 years of development being wiped out but the only meaningful measure of the true dimensions and impact of the crisis was the collapse of the rupiah, literally battering down living standards with every passing day. In largely Muslim Java, the island universe seemed steeped in prayer, anguish for current suffering, hope for a better tomorrow.

President Soeharto was being portrayed in the Western media as a tired old man, "bereft of ideas and mouthing the same old platitudes," said Britain's 'Financial Times,' his power base was said to be crumbling and, according to US economist, David Hale, the prospect was growing not only of riot but of revolution. President Soeharto himself warned that social issues could spark unrest and told his people to be more vigilant than ever against potentially divisive problems. 'Time' magazine on January 12, spoke about the New Order Government having broken an unspoken contract with the Indonesian people under the terms of which the Government delivered economically in exchange for the people's political quiescence. With fewer deliveries, the magazine argued, there was less need for the people to stay quiet.

Two months later, Indonesians who were deemed to count, again unanimously returned Soeharto to power - for his seventh five-year term. During his acceptance speech the President said pointedly that he would stand on the same spot in five year's time to make his report to the Assembly. Those who were close to him reported that the President was anything but tired and bereft of ideas. Those who may have dreamed of toppling him saw their chance disappear overnight.

Indonesia's economic crisis showed no let-up. Even at the end of January a Western diplomat was quoted by the 'Far Eastern Economic Review' as saying that the crisis had gone beyond reforms. "...more reforms are not the answer. It's too late in the day." Cees de Koning had earlier been quoted as saying that, economically speaking, in Indonesia it was "one minute to midnight." Singapore Prime Minister, Goh Chok Tong, now described the crisis affecting ASEAN as "the biggest test since the Second World War." - 'Financial Times,' UK, January 12, 1998.

Post-holiday news was mixed but very much dominated by people who desperately wanted to believe that the 'corner had been turned.' The flow of dollars into regional markets miraculously increased and share prices edged upwards. The Government's decision to halt temporarily the servicing of off-shore corporate debt was said to have brought : "new hope of survival for the country's economy." - 'Jakarta Post', February 3. The 'Jakarta Post' quoted Adnan Tan from BZW Niaga Securities as very wishfully saying: " A lot of funds from the US and Europe (have) poured into the region" looking for cheap local stocks, especially blue-chip companies with dollar earnings. More realistically, Tan warned: " Market confidence has improved but it has not recovered yet. Fundamentally, there hasn't been a change yet in the region's economy."

Reuters quoted ANZ Bank's Head of Asian Markets Research in Singapore, Daniel Lian, as saying: "Don't believe in the stock market rally we've had this week. There's more pain to come." The very next day stock prices fell again and the rupiah was only held above Rps 10,000 to the US dollar by renewed interventions by the Central Bank. Elsewhere in the issue, Standard Chartered Bank's Chief Treasury Economist was quoted as saying that no reliable change in currency values and stock prices could be expected before mid-1998. The market reality was that most foreign investors were adjusting their dollar holdings to Thailand's scrapping of its two tier currency system as well as covering short positions in regional stock markets. Just as the flow of dollars was momentarily turned on, and by wishful thinkers mistaken for a recovery, all too soon the dollar drought returned. The rupiah was substantially bolstered by Central Bank buying.

Meanwhile, to protect bank liquidity in Indonesia, Bank Indonesia Governor Soedradjad, and the Bank Restructuring Agency, announced that the growth of bank foreign exchange deposits and foreign exchange non-trade and trade related liabilities must be limited to a maximum of 2 percent per month. This news was also said to encourage the markets. More importantly, to protect the banks themselves, the two organisations announced that for the country's top 20 banks - about the number which many expected would survive any shake-out - only interest at 0.25 percent above the Jakarta Interbank offered rates could be charged. Lending rates immediately hovered above or below 20 percent. Equally immediately the new measures ran into a storm of criticism.

The 'Jakarta Post' quoted Banking Analyst, Rijanto Sastroatmodjo, as saying of the interest rate adjustment: "No interest rate level can really bring the funds back to the banks. The main problem is that public funds have become a scarcity in private banks now." From the Government's point of view, there was naturally the hope that the interest rate levelling combined with its earlier promise to guarantee bank deposits would restore public confidence in the banking sector as well as improve liquidity in the economy as a whole. Ferry Hartoyo, a Banking Analyst at Vickers Ballas Tamara, was quoted as saying that the most important factor in restoring confidence in the banking sector was to solve its problem of bad debt. "The policy on this matter is not clear," he was quoted as saying. While being interviewed, Hartoyo decided to take a major swipe both at Bank Indonesia and at the IMF. "Bank Indonesia has been inept in dealing with the real problems," he was quoted as saying, adding that it had solved "only a third of the factors creating the current financial crisis. The IMF programmes only serve the rich countries' interests," he is reported to have said.

Evidence of how poor most Indonesians were was now showing up increasingly in the form of sporadic riots. In Java, Nusa Tenggara and Sulawesi mobs went on the rampage to protest rising prices. The monthly inflation rate hit a 25-year high of nearly 7.00 percent. There was speculation that there could be no increase in minimum wage rates in 1998, already admitted by the Government to cover only 96 percent of basic needs. The minimum wage for Jakarta is Rps 172,500 or at Rps 10,000 to one US dollar, just US$17.25 per month. Even at Rps 5,000 to the dollar it would only rise to US$34,50. Per capita income had slumped nearly 80 percent since the crisis began. Reuters reported that market analysts now expected Indonesia's GDP growth to be not zero but minus 4 percent! The World Bank promised to disburse US$1 billion to Indonesia in February to assist drought-hit needy farmers and to procure medical supplies for public hospitals and rural health centres.

On February 8, there was a hint of 'official' confirmation of what many market participants and analysts had suspected since before Christmas - Indonesia might be forced by the collapsed rupiah to try to peg it through the use of a Currency Board. Confirmation that such a possibility was being discussed came, not from the Indonesian Government, but from IMF chief, Camdessus. The 'Jakarta Post' quoted him as saying in New York: " It's an option available but it's not the only one." He added: " If the (IMF) programme fails to restore the rupiah because of the lack of cooperation from the Government, then a Currency Board would not be the solution."

Here were the seeds of a conflict which was to drag on through the remainder of February and last until after the meeting of the Parliament between March 1 and 11. Indonesia was desperate to peg its currency because it believed that the IMF's 'medicine' had not worked. The IMF said that Indonesia could never afford and could never properly manage a Currency Board until reforms were carried out, and this, the Fund said, were being frustrated by the Government. Critics felt that the Government was thinking of introducing the Board merely to mask its unwillingness to carry out reform. Nothing was further from the truth.

Two days earlier, after a wait of six months, the team headed by Radius Prawiro reported on Indonesia's foreign debt - the problem which analysts had identified months before as the root of Indonesia's crisis. It was to be yet another month until, on March 10, Bank Indonesia announced that, by May 6, local banks must report all foreign debt exposure in excess of US$2 million. Toward the end of April the reporting was made the subject of a presidential decree. Observers wondered if the list would be made public, and with what consequences. The Government quickly announced that the list would not, in fact, be made public.

The offshore debt, Radius said, totalled US$137.42 billion of which US$63.46 billion was owed by the Government. The remainder of Radius statement should have been dynamite. He revealed that of the US$73.96 billion of private sector debt, only US$23.07 billion was in fact owed by private Indonesian companies. Included in this figure was US$11.9 billion of promissory notes. So, who owed the rest? The answer? Foreign firms and joint venture companies, firms which in theory, if not in practice, should be able to honour their commitments. At risk, so to speak, was a mere US$23 billion. Radius was quoted by the 'Jakarta Post' as saying with heavy emphasis: "So you may notice that the outlook of our corporate debts is not as bleak and scary as many have painted because the bulk of the debt is owed by foreign firms and joint venture companies."

What, then, had the markets been worried about? Had it all been rumour, after all? Was much of the crisis simply to be chalked down to a chronic lack of information and transparency from Indonesia's banking and financial sector managers and an equally chronic inability to reassure the markets? If Governor Soedradjad had gone before the media and said all this at the beginning, would it have changed the course of the crisis? Were those who said that Indonesia's was a tragedy that need never have happened, right?

Whatever the truth would later emerge to be, in early February, suggestions from Indonesia's private sector to the International Finance Corporation of the World Bank that it might help out troubled corporates now made sense: the sums involved might be nowhere near as large as previously feared. The IFC agreed to review the performance of its 42 Indonesian clients in case some indeed did need help.

By the second week of February, the second week of the Muslim holiday, all that apparently remained to know was the maturity schedules of the foreign debt. This was promised.

The trouble was that the markets refused to believe Radius. There had been speculation in the foreign media that Indonesia's offshore debt might total US$200 billion. It was known that by no means all debtors had reported to Radius or had even been asked to report. There could still be a mountain of unknown debt. This was clearly the market's suspicion and the reason for the non-reaction to what should otherwise have been good news. In London, even Camdessus seemed puzzled by the dull performance of the rupiah. Reuters quoted him as saying that not only the rupiah but other Asian currencies had fallen too far. "...these currencies have depreciated far more than is warranted or desirable." Camdessus defended the Fund's policy of high interest rates to shore-up currencies and was quoted as saying that the IMF had never intended to produce a large depreciation in currency values.

rates to shore-up currencies and was quoted as saying that the IMF had never intended to produce a large depreciation in currency values.

With the dollar again appreciating in value, Governor Soedradjad announced that the foreign exchange minimum reserve requirement had been lowered from 5 percent to 3 percent to improve foreign currency liquidity. In the banking sector, since the IMF Agreement had been signed two weeks earlier the Central Bank had concentrated on reassuring depositors and the overseas recipients of Indonesian letters of credit. Attempts had also been made to improve liquidity both to try to reduce pressure on the rupiah and to assist the country's beleaguered corporates.

Other measures the market wanted to see, namely an increase in bank capitalisation and a reduction in the number of banks after solving the problem of bank bad debt had not taken place. While it would have been wise to speed up measures in these respects, such measures were not contained in the IMF agreement which, instead, concentrated its focus on the more ideological targets of lifting restrictions on foreign bank branches and plans to merge and privatising the state banks. The arrest of four directors at Bank Indonesia seemed to indicate that at least the criminal aspects of bank supervision were receiving more attention. In the clamour for Indonesia to implement the IMF Agreement in full, it was nearly always forgotten that, in respect of banks, the deal was vague, not specific, as the markets required, if confidence in the banking system was to be rebuilt. Within Indonesia, bank reform was not so much a matter of pleasing the IMF as doing what it was prudent to do if banks hoped to stay in business.

Throughout the crisis in Indonesia, there had been several streams of information present at any one time, including the all important basic demands of the market. Side by side with this had been many misinterpretations of the market's demands, spawning countless false trails. And side by side with this and, to some extent feeding off it, had been a wide band of gossip, rumour and speculation, almost always with no basis in fact. In the case of banks, although no one could doubt that reform was essential, the mechanics of that reform had not been specified by the IMF. Yet many seemed to think that they had, suggesting that divisions existed between the IMF and the Government of Indone-

growing daily in importance, was the way in which the economic collapse brought out popular frustration with the long tenure of the New Order Government, especially its leader, President Soeharto. After Christmas the factual realities of the economic crisis became inextricably mixed up with widespread allegations in the domestic and foreign media that it was a failure of political leadership which had led to the total breakdown of the economy.

One person who was very fed up with the bad press was President Soeharto. But he was by no means alone. Indonesia's negative foreign press coverage had deeply wounded the pride and hurt the feelings of leading Indonesians in and around the Government. Of course, there were also other who felt that the foreign media criticism was entirely justified and that the Government was really to blame for the humiliations being heaped upon the country. President Soeharto had more serious concerns on his mind. On National Press Day, on February 9, he castigated the domestic media for reporting baseless rumours or news without taking into account whether they were accurate and their impact on the nation. The 'Jakarta Post' quoted him as saying: "Intentionally or unintentionally, the national media has actually also contributed to the unfavourable atmosphere for restoring (economic stability). There have been many cases recently that indicated how the people were easily made restless....(They) became irrational because they were provoked by media reports that were not proportional to the economic situation."

As the President spoke, one of the would-be candidates for his job, Amien Rais, was quoted as calling for "total reform" to heal Indonesia's crisis, including, "a totally new leadership, new ministers and new spirit." For the first time there was mention of bloodshed in bringing about change. Rais was quoted as saying in the 'Jakarta Post' on February 11: "Whether there is bloodshed or not" depends completely on the position taken by the Government. If it remains stubborn, turns a deaf ear to the demands or confronts such moves with counter demonstrations, bloodshed is unavoidable. Unfortunately, many say that bloodshed is a must and I am afraid that this will be a self-fulfilling prophesy."

On February 11, President Soeharto was quoted as warning Indonesians against groups plotting to destroy the nation's economy by engineering a dramatic fall in the rupiah against the US dollar. Earlier, Kwik Gian Kie had made a similar point. Amien Rais wrote in the 'Jakarta Post' on the same day: " I believe certain market forces and external powers hope to precipitate political change in Indonesia through economic pressures. Learning that the movement is politically motivated, I have repeatedly called for the nation, including entrepreneurs who were raised (up) by the state, to share the burden and work together to cope with the crisis." The President also called for national unity to destroy the plotters.

At last, on February 10, Bank Indonesia had announced that the minimum paid up capital requirement for domestic banks would be raised to US$125 million by the end of 1998, US$250 million by the end of 1999 and US$375 million by the year 2000. As a result, it was expected that the nation's 212 banks would reduce to a mere 28. At the time of the announcement, Governor Soedradjad revealed that only 10 or 11 banks possessed the requisite capital. Domestic funds would need access to new funds and these could only come from offshore. Yet access to Indonesia's banking industry remained restricted with foreign banks being allowed to own only 49 percent of a domestic bank and 85 percent of a joint venture bank. Soedradjad promised that changes would soon be forthcoming to make investment in Indonesian banks more attractive to foreign banks.

As with other reforms announced by the Government, a negative impression was again created a few days later when, responding to a plea from the Private National Banking Association, Soedradjad announced that the requirement for banks to hold US$250 billion would be postponed until the year 2000. Optimistically, the deadline for 1998 remained unchanged.

Although Indonesia's economic crisis was still severe, for the time being, in the second week of February, the rupiah strengthened. One reason may have been the statement by Radius Prawiro about the level of private debt. Another reason may have been the announcement of increased bank capitalisation with its promise of a solvent and stable banking system - despite the very big loose-end represented by continuing limitations on foreign bank participation. A very big reason was undoubtedly much firmer news about a currency peg. On Tuesday, February 11, the rupiah soared to the near incredible level of Rps 7,400 to 7,600 against the US dollar, after President Soeharto was reported as saying that the Government would soon announce new measures to stabilise the currency. The market took this as a reference to a Currency Board. Trading was thin and yet another reason for the strengthening rupiah may have been the selling of dollars to purchase rupiah. IMF Director, Kunio Saito, was quoted by Reuters as saying in Singapore, that Indonesia's economic reforms were a move in the right direction and were restoring market confidence. Saito was also quoted as saying that the idea of a currency peg was "worth exploring."

One thing that wasn't happening was the return of foreign investors. The 'Jakarta Post' quoted an analyst as saying: " How can we excpect foreign investors to stay long in the local market if political stability remains uncertain?" The paper said that price riots: "remained a barrier for most investors to make any long-term investment decisions in the country's market." College students in Sumatra and Sulawesi were at that very moment demonstrating against price hikes, one of the first occasions during which students had joined the growing protests and generally considered more alarming than riots by ordinary citizens. In Java, workers were rioting over raised tyre prices. President Soeharto ordered the Indonesian armed forces to take "tough measures" against "irresponsible people (seeking) to damage the nation's unity." - 'Jakarta Post', February 13.

The 'Jakarta Post', of course, was talking about indirect investment. On the eve of the New Year, State Minister of Investment, Sanyoto Sastrowardoyo, had announced that in 1997, the value of foreign direct investment approvals rose 13 percent, year on year, to a total of US$33.8 billion. Britain was the largest investor followed by Japan, Germany, Taiwan and Malaysia. Top sectors included: chemicals, transportation, pulp and paper, metal industries, electricity, gas and drinking water. Sanyoto was quoted as saying that, in 1998, for obvious reasons, he would favour labour intensive projects. Not so obvious was that the IMF was insisting on this approach - flying in the face of Indonesia's efforts to move up market and into high-tech, high value added industries. Most importantly, big offshore corporates were as confident about the long-term future of Indonesia as they were of other countries in the region. The downturn may have been a lot more than a 'glitch' or a 'blip' but eventually the bad times would pass and growth would be back. There was no sign of big foreign corporates quitting Indonesia, except in exceptional circumstances.

On February 9, President Soeharto was quoted as saying in Jakarta, using characteristically strong military language, that he hoped to "kill" speculators attacking Indonesia's currency. Earlier, he had discussed the Currency Board system with Professor Steve Hanke, the US pro-peg expert he had last met in Istanbul eight months earlier. Immediately a Currency Board began to seem like a serious possibility, analysts divided into two camps: those for and those against. The market simply took whatever steps were necessary to protect its investments, especially off-loading dollars. On Tuesday, February 10, the rupiah rose 30 percent since Monday, touching the Rps 7,000 to the US dollar mark. Whether a Currency Board would work in Indonesia and would be good for the country in all economic aspects was another matter. An editorial in the 'Jakarta Post' on February 11 said: "Such a system would be an easy target for currency speculators and huge foreign exchange reserves are needed to defend the chosen rate of exchange. Furthermore, many of the other factors required to successfully run a Currency Board system, such as a sound banking system, low inflation and good governance, are not yet present. Political independence for the CBS must also be guaranteed."

Supporters of the peg in Government and business simply wanted to see a halt to the decline in the rupiah and a return to more normal business conditions, indeed to enter a situation in which Indonesia's stalled businesses could resume. Critics said the peg would require massive reserves because every rupiah in circulation would have to be matched by a dollar and that the peg could lead to a surge of demand for dollars resulting in swingeing interest rates to continue defending the rupiah at its new pegged level - notionally Rps 5,000 to one US dollar. Moreover, neither the Central Bank nor anyone else would control interest rates which, instead, would be left to automatic adjustment by the market.

With the rupiah strengthening to up to Rps 6,000 to the US dollar, on February 11, Finance Minister, Mar'ie Muhammad, confirmed that Indonesia would introduce a Currency Board. The 'Jakarta Post' quoted the Minister as saying: "The primary objective of the system is to restore public confidence in the rupiah and the banking system. The Government will strictly control the growth of the money supply to curb inflation and to restore an orderly and stable economic condition." Steve Hanke confirmed, from his office in Baltimore, that he was finalising plans to implement a Currency Board in Indonesia. By now, Hanke had been appointed an adviser to the Economic and Monetary Resilience Council. The IMF directorate felt snubbed and spurned. Even as early as the very next day, February 12, market doubts about a Currency Board had outweighed its perceived benefits and the rupiah had slipped down again to Rps 9,000 to one US dollar.

There were widespread price riots in Java with reports of rioters attacking security forces with machetes and of the first fatalities, in Java and in Lombok, east of Bali. Security forces stepped up tracking down alleged hoarders of essential supplies including baby formula, cooking oil, instant noodles and flour, immediately releasing the items to the market to contain price rises. In some places troops sold kerosene at special low prices. Students at some Islamic boarding schools undertook to carry food into, even the remotest villages of East Java. In several places throughout Indonesia 'tycoons' distributed free food to the poor.

Significantly, expatriates now began to pour out of Indonesia, not because they wanted to leave particularly, but either because Indonesian companies could no longer afford their dollar salaries or because rupiah salaries made it impossible for them to service personal or family commitments abroad. A year ago there had been 100,000. By December, according to the Ministry of Manpower, there were only 48,000. More than 17,000 left for good during the Christmas and New Year holidays alone. For some of those remaining, the US, French and Australian embassies warned their nationals to be extra alert in case public security deteriorated. In the capital there was indeed a steady increase in media reports of robberies but the overall security situation remained normal.

Since expatriates earn up to US$15,000 per month, a few local voices had been raised drawing attention to how many billions of dollars Indonesia would save if the expats went home. This, of course, was not the point. Indonesia as much needed foreign expertise as it needed foreign loans and financial assistance. It has always been short of cash capital and human capital. According to the United Nations, Indonesia ranks 99th out of 175

This, of course, was not the point. Indonesia as much needed foreign expertise as it needed foreign loans and financial assistance. It has always been short of cash capital and human capital. According to the United Nations, Indonesia ranks 99th out of 175 countries, on the Agency's human development index.

No one can deny the achievement of the New Order Government in giving all Indonesia's children the opportunity to attend primary school, but an industrialising country with aspirations to high-tech cannot be run by primary school graduates. Also, the drop-out rate was alarmingly high, in some areas as much as 30 percent. Compulsory secondary education was only introduced in 1994 and the education sector as a whole has remained badly under funded and consequently under equipped and staffed. Teachers are poorly paid and are frequently forced by their financial circumstances to have more than one job, school books and teaching aids are inadequate, curricula are poor. To make matters worse, thousands of those who attend universities, almost always from wealthy families, choose not to work unless they can be immediately appointed to a supervisory or managerial position. Traditionally, the attitude taken to direct involvement in trade and industry by Indonesia's upper classes, especially in Java, has been negative. They were happy to supervise others or to be paid by others for allowing them to do the job. The result of all this is that Indonesia is seriously short of capable workers, management personnel and experts. The short-term answer: - expatriates. Now, many of the expatriates had left......... For the long-term, at the end of February, the Indonesian Government announced that foreign universities would be allowed to operate in Indonesia. With fewer students able to afford study overseas this seemed wise indeed.

The Government was desperate and Steve Hanke looked like a gift from God. Jesuit in his promotion of Currency Boards, Hanke was a man with a mission, whose sales-pitch fell on unusually receptive ears. Pictured with President Soeharto on February 13, the President was smiling broadly with the smile of someone who sensed that he had at last found a secret weapon which could be used to 'kill" the speculators ruining Indonesia. But the more enthusiastic the President became, the more skeptical became the markets .

For the first time, the IMF was reported as condemning the introduction of a Currency Board to Indonesia. "We have concluded that a lot of options need to be in place before a Currency Board would make sense," the 'Jakarta Post' quoted Stanley Fischer as saying on February 13. On the 15th, Michel Camdessus wrote formally to President Soeharto cautioning him about the drawbacks of pegging the rupiah against the dollar and threatening to terminate the IMF's so-called bailout. This letter must have infuriated the entire Government. For the first time, there was talk now in the media of a "standoff" between the Government of Indonesia and the IMF. US Treasury Secretary, Robert Rubin, added his voice to the chorus of dissenters. ASEAN economists, meeting in Manila, also condemned the idea as likely to "aggravate the regions financial crisis." The 'Post' quoted Asian development Bank Institute Dean, Jesus Estanislao, as saying: "The contagion effect of the financial crisis in southeast Asia stemmed from having stubbornly pegged interest rates at unrealistic exchange rate levels. Why would anyone want to repeat the problem?" Australia urged Indonesia to take the IMF 'medicine' and abandon the Currency Board. German Finance Minister, Theo Waigel, repeated the thought. President Clinton rang President Soeharto again to voice his concerns.

Meanwhile, after canvassing all factions in the House of Representatives, House Speaker, Harmoko, was quoted by the 'Jakarta Post' as saying: " I have talked to all the four factions of the House and all came out in support of the CBS (Currency Board system) as they are confident the system will stabilise the rupiah rate and restore certainty for economic and business activities.

Japan also poured cold water on the peg plan but, instead, suggested pegging the rupiah against a basket of currencies. According to the 'Jakarta Post', the suggestion came from none other than IMF Executive Director for Japan, Yukio Yoshimura. In Indonesia, fears were now made public that a Currency Board would force many more banks to the wall, intensifying panic and uncertainty. It was feared that if interest rates skyrocketed in the wake of dollar demand, economic and business activity would be harmed severely instead of helped considerably. Kwik Kian Gie wrote in the Jakarta Post' on February 17, that a peg would eat up most of Indonesia's foreign currency reserves, perhaps requiring as much as US$15.6 billion to back Indonesia's base money, estimated at Rps 78.3 trillion. In mid-

The peg issue had become very personalised to the President. It seemed to be largely his initiative and whether it was the Finance Minister, the Central Bank governor, other ministers or members of special committees, such as the Council for Economic and Monetary Resilience, as the Constitution, in fact, required, all looked to him for leadership and approval. The President was repeatedly quoted as saying that a Currency Board was the best and least risky solution to stabilise the rupiah. Anticipating a Currency Board, the rupiah had remained 'stable'. Even if it was never implemented, just talking about a peg kept dealers from holding on to too many dollars.

Seeing the bind in which Indonesia found itself, governors of southeast Asian Central Banks, meeting in Bali, were reported as asking the IMF to be flexible toward Indonesia. This was the first time that such a plea had been made. Others were to follow. In an unrelated development, Camdessus was quoted as saying in Washington that Indonesia should stop thinking about a Currency Board and get on with implementing the IMF reforms.

There were, of course, often hard and fast reasons why reforms could not proceed to the extent or to the timetable proposed by the IMF. It was not the Fund but Indonesian politicians and business leaders who had to wrestle daily with the on-the-ground problems of price-related riots (which affected subsidies), problems of shortages of essential items (which to some extent affected BULOG), high interest rates (which affected the entire business world, especially banks and corporates), bank rationalization (at a time when banks lacked sufficient capital and where increased capitalisation and even the Currency Board threatened large scale collapse). Indonesia wanted to be saved from complete collapse, with all the terrifying social and political consequences that would have. It HAD to be saved. Yet the IMF was not saving it. Nothing the Fund proposed worked or at times even seemed relevant.

There were also bureaucratic hurdles. As Emil Salim pointed out in a column in the 'Jakarta Post' on February 16, there were doubtless ministers gung ho about reform and others who wanted to move more slowly, if at all. And there were almost certainly legions of lower level officials who found it difficult to abandon their old ways. This wrestling between modernists and traditionalists and the inertia at lower levels of the bureaucracy did nothing to help the Government either satisfy the IMF or make improvements to the operation of the economy, which would lower costs and enhance efficiency and competitiveness - desirable under any circumstances.

Meanwhile, at the University of Indonesia campus at Depok, around 2,000 students demonstrated in favour of guaranteed supplies of food, jobs, lower prices and political reform. 'The Jakarta Post' carried a report that the students were demanding the resignation of the New Order Government for failing to keep the people's mandate. More people-based riots (as opposed to students) were reported as taking place in Sulawesi and Sumatra.

On Tuesday, February 17, President Soeharto honourably dismissed Bank Indonesia Governor Soedradjad from his duties at the Central Bank, replacing him with US trained Sjahril Sabirin, 55, a Bank director since 1997. Sjaril had spent three years at the World Bank in Washington returning to Indonesia in 1996. Otherwise, since completing his university studies, he had worked in various capacities for Bank Indonesia, an institution the new Governor was quoted as saying he knew "very well."

On February 20, the 'Jakarta Post' quoted the ex-governor as saying that he knew that he had failed to contain the monetary crisis or to restore confidence in the banking system. He explained that he had done his best. The ex-governor was quoted as saying: " We continuously tried to tackle problems but problems were followed by other problems." And, sadly: " I thought that we were building a prudent system. Nobody knew that, in one day, it could disappear. It is like you are building a sand castle on the beach and suddenly there is a big wave that wipes out everything." He was quoted as identifying the main cause of Indonesia's economic problems as greatly weakened public confidence resulting in the withdrawal of funds from banks and a weakening banking sector plagued by domestic and offshore debt.

While Soedradjad had not been a vigorous Central Bank governor, even allowing corruption to flourish under his nose, there was widespread speculation that he had been released ahead of his full term because he opposed the introduction of a Currency Board. In fact, this may not have been the case at all because the new governor was soon quoted in 'Ummat' magazine as saying of the Currency Board: "At this moment, it's an interesting alternative to help us with the crisis but the Government is still looking into it."

At prayers on Friday, February 21, President Soeharto was reported as telling visiting Yemeni President, Ali Abdullah Saleh, that the crisis had shown graphically that Indonesia's economic resilience was not yet strong enough to resist external pressures. Those suffering from this lack of resilience continued their sporadic lootings, rioting and protests, with students from no fewer than ten universities rallying in the central Java city of Yogyakarta, demanding adequate supplies of basic commodities and affordable prices. The demonstrators were said to have specifically kept their attention away from political issues, preferring instead merely to draw attention to the plight of Indonesia's suffering poor.

On February 21, something notable happened to the rupiah - for the first time in almost eight months. The 'Jakarta Post' quoted a dealer as saying: " The speculative interest in the rupiah is not there any more. The rupiah seems to have found an equilibrium at Rps 9,000 to Rps 9,500 to the US dollar." This was to remain true until after the Presidential and vice-presidential elections in March. On the one hand, Indonesians could be thankful that things were not getting worse. On the other, an exchange rate of Rps 10,000 to the US dollar was a far cry from the Rps 2,400 that it had been back in June, 1997. Business distress was as painful as ever, with the social consequences and even the political consequences of this pain becoming daily more apparent as there were more and more student demonstrations and increasing incidents of looting, rioting and strikes called to protest price hikes or shortages.

On a sounding-out mission in Tokyo, KADIN Chairman, Aburizal Bakrie was reported to have asked his Japanese counterpart if Japan would help Indonesia should the country run out of foreign currency reserves as a result of implementing a Currency Board. One way or another the answer was said to have been 'No'. Indonesia had earlier asked the Japanese Government to help it roll-over private sector debts owed to Japanese banks and the answer had also been "No." At over US$25 billion, Japan was Indonesia's largest creditor and had growing problems with its own banks. Japan's banking system was going through its own crisis and domestic growth was weak. By the end of the first quarter of 1998, Japan's bad bank debt was estimated at an incredible 40 percent of bank operating profit. Exports to Asia were slumping and were expected to slump further. It was a bad time to request money. Unsurprisingly, even by the following March, no agreement had been reached with Japanese lenders to roll-over debt. And Japan had taken as tough a line as the IMF by insisting that Indonesia implement the reforms agreed with the IMF in full. Analysts generally felt that Tokyo had enough problems with Washington as it was and would not want to annoy the US further by appearing to undermine the IMF in Indonesia with offers of additional aid.

At a meeting in London ending February 22, the Group of Seven, including the US, Britain, France, Germany, Italy and Canada turned on their Japanese colleague to demand more action from Japan to boost its economy and strengthen the Yen. Japan got the message at last and in April unveiled a US$155 billion expansion package. The weak Yen was a constant thorn in the side of the US because it discriminated against foreign imports to Japan. Meanwhile, Japan's trade surplus with the rest of the world continued to skyrocket infuriatingly. Japan was already under attack and had no intention of allowing additional help for Indonesia to become yet another thorny issue. Japan fought back feebly by pointing out that, in fact, it was trying to be helpful but its economic plight, the measures taken to improve the economy and even the cultural background in Japan were simply not understood by the West. On March 5, the 'Far Eastern Economic Review' quoted Japanese Finance Minister, Hikaru Matsunaga, as saying: "The Americans are idiots - they don't understand a thing. What are they after anyway?s If they're trying to weaken our Government and make our economy go downhill that's what they're getting."

Frustration and anger aside, to play safe, Tokyo emphasised repeatedly that whatever role it played would be discharged only as part of successive agreements with the IMF. US Treasury Secretary, Robert Rubin, had described Indonesia's "sustained adherence" to the IMF agreements as a "crucial step" and he added that some of the reforms would involve "wrenching changes." Efforts to persuade Japan to convince the IMF to ease its conditions for Indonesia and make some of the changes less wrenching similarly fell on deaf ears. In any case, greater transparency, equitability, certainty and opportunity in Indonesia were clearly in Japan's interest.

While Japan did not want to do anything to undermine the IMF, in fact a little extra cash was forthcoming, for trade credits, insurance against bankruptcy and a token contribution to development funds. The whole package, announced in the third week of February, amounted to US$2.36 billion. As in the case of its defence against the G-7, Reuters reported that, in granting the funds, Japan was eager to counter criticism that it was not doing enough to help rescue Asia's troubled economies. In March a further US$8.2 million was advanced to Indonesia to help Indonesia counteract shortages of medicine and price increases. Most of the funds were advanced against the US$8 billion promised by Japan as part of the IMF's rescue package, not new disbursements.

Japan was in a difficult position: it did not want to be perceived by Indonesia as unhelpful - although this was largely inevitable. And it did not want to be seen by the US as doing anything to undermine the IMF and, indirectly, US programmes and policies.

On February 20, US President 106 Clinton had telephoned President Soeharto for the second time in a week to urge him to implement the IMF reforms in full.

In Jakarta there seemed to be some new element of wavering about a Currency Board. The Finance Minister was quoted as saying that nothing had been decided while Indonesia's Research and Technology Minister, B.J. Habibie, was quoted as telling the German magazine, 'Der Spiegel,' on February 20, that he thought a Currency Board would only be applied as a brake in case speculation against the rupiah continued.

Despite being a holiday month, February had been busy in Indonesia as the Government twisted this way and that, tried this and that, rushed from one problem to another to try to achieve what alone could solve the crisis - the stabilisation of the rupiah. The country's leaders were shocked and panicked. What had gone wrong? What should they do? The advice of the foreign business community resident in Indonesia had been sought; there were long meetings with the representatives of foreign chambers of commerce and heads of foreign banks. The foreigners were invited to speak frankly. Given Indonesia's allegedly strong fundamentals, such was the official and unofficial bewilderment at economic events that even whispers of plots to destabilise the currency and topple the President began to emerge. Society became more restless and more desperate.

President Soeharto said gloomily that perhaps countries like Indonesia were too weak yet to survive the white heat of unfettered global competition. Not only the President but the Government and many more in the 'establishment' were puzzled and depressed. Steve Hanke's Currency Board seemed like deliverance from a fate worse than death. But few experts, at home or abroad, agreed with it and the more it was looked into the more pitfalls there seemed. The IMF was especially angry and insisted that only its reforms represented the road ahead, a refrain chorused by all its leading supporters. The problem was that, since there had been no cure of the rupiah's sickness, Indonesians simply couldn't see or understand how the IMF recommendations could be the only solution. They would do what they were told, if they had to, but they wanted and needed IMF-Plus, the 'Plus' being some way of halting the slide of the rupiah.

The IMF's relationship with Indonesia had soured progressively until, at the end of February, ABN-AMRO's, Eugene Galbraith, could be quoted by the 'Jakarta Post' as placing " a large share of the blame for Indonesia's woes on the IMF, which he said had handled the situation badly. "While the IMF's prescriptions to steady the staggering Indonesian economy were 'uncontroversial', its (the IMF's) way of dealing with the country's leaders undermined their authority and failed to recognise political realities." Galbraith described the IMF as 'petulant' in its early dealings with the country over the Asian crisis. "On the topic of the Currency Board, the way the IMF dealt with Indonesia was disgraceful. Giving an ultimatum to a sovereign nation does not create a fertile environment for good political dialogue."

It could now be seen that the IMF's relationship with Indonesia broke down into several parts. At the level of behaviour, as Galbraith said, the record of the Fund's officials had not been good. They did not understand Indonesia or Indonesians. Its structural reforms, while capable of imposing hitherto unimaginable 'soundness' on Indonesia's economy , seemed to the Indonesians to be irrelevant in the short-term and, in some cases, in any term. Knowing themselves, they feared some of the legal and regulatory reforms would take years to introduce - the reason why there are so many presidential and ministerial decrees in Indonesia. Finally, there were the Fund's specific measures relating to money supply, interest rates, the state budget, measures to decrease costs, steps to increase revenue. Some seemed harmful, others unlikely to solve the immediate crisis.

It has to be borne in mind that the Government of Indonesia believed that it was facing complete economic collapse with all its terrible social and political consequences. It felt that if solutions could be identified embodying the idea of 'salvage' they should be tried first. The Government meant well. Culturally and traditionally, Indonesians must help other Indonesians. Crisp, Yankee-style reforms inflicted licketysplit on a suffering nation were simply not in its book of options.

Controlling Indonesia's money supply had proved difficult. Of course, the Government agreed with the IMF that, if hyperinflation was to be avoided, the money supply must be fairly rigorously controlled. The Fund advised that the broad money supply should be held at 16 percent throughout 1998. But, in December, 1997, and January, 1998, it had risen by an average of 10 percent-a-month as the Government printed more money in a bid to try to maintain liquidity. Foreign observers were talking about the money supply being "out of control." Inflation was rising and the IMF warned of the prospect of hyperinflation unless the money supply was cut. High interest rates were one way of achieving this but high interest rates were devastating Indonesian business and making its problems immeasurably worse. The Government was between a rock and a hard place. If it kept interest rates high it destroyed the corporates but staved off inflation. If it increased the money supply it saved the banking system but risked hyper-inflation. It was a genuine disagreement. The Fund meant well, the Indonesian Government meant well. Critics feared and suspected that the Government was acting simply to save sick or dead banks owned and run by cronies of the regime.

In the long-term, in these respects, the Fund was highly likely to be right. For the Government, there was no choice. Insolvent banks and corporates had to be allowed to go to the wall - run by cronies or not. The alternative was a banking system riddled with debt and an economy wracked by inflation. Typical of

Indonesia's approach, the Government seemed to manoeuvre to avoid the harsh reality until the bitter end, until the April agreement with the IMF forced its hand.

Indeed, despite its doubts, the Government of Indonesia genuinely felt that it had done a good job in executing the January Agreement. If you sit down with the IMF's list of 50 items and put ticks or crosses against those the Government of Indonesia had, or thought it had, carried out and the letters "LT" against those which seem long-term, you will see that the ticks predominate. This was why the Government of Indonesia found it difficult to understand why so many people accused it of not carrying out the reforms. It was why the 'Asian Wall Street Journal' was able to say on March 5: " Quite a large number of the 50 points agreed to with the IMF have been gone through."

Anything relating to subsidies, to measures which could raise consumer prices or to the creation of shortages of items considered to be essential, such as palm oil had not been actioned or had been actioned partially. With no system of social security, no social safety nets, millions of poor people and a real fear of the consequences of shortages of items deemed essential the Government of Indonesia simply could not act. It would have been irresponsible to act. It would have courted certain unrest. Later, when it had developed some understanding of the specific realities in Indonesia, the Fund would relent somewhat on issues which threatened to raise prices or create shortages.

The work of privatisation of state companies seemed not to have been speeded up, and would not be, until after March elections and the appointment of a new cabinet. Long-term fiscal and banking reforms would similarly have to wait for the new Government. Again, the Fund and the world, misunderstood the importance of the March political process and of its impact on the implementation of Government promises. In the run-up to the elections and the appointment of the new cabinet, Government effectively came to a halt. Later, the IMF realised this and it was for this reason - not, as the world media alleged, to somehow punish Indonesia - that it announced that the Fund's March review would be delayed and, consequently, the disbursement of funds postponed.

Although dismantling monopolies may not have seemed a priority to the Government, it was for the IMF. In the case of BULOG, the Government's hesitation would eventually be understood. But, in respect of the clove and plywood monopolies, especially cloves, Government enforcement of the termination appears to have been weak and, to the world at large, the monopolies seemed to continue in various forms long after the Government stressed that they had been dismantled.

IMF anger about alleged Indonesian Government foot-dragging over subsidies and legal and regulatory reform brought down a storm of condemnation on Indonesia's head. But there were reasons - the prospect of social unrest, the imminence of a new Government, the uncomfortable speed with which everything seemed to have to be done. While the Government of Indonesia had been perpetually accused by the IMF and many others of being slow in its implementation of the IMF Agreement, in fact, against the background of the traditional pace of change in Indonesia, changes had been introduced practically at the speed of light. Such was the seriousness of the situation. Such was the urgency of the Government's approach.

So, were the directors of the IMF completely ignorant? Or was their real agenda, as some Indonesians suspected, to topple the New Order Government, especially its leader? In case anyone thinks this is far fetched, Malaysian Prime Minister, Mahathir Mohammad, had had the same thought. Back in September, 1997, as the currency crisis had ravaged Malaysia, Dr Mahathir had said: " There is a definite attempt by certain Western media and some fund managers to get rid of me....As far as my resignation is concerned, it will be a futile attempt."

In the case of President Soeharto, there was no need for suspicions. The Western press was rampant in its calls for him to resign. The British 'Economist' was the most direct of them all with a front page picture of the President alongside the headline 'Stand Down, Soeharto". With the March presidential election only days away, President Soeharto had different ideas and, like Dr. Mahathir, had no intention of resigning or otherwise fading away.

Against a noisy backdrop of widespread accusations that Indonesia was not implementing the IMF reforms, on February 22, it was quietly announced that the Government had ordered all limited companies with assets of more than US$5.5 million to publish their annual financial reports. The reports must be audited by public accountants. The reform was good news for foreign investors who had complained many times about the difficulty in valuing Indonesian companies under circumstances where such basic data was missing or suspect.

On the eve of the General Session of the People's Consultative Assembly , as it had been for months now, the focus of the nation's attention was fixed firmly on the rupiah. Among the first pronouncements of the new Central Bank governor, Sjahril Sabirin, the 'Jakarta Post' quoted him as saying: " Our focus in the days and weeks to come is to create a stable and affordable rupiah exchange rate level." While stressing that no decision had been made about a Currency Board, the tone of Sjahril's comments suggested strongly that the Government still saw it as the only effective solution. There was a general feeling that if the IMF didn't agree "it should come up with other alternatives." Kwik Kian Gie suggested returning to the system of fixed exchange rates which Indonesia had followed for 25 years after 1967, with the conversion rate being set at Rps 5,000 to the dollar. Kwik argued that the IMF should earmark some of its funds to make good any short fall in foreign reserves following a possible rush for dollars. He estimated the assistance needed to be in the region of US$ 20 billion. The principal benefit would be, aside form stabilising the rupiah exchange rate, that there would be no need for a Currency Board. Meanwhile, the prospect of a Currency Board continued to keep the rupiah 'stable' at around Rps 10,000 to the dollar. It could have been worse!

CHAPTER NINE

Australia
Breaks Ranks

Facing "the greatest single challenge for 30 years", Australia now substantially broke ranks with 'the West' when statements began to be made and articles to appear, in effect, defending Indonesia and condemning aspects of the IMF's rescue package. Indonesia had been caught from the beginning on the hook of the IMF's insistence that it apply long-term and often irrelevant solutions to short-term problems. Writing in the 'Jakarta Post', Colm Kearney, Professor of Finance and Economics at Sydney's University of Technology showed conclusively that Michel Camdessus was perfectly aware of the very long-term nature of the reforms he wished to see enacted in Indonesia, many of which had been imposed by the IMF rather than suggested voluntarily by Indonesia. He quoted Camdessus as telling the Bretton Wood's Committee in Washington on February 13: "Taken together, these reforms will require a vast change in domestic business practices, corporate culture and Government behaviour. Of course, all of this will take time." A "vast change," over "time." At the end of April negotiations in Jakarta, IMF chief negotiator, Hubert Neiss, would tell an interviewer on state television that the long-term structural reforms were needed to restore 'confidence'. It was clear that he, too, knew that they did not represent any kind of short-term solution.

Stating the obvious and echoing the Indonesian Government's own conclusions, Kearney went on: "The IMF's Indonesian programme did not succeed in stabilising the rupiah and the Indonesian Government is well aware that a stable rupiah is necessary in order to facilitate the real sector reform agenda.

The Indonesian Government's proposal for a Currency Board should be seen as a genuine attempt to buy time on the financial reform agenda while it gets on with implementing the much needed real-sector reforms. The proposal's strength lies in its recognition of the need to secure a workable sequencing of the financial and real reforms. This aspect of the proposal makes perfect sense." In other words the IMF was trying to put the cart very far in front of the proverbial horse.

Kearney's comments are so apposite and so strong that it is worth quoting him at length: "The IMF has not responded helpfully to the Indonesian Government's proposal to stabilise the rupiah. It has demonstrated insensitivity to the plight of the Indonesian people and the genuine attempts of its Government to stabilise the exchange rate in response to a battering from the international financial markets. It has evidently interpreted the Currency Board proposal in a negative light as an attempt to postpone the much-needed real sector reforms."

Kearney went on to accuse the IMF of trying to meddle in Indonesia's internal politics through a public comment by Stanley Fischer, clearly aimed at B.J. Habibie, to the effect that the rupiah had been hit by suggestions that Indonesia could select a vice- president whose "devotion to new ways of doing things is limited." And he cited the letter leaked from the IMF, allegedly threatening to withhold disbursements of promised funds if the Currency Board proposal was pursued.

He wrote: " The evidence is entirely consistent with the interpretation that the IMF had attempted to exert political pressure on the Indonesian Government to sequence its financial and economic reforms according to the IMF's own preferences. This is inappropriate and unhelpful for a number of reasons."

Kearney listed the reasons, at the top of the list that the IMF's approach was "neither a polite nor productive way of doing business." Anyone who had seen the photograph of Camdessus standing over President Soeharto could easily empathise with this.

Most telling of all he showed how the approach contravened the Fund's own stated purposes which, he said, included (Article 1 (V)): "To give confidence to members by making the general resources of the Fund temporarily available to them under adequate safeguards, thus providing them with

170

opportunity to correct maladjustments in their balance of payments without resorting to measures destructive of national and international prosperity." Kearney also mentioned Article 1 (iii) of the Fund's guidelines requiring it to promote exchange stability.

He went on: " Specifically, the IMF's response to the Currency Board proposal did not help stabilise the rupiah, which is partly what the Government was trying to do. Also, the threat of withholding the loan package did nothing to assist the Government in its task of stabilising the economy with minimum destruction to national and international prosperity." He concluded: "The IMF's preference in terms of the sequencing and timing of financial and economic reforms appears to be neither well formulated in theory nor sufficiently worked through in practice. It has demonstrated little sensitivity to the complex issues involved in implementing the reforms. It is therefore ill-placed to justify its attempts to railroad through its own preferences. More sensitivity is required."

For whatever reasons, and most of them are quite obvious, Australia was to become one of Indonesia's few champions, together with friends from ASEAN. Later, Indonesia would single out its friends for thanks.

Kearney's message was quite clear. The IMF had taken advantage of the crisis in Indonesia to try to ram through its own agenda, stirring up political unrest when the Government was unable to comply with its demands and bringing down upon them a storm of ill-informed and almost entirely negative media attention. It would take very little to prove that a combination of IMF ideological dogma and cultural misunderstanding (or arrogance) had done more to depress confidence in Indonesia than any other single factor.

Mistakes, omissions, and careless, or at least over-hurried, implementation of reforms on the Indonesian side had certainly not helped. President Soeharto himself admitted this soon after the Presidential election. "Various Government policies aimed at handling the crisis have not fully succeeded," the 'Jakarta Post quoted him as saying in a speech read out on March 31 by the governors of all Indonesia's 27 provinces. As if to give the truth to his admission, more or less simultaneously the new Central Bank governor revealed that figures given authoritatively by radius Prawiro to describe the country's foreign debt had not been quite right. Fortunately, at US$136.09 billion the overall debt was marginally lower than announced previously (US$ 137.42 billion) but the bad news was that private offshore debt owed by Indonesian companies stood at US$30.12 billion rather than the US$23,07 billion announced by Radius. Total private debt was described as US$68.31 billion, lower than the US$ 73.96 billion announced earlier. Government debt was said to stand at US$67.77 billion, higher than the US$ 63.46 billion announced by Radius. Since Bank Indonesia had not been recording offshore private borrowings we can easily understand that, as the work of Radius's committee went on, a more complete picture of the debt emerged. But how did the Bank miscalculate Government debt?

Whether it was Indonesian Government ineptitude, IMF ineptitude or ineptitude on the part of Indonesia's imprudent foreign borrowers, the economy of Indonesia showed little, if any, sign of improvement. In March, observers were beginning to write that the worst of the economic crisis which had swept the region since the previous June seemed almost over " except in Indonesia." Indonesians themselves could see improvements in Thailand and South Korea and asked themselves: "Why not here?"

Thousands of students demonstrating against rising prices at campuses across the country thought they had the answer: "The country's bankruptcy has been caused by the misdeeds of the Government," the 'Jakarta Post' quoted students at the University of Indonesia as saying. Earlier the students had spray-painted out a reference to the Government from a sign which had originally read: " Welcome to the Campus of the struggle for New Order." Significantly, Indonesia's Minister of Defence and Security, Edi Sudradjat was quoted by the 'Jakarta Post' as saying that it was natural for people living in a democratic society to have different opinions. He was quoted as calling "constructive" some of the opinions expressed by the demonstrators. Different groups wanted different things but demands centred on lowering prices, ending corruption, collusion and nepotism and empowering the people and their representatives.

The thinking in some of Australia's ivory towers now reached the Government. Foreign Minister, Alexander Downer said in Adelaide that the IMF should be more sensitive to the social environment in Indonesia. Even as he spoke the IMF was making its now characteristically bombastic and belligerent statements.

Camdessus was reported as saying in Paris: " At this moment it is the view of the IMF, supported by the entire world community that the Currency Board medicine would kill the Indonesian patient." A few days later, David Nellor, Deputy Director of the IMF's Asia Pacific office was quoted as saying that the Fund might "allow" Indonesia to have a Currency Board once the reforms agreed with the IMF were implemented. "There may be a follow-up to the package which would consist of the Currency Board," AFP quoted him as saying. If IMF officials weren't talking to and listening to Indonesia were they even talking to each other?

Of course, Indonesia had at no time said that it was going ahead with the Currency Board - although it was no secret that it wanted to. There seemed no other way to rescue the rupiah and the economy. Certainly not by means of the packages suggested by the IMF.

Like a repeatedly played record, US White House spokesman, Mike McCurry was quoted as saying: "It (the crisis in Indonesia) remains a serious situation and it is important for the Government of Indonesia to promulgate the reform programme." US Trade Representative, Charlene Barshefsky was quoted as adding: " It is very important that Indonesia reestablish confidence by enacting and fully implementing the reforms to which it has committed."

President Soeharto was in a corner. He had implemented as much as possible as fast as possible of the IMF package. But, it was not working. A Currency Board looked like the one straw that could be grasped, the last life jacket on a sinking ship. All four factions of the House of representatives were pressing for a fixed exchange rate by some means or other. If the means turned out to be a Currency Board there were strong warnings that it should only be introduced after "thorough preparations." Of course, if a Currency Board would really do more harm than good the President knew that it would have to be abandoned. But he wanted to go every last mile to find out as long as a peg seemed the only chance to stave off disaster.

The IMF's man in Jakarta, Prabharkar Narvekar, seemed to know better than his boss that no decision had been made about introducing a Currency Board. He was quoted as saying that the President and his officials were merely studying it. The world didn't seem to understand this, or perhaps didn't want to understand. President Soeharto was portrayed as a dictator who, despite the record number of reforms already enacted and in process, had set his face firmly against needed reforms and in favour of a quick-fix gimmick which might wreck the economy.

The Australians most of all realised the depth and breadth of the misunderstandings between Indonesia and the IMF, and increasingly raised their voices in favour of the two groups getting together around a table and for the IMF to make a genuine and sincere attempt to better understand Indonesia. Downer spoke of the need to "develop a relationship" - as if this had not been done and the two parties had taken 'sides.'

Even in Indonesia, the press and sections of the 'intelligentsia' were in full cry against the Government for its alleged failure to implement the reforms agreed with the IMF. Asked the 'Jakarta Post' in a leader on February 26: "Has the Government executed the reforms to which it is now committed in a firm and consistent manner? The answer, after scrutinising the 50 points of reform contained in the IMF agreement, is a resounding no." Actually, the answer was a resounding: 'partially.'

On February 25, an IMF team arrived in Jakarta to review achievements. By the end of the week there was some progress. Radius Prawiro, Chairman of the Corporate Foreign Debt Settlement Team, announced that the Fund, the World Bank and the Asian Development Bank would provide technical assistance to Indonesia in handling the problem of its offshore private debt. Many wondered why they couldn't have made this invaluable offer months before! He also announced imminent reform of some of Indonesia's key laws and regulations relating to business, notably: contract enforcement, the seizure and sale of collateral and bankruptcy.

At the end of February, for the first time, reports began appearing in the regional press about nerves and jitters being felt in Singapore, Malaysia and Australia about the possibility of waves of refugees fleeing Indonesia as its economy went down. Australian Government sources reported a surge in immigration applications. Standard & Poor further downgraded its ratings on 15 Indonesian banks. Others were put on Credit Watch. The banks included many, if not most, of Indonesia's leading and strongest banks, private and public. The Agency said that its latest downgrading reflected fears about the Government's decision to guarantee bank deposits, about the increase in minimum bank capitalisation and about continuing market uncertainty.

While it can cogently be argued that business needs access to accurate information about markets and players and, while it certainly could not be argued that the various ratings agencies have been proved wrong in their warnings and forecasts, nevertheless, persistent negative statements and downgrading did nothing to help restore confidence in Indonesia or anywhere else wracked by the crisis. On the contrary, there cannot be a shadow of a doubt that negative ratings made markets even more bearish and cautious.

As the opening approached on March 1 of the General Session of the People's General Assembly, the reforms agreed with the IMF and the possibility of a Currency Board remained in process. There was a feeling among markets and observers that outgoing ministers would naturally be reluctant to go much further along the road to reform; in a week or so they might be replaced. And there was the sense that Indonesia's relations with the IMF were deadlocked with no hint of what might unjam them. The domestic media expressed open skepticism about whether the Assembly would make even a small contribution toward helping solve Indonesia's economic problems while students and others tried until the last to force the Assembly to devote substantial time to the crisis and to possible solutions.

The President was undoubtedly looking forward to the election. He had been the target of an unprecedented barrage of demands to resign or retire and his Government subjected to the most fundamental criticisms. What he needed now was a reaffirmation that he was still Indonesia's favourite son, that the mandate of power was still his. His nomination was already assured and the armed forces had specifically said that their informal sounding-out of opinion at grass-roots level across Indonesia indicated that this was the choice most people wanted. The foreign media were saying that President Soeharto had worn out his welcome. If the President now secured a unanimous, resounding mandate for a new five-year term, some of the ground would be cut from under his critics' feet, at home and abroad.

The first step on the road to obtaining a renewed mandate was the presentation to the General Assembly of the President's accountability report. Speaking realistically and candidly about economic and social challenges faced by Indonesia, the President said: "Last year, we suffered from one accident after another on land, at sea and in the air. Our economic lifeline began to be compromised. We were also subjected to a long drought. Extremely vast areas of our bush and forests caught fire. This resulted in a decline in the production of crops, particularly foodstuffs and plantations. But we had to go through a much harder trial. Since the middle of last year monetary turmoil has hit us unexpectedly." There it was. In a few paragraphs of a single speech. The monetary crisis had been "unexpected" and had puzzled everyone as much as a solution had eluded everyone. Large tracts of the country had burnt, food supplies were compromised. A succession of accidents had plagued Indonesia. The President continued: " This region was engulfed in a financial crisis. Then it eventually became more serious, more widespread and more lasting than anybody could have imagined. And yet our economic fundamentals were quite strong at the time. As a matter of fact many experts believe that the depreciation of our rupiah is absolutely unreasonable." Another succinct paragraph, summarising exactly what had happened and the attitude to it of Indonesia's leaders. Given Indonesia's strong fundamentals, no one could understand why the rupiah fell so far and the crisis lasted so long. This combination of unexpectedness and inexplicability constantly underlay Indonesia's apparently slow response to events. The scale of the impending disaster had simply been unimaginable.

The President was highly appreciative of the assistance given to Indonesia by international institutions and by friendly countries but he struck a note of keen realism as well as defending Indonesia's sovereignty when he said: " ....the burden of responsibility (for solving the crisis) rests precisely on our own shoulders. It is precisely our own action which determines whether we succeed or fail in overcoming the present crisis." It was clear from these remarks that the President fully realised the necessity for Indonesia to embark upon a deep-going and far-reaching programme of reform and he described some of the steps necessary as "difficult and painful." In the international media he and his Government were consistently described as being lukewarm and inconsistent about reform, yet the President's accountability speech left no one in the slightest doubt that he fully understood what was at stake.

He went on: "The main objective of our economic reform and restructuring programme is to restore confidence in our currency, in our financial institutions and in the future of our economy. It is extremely important to restore confidence. It is precisely the loss of confidence that becomes the primary cause of the numerous difficult problems we are facing today. The serious implementation of this programme will hopefully restore the confidence of economic players at home and abroad." The President had referred to "institutions" and to the economy as a whole. His intention was clear. His support for the IMF clean-up of aspects of Indonesia's legal and regulatory environment was clear. He did not add the obvious rider that these matters would be the responsibility of a new Government and that implementation must wait 'till then - now only a few days away.

The President had underlined his seriousness about reform and, by implication, the seriousness of his new cabinet and Government. To ram home the point, and also reflecting Indonesia's sincerely held belief, referring to Indonesia's Agreement with the IMF, President Soeharto added: " In accordance with the set schedule, we have carried out parts of the programme while the other parts will follow later. We are firmly committed to implement this programme in its entirety." A few sentences later, the President repeated again: " I have started and will continue to implement the economic and financial reforms which have the support of the IMF." His repetition of this key point shows the depth of his concerns that people weren't listening, important people, such as officials of the IMF and leaders of powerful and influential foreign Governments. The foreign media especially seemed not to want to hear or to believe.

Describing the reforms under way, the President mentioned the Government guarantee of bank deposits, bank restructuring and rehabilitation, steps to ensure the unhindered continuance of foreign trade, measures to enable and encourage foreign investment and the abolition of monopolies and privileges as well as the cessation of funds for either the national car or for the aircraft industry - funds which many thought would come either to be a bad debt (in the case of the Timor car) or an endless financial drain with little prospect of profit (in the case of IPTN).

Pointing up his differences with the IMF, President

Soeharto said: " Despite the fact that we already have, and have started to carry out clear and fundamental reforms and restructuring programmes, there are no signs yet that the situation has improved. On the contrary the people's life is becoming more difficult." Corporations, he said, were forced to reduce their activities, unemployment was growing, prices "skyrocketing." What was a consequence of this - not perhaps entirely visible or understood by foreign experts who only stayed briefly in the capital city at 5-star hotels before returning to what was, in effect, another world, among the developed countries? "The public becomes restless. Even the slightest misunderstanding sparks greater unrest. The situation becomes even worse when there are individuals who fish in the muddy water."

Anyone who knows Indonesia also knows how prevalent and dangerous rumour can be, how easily misunderstandings develop and how dangerously volatile and explosive the population can be. One of the Government's nightmares was undoubtedly of an orgy of destruction by rampaging mobs after which there would still be no solution to Indonesia's economic problems and even less chance of a return of international business confidence.

A short time later, he repeated for a second time the thought: " ...there are no signs of improvement yet." Did the foreign experts and Government leaders really understand Indonesia's position? They were doing as much as they could as fast as they could under crisis conditions but still the economy was going down and the sufferings of the people were going up. Did no one understand how potentially explosive this was? It was an equation which without the shadow of a doubt could see Indonesia explode in flames. the President promised; " I shall not hesitate to do whatever possible to overcome the situation in order to alleviate the increasingly heavy burden on the people's life."

The President now hit firmly on the head the nail of contention with the IMF and the root problem bedevilling the economy: "The key problem is the stabilisation of the exchange rate of our rupiah at a reasonable level. Unless this is achieved, I do not see any possibility of improvement within a short period of time. This is why I have asked the IMF and other heads of Governments to assist us to find a more appropriate alternative. I refer to the more appropriate concept as IMF-Plus." The President revealed that "I, myself" am "carefully and cautiously" contemplating the introduction of a Currency Board. If anyone else had any other solution for halting the slide of the rupiah they had certainly been very quiet about it. It was all very well for foreigners to talk about reforms which would make Indonesia "stronger" in "two to three years" but President Soeharto and the Government had to find a solution as quickly as humanly possible or face the risk of chaos, a risk which grew every day the crisis continued, with every new price increase, with every new redundancy, with every new imported goods shortage. Factory and office workers, housewives, children, the sick, students - all were affected and some were increasingly vociferous.

The President referred to measures being taken by the Government to try to safeguard Indonesia's millions of poor people through job creation programmes, to try to help skilled people who had lost their jobs with entrepreneurial training and to try to increase the supply of food through more efficient farming and the bringing into cultivation of industrial and marginal lands. Touching on another thorny discussion point with the IMF, the President said pointedly: " To facilitate (...) distribution, to provide certainty, and to maintain a stable and reasonable price, the Government provides subsidies for imported food and medicine. These subsidies are covered by the state budget."

Though his accountability speech was understandably underscored by his worries about the impact of the crisis on Indonesia, an impact which had slashed the country's spectacular average 7.1 percent per annum growth to only 4.7 percent in 1997, he nevertheless launched into an exhaustive summary of the Government's impressive achievements in spurring development, encouraging investment, stimulating industrial growth, improving agriculture, providing employment, raising incomes, reducing poverty and enhancing the education and health of the people. Virtually every achievement was ignored by the international media, still in full cry for his resignation and even by sections of Indonesian society, such as its students, frustrated by the severity of the crisis and believing corruption, collusion and nepotism under the New Order Government to be to blame. The President called this scapegoatism. At the end of his hour-long speech he commented: " It is useless to look for a scapegoat. It is far more useful for us to conduct introspection. We may find a

179

blessing in disguise from this hardship. "

Earlier, discussing the twin impact of globalisation and the monetary crisis on Indonesia, President Soeharto said: "Apparently our economic resilience was not strong enough to withstand such an external blow. Moreover, apart from external influences, some of the hardship we are suffering today is due to our own internal weakness. With full awareness, we must have the courage to acknowledge our own weakness and shortcomings. We look for strength from this weakness."

Addressing Indonesia's weakness would be the hardest task of all and certainly not something that could be achieved overnight merely by signing an agreement with the IMF or other foreign players in Indonesia's economic drama. Yet, the Government had clearly to share the heavy burden of blame - admissions of which would tilt it close to some of the positions of its critics. Lack of adequate guidance, lack of adequate organisation, lack of adequate regulation, lack of adequate legal frameworks, lack of adequate supervision, lack of adequate and impartially imposed penalties upon wrongdoers, partiality, favouritism, collusion, corruption - were these not all areas in which a good Government would be expected to exercise strong ethical as well as practical leadership? Many Indonesians now thought that they were, and many doubted that, after 30 years, the New Order Government could switch from a benign presence to an evangelising force capable of reshaping Indonesia's distorted structures and winning back the international confidence which the crisis had destroyed. Until the crisis hit, Indonesia had looked like a sparkling island of miraculous and well managed growth in the tropical seas. But when the water levels went down many of the piers and polls beneath the island were revealed to be rotten stumps.

Mindful of the public mood, in the wake of the speech, the leaders of the United Development Party (PPP) and of the Indonesian Democratic Party (PDI), both criticised the President for concentrating only on economic matters and failing to mention any need for political change, including, PDI chief, Soerjadi who was quoted as saying: " corruption..collusion and business monopolies" were at the root of the present crisis. While, 11 days later, the once-in-five-years Assembly would come to an end, students at campuses across Indonesia refused to let the issue die. Wherever there were demonstrations there were banners calling for an end to corruption, collusion and nepotism - a demand which many thought had heightened relevance once the new cabinet was announced. The demonstrators were still tolerated and even encouraged by the security forces so long as they did not stray off campus and some faculty members stood behind their pupils. Some demonstrators requested a dialogue with the representatives now meeting in General Assembly. The appointment of a new cabinet by President Soeharto was now only days away. On the campuses students now included in their demands that " the Government form a cabinet with members who have good moral reputations."

Although the PPP eventually agreed to accept the President's accountability address it did so with reservations, reservations which exactly mirrored the feelings of many Indonesians, many of whom had transformed the PPP into a significant political force during 1997's general election, following the eclipse of the PDI - 89 seats out of 1,000 (500 elected) compared to the PDI's 11- down from 56 at the last election. PPP faction leader, Jusuf Syakir, was quoted by the 'Jakarta Post' as saying: "Many have lauded Indonesia's successful development programmes, but when economic crisis prevails in the region, it is proven that we suffer the most compared to other countries. There must be something wrong with us. We think that corruption, collusion and monopolistic practices that have reached out to the lowest administrative level must be blamed for the prolonged crisis. This is the situation we have to change." Rightly or wrongly, this was an accurate reflection of much popular thinking. Jusuf went on to recommend that those selected for inclusion in the new cabinet should only be those "who could help carflry out good governance."

The Government's room to manoeuvre with the IMF was increasingly limited. Reflecting rising prices, inflation in February reached nearly 13 percent in the month and fears were expressed about the effect on fuel, power and transport prices of going ahead with the IMF Agreement to remove subsidies. Other fears were expressed about the possible rescindment of the ban on palm oil exports, a move which it was said would send cooking oil prices skywards. Meanwhile, the foreign media called for the ban to be lifted, mistaking its intention and even mistaking the industry's structure, describing the ban as a new "monopoly."

Meanwhile, as seemingly the whole world criticised the introduction of a Currency Board in Indonesia, stock market prices rose in response to President Soeharto's IMF-Plus plan. The 'Jakarta Post' quoted David Chnag, Head of Research at Trimegah Securities, as saying that, "rising inflation and the unstable rupiah rate against the American dollar were the country's most urgent issues in the short-term, before proceeding to the implementation of long-term reforms agreed to with the IMF." The market saw what the President saw. The IMF's suggestions were long-term. Indonesia's needs were short-term. The 'Jakarta Post' went on: " Most stock analysts in Jakarta shared a common view that pairing the IMF reforms with some other elements, such as pegging the rupiah to a foreign currency at a fixed exchange rate, would improve the country's ailing economy."

Tjandra Kartika, Head of Research at Mashill Jaya Securities, was quoted as saying that the market was speculating "that the IMF-Plus plan would include a fixed exchange rate for the rupiah and a new programme for rescheduling and reducing Indonesia's mounting foreign debt. This is really positive for the market because the Government addressed both the (country's) short-term and long-term problems at one time. The market welcomes the Government's strong commitment to introduce new bold measures to complement the IMF reform package."

In his accountability speech, the President had been careful to describe the deal with the IMF as having been agreed with them, implying that it was not imposed - a notion almost certain to ignite nationalist sensibilities. By now, however, the deal was commonly referred to as being the IMF's. While the debate raged, Indonesia's foreign currency reserves slumped further to US$ 16.33 billion, not enough by themselves to back a Currency Board.

When former US Vice-President, Walter Mondale, walked through President Soeharto's door on March 3, sent as a special envoy by President Clinton to persuade him to fully implement the IMF reform package, the President looked decidedly strained. With all the pressures upon him to go beyond the package and, after the many times he had stressed that the package had not worked, here was Mondale to press the same ineffective course upon him once again. By all accounts Mondale's case was weak. He was reported to have told the President that Thailand and South Korea were on the road to recovery because they had followed IMF advice. Why not Indonesia? The President was under the impression that, as far as possible in the time available, Indonesia had followed the IMF programme. This meeting represented a serious disjunction. Mondale was said to have complained later, at a press briefing in Dallas, Texas, that he could not illicit a firm decision from the President about proceeding with the IMF reforms or about the prospect of a Currency Board. How could he? The President could not at this stage afford to spurn an apparently viable option. It was an impossible request. Mondale's report fanned international negative opinion against President Soeharto. After meeting President Soeharto in Jakarta, Mondale was quoted as saying: "It's our view that the way to deal with the severe currency problems here is to deal with the underlying forces that are driving the rupiah towards its weakness. There are no quick fixes that provide an alternative."

The 'Jakarta Post' agreed. In a leader on March 4, the paper said: "There is no quick solution to gaining confidence, or to ending the currency crisis" (words which would seem profoundly prophetic when agreement was finally reached with the IMF a month later.) "Confidence is earned through prudence, wise policies backed up by efficient and consistent implementation and fair and honest conduct. These principles are the basic elements of good governance. Without the support of public confidence, any fixed exchange rate regime will lack credibility. It might be effective in the short-term, but only momentarily, buying a small amount of time before the foundations of our modern economic system collapsed."

Events surrounding the prospect of a Currency Board were gathering pace. Towards the end of February, Steve Hanke had been a frequent visitor to President Soeharto's residence at Jalan Cendana, Jakarta. At one stage, interviews with Hanke explaining his system, had been aired nightly for four consecutive nights by state television. The rupiah kept to its Rps 10,000 to the US dollar level. Back in Washington, Hanke was quoted as admitting that the operation of a Currency Board in Indonesia would need to be "more ambitious" than elsewhere because of "weaknesses in the banking system" - the very fears voiced most often by the board's critics.

It now emerged rather casually in the media that President Soeharto's IMF-Plus package was not merely the IMF-Plus a Currency Board. On March 4, the 'Jakarta Post' alleged that such a package would include, large-scale privatisation of state companies, a bankruptcy code and the reduction and rescheduling of external debt. It would be no understatement to say that the Government was feeling increasingly desperate.

US Commerce Secretary, William Daley, was quoted as saying two days earlier: "Indonesia clearly has the most significant problems (in ASEAN). The currency devaluation has made importing food difficult and forest fires are exacerbating the country's problems. Economic unrest is now spilling over into the political realm, with legitimate fears of widespread ethnic violence."

Around Indonesia, a handful of students tried to stage hunger strikes in support of political reforms. But as the days ticked past more and more students joined the campus rallies until thousands were involved - possibly as many as 10,000 nationwide. Seeing that there was now no chance of the General Assembly discussing the very serious issues facing the country, student leaders condemned the whole affair as "stage managed" and demanded a "new president." As usual, the security forces restricted the students to their respective campuses and there appeared to be no witch-hunt of leaders or follow-up arrests.

Within the Assembly, mindful of the new support it had won less than a year before which had transformed it into the second largest faction in the Assembly with nearly 90 seats, the PPP refused to approve President Soeharto's accountability speech - also one of the students' demands. The party said that the speech had failed to adequately explain the current economic crisis or to discuss the problems of poor law enforcement, bureaucratic corruption and the "painfully slow pace of political change."

Meanwhile GOLKAR and ABRI, the two elements in the Governing 'coalition' representing the people, the bureaucracy and the armed forces, were pushing for the President to be given additional powers to deal with any "groups or individuals seeking to undermine the state." It did the Government little good that some of the first people to be tried in connection with unlawful activities arising from the crisis were women who had publicly protested over rising prices of milk for babies. In the packed Jakarta courtroom, sympathisers wept and sang patriotic songs.

Inside the General Assembly the dominant GOLKAR and ABRI factions promised political reform. GOLKAR's Nazaruddin Syamsudin was quoted by the 'Jakarta Post' as saying: " GOLKAR is ready to (introduce) reform now that the people are ready..(but not) revolutionary reform (which) changes the political structures." - precisely the element people wanted to see changed. GOLKAR colleague, Rully Chairul Azwar, was quoted in the same report as saying that the changes could take place during "the next five years." Student leaders said they hoped that any changes would be "real" and not "artificial."

Gloom in the corridors of Indonesian power must certainly have been deepened at the end of the first week of March by the arrival of bad news from Washington. Deputy US Treasury Secretary, Lawrence Summers, was quoted as saying that the US would oppose additional IMF funds for Indonesia until such times as it was clear that its Government intended to fully implement the package of measures agreed with the IMF including "banks, budgets, monetary policy and structural reform." He also called for the elimination of "crony capitalism" to help stabilise the rupiah. The IMF had advanced US$3 billion to Indonesia soon after January 15 and a further US$3 billion was due to be paid on March 15 - subject to progress.

Crony capitalism as such was not part of the IMF agreement. How could it be? A way of life could not be wiped out merely by signing an agreement. Steps had been taken to eliminate the three monopolies targeted by the IMF - cloves, plywood and most of the essential items previously controlled by BULOG, the state Logistics Agency. In relation to BULOG there were special concerns relating to the social and political consequences of removing subsidies but the Government seems to have believed that the cloves and plywood monopolies had been totally dismantled. Indeed, it constantly reiterated that this was the case. The problem was that evidence kept popping up to show that aspects of the monopolies were still functioning or that new monopolistic practices had been put in place. BULOG had retained its monopoly over rice, the basic staple of the diet of every Indonesian, rich or poor, but anyone could now import such items as sugar, wheat flour, soybeans and cooking oil. But great care

monopolistic practices had been put in place. BULOG had retained its monopoly over rice, the basic staple of the diet of every Indonesian, rich or poor, but anyone could now import such items as sugar, wheat flour, soybeans and cooking oil. But great care had to be taken about the price at which these goods were offered it the market under conditions of falling purchasing power and rising poverty. Minister/State Secretary, Moerdiono, was quoted by the 'Jakarta Post' as saying: " ...the Government sees it as quite essential to continue subsidising the prices of these basic staples to help the common people." The subsidy covered the difference between the prevailing rupiah exchange rate and the Rps 5,000 to the US dollar rate fixed by the Government in the state budget.

On the good news side, Minister of Industry and Trade, Tunky Ariwibowo announced that in 1997 Indonesia's trade surplus had soared by almost 71 percent to reach US$ 11.77 billion. Imports fell marginally from US$42.87 billion to US$ 41.66 billion. But the dramatic increase in exports was by no means a complete victory. Many exports included imported materials and foreign banks were still refusing to honour letters of credit from Indonesia even if issued by the Central Bank. As with so many other elements of the crisis, efforts to put together multilateral trade finance guarantees had moved very, very slowly. As with so many other aspects of the crisis there had been much talk but only very limited action.

On March 5, the European Union's special envoy arrived in Jakarta, but not with any encouraging news. Britain's Junior Foreign Minister, Derek Fatchett said that Indonesia must obey the IMF's recommendations to the letter. He was quoted as saying that he disagreed with President Soeharto and most Indonesians' assessment that the IMF package had failed to solve the economic crisis. Using the analogy of a patient failing to take medicine as prescribed by a doctor, he seemed to blame the ongoing crisis on Indonesia's alleged failure to implement the agreement with the IMF, consistently, wholeheartedly and completely. He was also quoted as opposing the introduction of a Currency Board. From Indonesia's point of view more harsh words and no solutions. The rupiah and the Jakarta stock market slumped.

Reflecting the desperation in Government and business alike, KADIN Chairman, Aburizal Bakrie was quoted as

reforms." Supporting the IMF-Plus concept Bakrie was quoted as saying that: " the most important step toward salvaging Indonesia's wrecked economy was not scrapping monopolies and other restrictive trade practices as prescribed by the IMF, but stabilising the rupiah." While the international media seemed to want to pin responsibility for the IMF-Plus idea on President Soeharto exclusively, Bakrie's statement made it clear that, with corporate survival at stake in a dying economy, captains of industry also believed that much more was needed, more urgently, than the IMF's 'medicine'.

Events in Thailand seemed to highlight the extent to which the IMF's involvement in local economies was in substantial part 'smoke and mirrors.' After the storm of publicity about how the IMF had 'bailed-out" or otherwise "rescued" Thailand, on March 5, Reuters reported that less than US$3 billion from a total promise of US$ 17 billion had in fact been loaned to Thailand. The IMF had advised Thailand to strengthen its financial system but, with adequate foreign reserves of its own, after a clean-up of the banking and financial services sectors, Thailand appeared to have done much to pull itself up by its own bootstraps. Aburizal Bakrie was clearly wondering whether Indonesia might not be better off to do the same thing and sacrifice what many saw as unwarranted interference from the IMF amounting to neo-colonialism - an extremely sensitive topic in Indonesia.

Indonesia's economic crisis had now dragged on for almost nine months, with no sign of any solution and, as ex-Central Bank governor Soedradjad had once said, with problems leading to more problems on every side. While most domestic eyes were focused on the General Assembly and Indonesians and foreigners alike thought they saw Indonesia and the IMF, eyeball to eyeball, on the brink of confrontation, another drama was quietly but dangerously playing in the banking system.

The corporates were very quiet largely because those who owed major offshore debts were not paying their bills. The banks were very quiet but bad debts were thought to have risen to at least 15 percent just when the banks themselves faced having to repay foreign loans or, worse still, in the case of some of the state banks, to meet huge losses incurred in currency trading at the end of 1997, undertaken at the request of the Central Bank to help shore up the rupiah. Corporates could not pay their bills, lenders refused to roll-over or renew, domestic banks were in no position to extend new loans. Mergers which might have strengthened ailing banks had come almost to a complete standstill, meaning, that with each passing day, bank liquidity became tighter and the prospects of insolvency greater. Foreign banks had long cut their credit lines to all but Indonesia's strongest banks. Private banks launched into an interest rate war which saw deposit rates hit 65 percent in a bid to increase bank liquidity. The IMF team, in Jakarta since the last week of February, was known to be going over the banking sector with a fine tooth comb.

Two weeks after their arrival, state-owned Bank Expor-Impor Indonesia revealed hefty potential losses as a result of allegedly trying to force the rupiah rate upwards by offering to sell US$ futures at Rps 2.725 to the US dollar. Their exposure was US$2.2 billion. Bank President Kodradi was quoted as reassuring the public by saying: "We continue to operate normally and we are able to meet all our obligations." In an unconnected case, two bank officials were arrested for falsifying records and taking bribes. He said that the Bank would still enjoy a small before tax profit in 1997. Suppressed anxieties about the banking system began to ripple to the surface.

Despite the Government's guarantee of all deposits, bank customers were getting more nervous. The Indonesia Bank Restructuring Agency was silent. Was this because all attention was now focused on the General Assembly, because the agency was less active than anticipated or because major problems loomed? Time would tell.

Market fears that a second tranche of IMF money from the IMF would not be released now came to reality. With the General Assembly still going on in Jakarta and Indonesia effectively without a Government, on March 6, the IMF announced from Washington that there would be no further discussion of more cash for Indonesia until April, when a new Government would have taken office and there had been time for its officials to discuss latest developments with the new team. The world press seemed to interpret the delay as some kind of punishment for Indonesia. In fact it reflected the reality that there was temporarily no Government in Jakarta. Other than delay what else could be done? The money could not realistically be given because there were still many uncertainties and still much information lacking about a highly volatile and rapidly changing economic situation. The fact that all normal Government business seemed to have come to a stop during the General Assembly did not help matters.

Outgoing Foreign Minister, Ali Alatas, while confirming that Indonesia wanted to implement its agreement with the IMF in full, explained: " We need time before we can start implementing them (the reforms) because the nation is currently concentrating on the constitutional process of the General Session." He was quoted as adding that the reforms would resume after a new cabinet was formed. The IMF accepted the reality of this and its team went quietly on with its investigatory work in Jakarta. The world saw only more procrastination in Jakarta.

The New Order Government is exceptionally proud of having honoured all international agreements and obligations. It was greatly offensive to be told daily that in the case of the IMF Agreement this was far from being the case. Hence the tireless reiteration by the President and his ministers that Indonesia would implement the deal in full. But there was a problem.

To the world outside, the IMF Agreement had not been implemented in full. The Agreement had been signed under panic conditions and Indonesians do not perform well under any level of stress. Perhaps, at the moment of signing, Indonesia had not realised that some of the conditions were inoperable because they were politically and socially unacceptable, even downright threatening to national stability. Speed had been of the essence. Complex matters had to be simplified and made the subject of immediate action. One can easily guess that all requisite information might not have been to hand. Snippets of information pointing in this direction later emerged in dribs and drabs in the media. Trust was high. Policing and enforcement appears to have been weak. While the Government pushed in one direction, some of those it sought to move pushed back, either inwittingly or deliberately. The unfortunate result was that the dismantling of the clove and plywood monopolies was viewed as only partial.

Another problem was that, in their ignorance of the real situation in Indonesia, the IMF's directors had unknowingly insisted on some measures which, later, with greater knowledge, they would themselves come to see either as impractical or inimical. The fact that the IMF had admitted its lack of detailed knowledge of Asian economies is a measure of its arrogance in imposing its so-called solutions to Asian regional problems. In early March, the Fund, backed by leaders of the developed countries and by most international media, insisted that Indonesia stop its foot dragging and gulp down the IMF's 'medicine' in full. Indonesia simply couldn't do it. It was too dangerous and could only lead to frightening levels of chaos. Anyway, it believed it had already swallowed hefty doses in record time.

Indonesia seemed incapable of explaining; the IMF seemed incapable of understanding. The world media portrayed this comprehension gap as a stand-off, as stubborn Indonesia refusing to carry out the well intentioned advice of the IMF - mostly because the Government was in some way trying to protect its or its supporters vested interests - the crony capitalism, corruption line.

Whether or not President Soeharto really had been waiting to draw renewed strength from his confirmation for a seventh term of office, on the very day of the announcement of his acceptance of renomination, a new, tough, line seemed to be taken with the IMF. The President was quoted as saying that some of the IMF's recommendations were against Indonesia's 1945 Constitution, which he was sworn to implement "to the letter." President Soeharto was said to be chiefly concerned about Article 33 which stipulates that: "The economy shall be organised as a common endeavour based upon the principle of the family system. Branches of production which are important for the state and which affect the life of most people shall be controlled by the state. Land and water and the natural riches contained therein shall be controlled by the state and shall be made use of by the people." The President was quoted as saying that the IMF's package for Indonesia was based on 'Liberal' principles and therefore not consistent with the family approach taken in Indonesia - 'Liberal' meaning free market.

To the world press, President Soeharto's citing of the Constitution seemed a mere flimsy excuse for continued alleged foot dragging.

Article 33 is an interesting clause. It reflects a typically Asian view of the family as a basis for social and economic organisation which has its counterpart in district Government structures and even in the Indonesian state ideology of Pancasila. It should not be supposed that because many Indonesians want more political empowerment this also means that they want to throw out Pancasila. The two are not mutually exclusive. Within this family environment are notions of mutual assistance and of sharing, also deeply embedded in traditional Indonesian culture. Article 33 also reflects the sharp desire to achieve and exercise full sovereignty in a country just wrested from an occupying colonial power, which had to be pushed out by armed force. Given the politics of the day, it also reflects socialist thinking that the state should control key strategic resources and basic necessities for the good of the people. If it was true that the President had cited Article 33 of the Constitution he did not have in his mind state ownership of companies. A privatisation plan had been in place for some time and would soon be given an injection of new life. What he would have had in mind were the subsidies which the Government had for long used to ensure that even the poorest people had access to basic necessities. It was not an excuse. It was a reflection of one of the most basic beliefs of all Indonesia's Governments, whether old or new. It is also a reflection of the paternal relationship in which Indonesia's Government and corporate leaders still stand in relation to their people, better off than they were 30 years ago, but still poorly educated and often too poor to survive unaided. The President knew that he had to help them through the crisis but he could see from international media criticism that if he, himself, called for subsidies to be continued the same media would heap more criticism on him for being uncooperative. Citing the Coznstitution gave objectivity to his insistence that subsidies could not be eliminated while the crisis was at its height.

The fact that the President had requested emergency powers was taken as a sign that the elderly general was becoming more authoritarian. It was more a response to reality. In any case, he had possessed such powers throughout five of the six previous Governments. Indonesians are an extraordinarily patient people. But living through an economic crisis so severe that it has been compared to war, aggravated by drought and with domestic and foreign media fanning growing flames of political unrest the President's nightmare may have been the prospect of an explosion of probably bloody violence akin to a national amok which could only be halted by quick and decisive action. Those who don't know the temperament of the Indonesian people, can have no concept of what a national amok might mean. An amok is an uncontrollable frenzy, stemming from a sense of total hopelessness, which usually end in the death of those running amok or in the death of their enemies. It may be no accident that the President had appealed several times for people not to lose hope about a crisis which seemed to have no solution. Perhaps, fortunately for the Government, nobody else really had a solution.

CHAPTER TEN

The Electronic Herd

In the storm of activity aimed at solving the crisis, not only in Indonesia but around the region, international attention had been focused almost exclusively on what was being done, how quickly and with what effect. Within the region, there was a persistent belief that some of the countries had been victims of some of the early steps towards globalisation, particularly the unfettered movement of capital. In others there was an equally persistent belief that the IMF's medicine had not always been helpful.

Thailand's Deputy Prime Minister, Supachai Panitchpakdi, was quoted as saying: " The IMF measures have not always shown the right result." He was quoted as blaming the Fund for helping to create damaging deflationary conditions. But then he went on to touch on a subject which seemed almost to have been forgotten - currency speculation. To the apparent cost of the Malaysian Ringgit, Prime Minister Mahathir had been the first man to strongly criticise uncontrolled capital movements around the globe and uncontrolled speculation in currencies. One of the features of these movements and speculations was the way in which perceptions influenced markets. If 'sentiment' became negative, herd-like, massive funds could flow out of a market as quickly, if not more quickly, than they had flowed in. Suspecting the development of negative sentiment in a market, currency speculators could make a killing. The Thai Minister was quoted as also saying: " Fluctuations in currencies are determined excessively by moods and financial markets." - in other words by perceptions which may or may not have any basis in fact and by market operators sniffing profits to be made at whatever cost to someone else. The Minister went on to note that regional currency fluctuations seem to have been exaggerated by the "excessive role of international fund flows over trade considerations."

When Dr. Mahathir had first discharged his broadside against speculators back in September, 1997, the international media, especially in the West, made him look like a crank and a figure of fun. But the issue he had raised would not go away. As more people carried out more analyses of the causes of the crisis the role of international investment funds, hedge funds and speculators was seen to be paramount - not marginal or inconsequential.

In Indonesia, the depth of the economic crisis had been blamed on corporate and Government ineptitude and corruption but, writing in the 'Jakarta Post', ABN-AMRO Bank's, Cees de Koning, defined what had not caused the crisis. He wrote: "It was not a crisis of domestic Government spending or excessive Government consumption, it was not a domestic inflation crisis, either on the domestic wage front or caused by domestic price developments. It was also not due to a lack of international competitiveness, which would have made Indonesian exports grow slowly or decline. It was not even a local banking crisis, notwithstanding that some banks were clearly undercapitalised and not always prudently managed. It became a banking crisis in the later stages of the crisis. It was not even a crisis caused by inefficiencies in the Indonesian economy, notwithstanding that greater efficiency is always desirable. Finally, it was not even a rupiah crisis, which would have been caused by excessive local rupiah money supply growth, or other domestic factors. The crisis erupted because of the changes in risk perceptions by the parties involved." There it was again, that word: "perceptions."

In the wake of the Thai crisis, investors had suspected bad tidings from Indonesia and begun to liquidate their positions. Speculators, foreseeing a plunge in the value of the rupiah, had bet on it, making fat profits and forcing down the currency in the process. In the midst of all this it came to be known that Indonesian corporates had incurred excessive short-term offshore borrowings, which were increasingly difficult to repay as the rupiah plummeted. And on top of this was the dollar drought which kept the trend of US dollar value rising while other currencies were falling.

Dr. Mahathir's comments about speculators seemed to have been aimed at George Soros and, from the words used, it is probable that the Malaysian Prime Minister had done his homework well and read up on Soros. Even if it was true that no one person could or should be blamed for Asia's crisis, the Soros story makes informative and frightening reading. In case you are thinking that currency speculators are mere gnats in the market, bear in mind that George Soros, by his own admission, compared himself to a god and in 1992 won himself the reputation of being the man who broke the Bank of England. Not exactly the thinking and achievement of a market gnat!

Bearing in mind that, in the context of the cause of the crisis in Asia, there is general agreement that it was triggered by 'sentiment' and changed 'perceptions' it is at least interesting that Soros' theory of what drove markets was that it was not logic but "Psychology...more precisely, the herd instinct." With their superstition-prone, panicky inhabitants, shallow planning, limited forward thinking and tenuous acquaintance with lateral reasoning, what countries could have been more perfect candidates to provide unrivalled examples of the herd instinct at work that those of Asia? As someone remarked, the region was a lamb with its neck stuck out ready to be slaughtered. We have only to look at how foreign investors and speculators reacted to brush aside all doubts that Soros was right.

In his 'The Alchemy of Finance' discussing the buying and selling of securities, Soros wrote: "When events have thinking participants, the subject matter is no longer confined to facts but also includes the participant's perceptions. The chain of causation does not lead directly from fact to fact but from fact to perception and from perception to fact."

Soros was quoted as saying by Robert Slater in his SOROS: The Unauthorised Biography:" The bias of investors towards a stock, whether positive or negative, causes the price to rise or fall." Not merely a stock but a currency, too, he might have added. Frighteningly, Slater went on to explain that there was often a divergence between perception and reality. "When the divergence was large, perception and reality were far removed from one another. No mechanism existed to push them close together. Indeed, forces were at play to keep them far apart." Was that the position in which Indonesia had so shockingly and abruptly found itself? Quoting Soros, Slater continued: " Sometimes, he (Soros) said, financial markets might affect the fundamentals (of the economy) even though they are supposed only to reflect them. When that happens markets enter into a state of dynamic disequilibrium, and behave quite differently from what would be considered normal by the theory of efficient markets. Such boom/bust sequences do not occur frequently. When they do, because they influence the economy's fundamentals, they are disruptive. A boom/bust sequence can happen only when a market is dominated by trend-following behaviour. By trend-following behaviour I mean people buying in response to a rise in prices and selling in response to a fall in prices in a self-reinforcing manner."

For Indonesian observers, doesn't it all sound only too familiar? Hadn't they seen the crisis in Indonesia precisely feed on itself. Quoting Soros, Slater commented: " Feeding on themselves was another way of saying that investors had gotten themselves into a blind frenzy, or a herblike mentality. And markets that feed on their own frenzy always overreact. That overreaction - pushing towards the extremes - causes a boom/bust sequence." Weren't these the very words and phrases observers had seen applied to the situation in Indonesia - panic, frenzy, overreaction, overshooting etc., etc.

When the British pound sterling came under siege in 1992, Slater wrote that the effects and implications were so serious that the cabinet felt itself to be at war. Sterling began to be sold "like water running out of a tap." Interest rates went from "10 to 12 to 15 percent in one day." The British Prime Minister, John Major, was constantly on the 'phone to world leaders. Eventually the pound was devalued, Britain had to dishonour promises made at Maastricht and was forced to withdraw from the European Exchange Rate Mechanism and put on hold plans for any early support for a European Central Bank and a single European currency. The parallels with events in Jakarta are striking!

How much power did the money markets have to bring about this kind of devastation? Slater says up to US$1 trillion per day - with its movement greatly and dangerously facilitated by deregulation and developments in technology! Against sums like this what chance had the Baht or the rupiah or the Peso! Slater said that: "In the early 1990s, hedge funds, the largest and least regulated sector of the financial markets, dominated high finance." He quoted 'The Wall Street Journal' as dubbing them: "Wall Street's newest great casino."

How might a serious man like Indonesia's President Soeharto feel at the thought that 30 years of development had been wiped out by people who acted as if the money markets were a casino! On this point the President had little need to speak. Dr Mahathir had said it all already. As Dr. Mahathir had done, Slater quoted 'Business Week' as terming these speculators "gunslingers" - unrecognised, freewheeling and often far better as investors than their conventional counterparts." And far more dangerous. Media reports of southeast Asian regional market transactions throughout the crisis had described fund managers as "aggressive." Slater explains why. "Hedge fund managers have great incentives to use these tools (that they have) to push for profits. No matter how their assets perform, conventional managers receive a fee of about 1 percent of assets. They have, therefore, no compelling, personal incentive to act aggressively. Hedge fund managers, in contrast, typically receive 20 percent of the fund's profits. They have every reason in the world to bring in earnings."

How much damage did Soros think the combined attack of the speculators had wrought? " The net effect is a breakdown of the system, instability and a negative effect on the economy, the size of which we don't know, but it could be very, very serious. Instability is always bad. It may be bad - it may be good for a few people like me who are instability analysts, but it is really bad for the economy." Like the British cabinet, the Indonesian cabinet had long felt itself to be at war against an unseen enemy. The steps in the crisis in Indonesia had unfolded in much the same way as in the UK, albeit with infinitely greater damage to the economy. And at the end of the day there could be said to be a meeting of the minds between George Soros and President Soeharto. Stability in the end seemed to be the exclusive key to survival and recovery.

Soros went on: " I have not even the shadow of remorse for making a profit out of the devaluation of the pound. As it happens, devaluation has probably turned out to be for the good. But the point is: I didn't speculate against the pound to help

England.I didn't do it to hurt England. I did it to make money."
According to the vengeful British media the speculators had cost
every British taxpayer £25 and every man, women and child in the
Kingdom £12.50. The world now knows the identity of a few of the
mega-players in that global casino known as the money market.
But most are anonymous. In his book about the impact of the
currency crisis in Malaysia, 'Black September', author Ranjit Gill
quotes the following: "The global market today is an electronic
herd of anonymous stocks, bonds and currency traders, sitting
behind computer screens. The electronic herd only recognises its
own rules. They stipulate what savings rate your country should
have, what level of interests rates, what deficit to GDP ration, and
what level of current account deficit. You keep looking for someone to complain to, someone to take the heat off your markets.
Well, guess what, there's no one....." Gill adds: "One wonders..."

Many people in Indonesia had also wondered. Many
in Malaysia had wondered. If it was possible to unleash havoc
equivalent to war by means of bottomless oceans of money and
clever market tactics would it not be possible to achieve the same
result in circumstances of perpetually thin trading? On balance,
Indonesia's problems look like the work of the "anonymous herd"
but, as Gill says, people are still wondering...

At the end of February, Singapore had drawn attention to the need to regulate the activities of huge international
investment funds. Now, on March 9, Singapore Prime Minister,
Goh Chok Tong, an economist, weighed in again, being quoted
calling for new rules to prevent destabilising global capital flows.
Goh was quoted as saying: "This destabilising effect of quick fund
transfers, based on analysts' reports, and sometimes on rumours,
is a new phenomenon which the IMF has got to tackle. In future the
IMF may have to look at new ways of doing things, new rules to
prevent these currency transfers from destabilising the whole
system." Why he should have thought that the IMF would be
responsive to this plea was a mystery, given the Fund's zeal in
pushing for untrammelled money flows around the world, a zeal
fully backed by Washington.

The Government of Indonesia certainly thought that
a new approach was needed from the IMF. There was a sense of
collective hurt among the members of the People's Consultative
Assembly. There was talk of the IMF "forcing" impossible de-

mands on Indonesia, of a loss of sovereignty and of a loss of dignity. "The rupiah may crumble but our dignity must not," one Assemblyman was quoted as saying.

From Australia, the bilateral business council National President, Rob Hogarth, defended Indonesia. He was quoted in Malaysia's 'Sunday Star,' on March 22, as "critical of Western commentators, the foreign merchant banks and US Government agencies for calling on Soeharto to stand down (and for telling the Government that) they must do this and they must do that." He was quoted as continuing: "These people have to get off their wagons. It has nothing to do with them. Sure, they can have an opinion, but they cannot say to a sovereign country this is what you must do. You can't change the cultural values of Indonesia. You can go through some reforms. You can change a lot of laws and, to some extent, people's attitudes in the way they are prepared to conduct themselves. But you can't change people's culture. This is the conflict that is going on in Indonesia. It is under pressure from the outside, which is largely misunderstood. We've got many Indonesian business people feeling besieged. And they are desperate. They can't believe what is happening. The situation has changed so quickly and so dramatically. I think it's a vicious circle. We've got political, social and economic problems revolving around in a circle with no obvious resolution. And in the middle is the President fighting with the IMF. In many ways the President is right to stand up and fight to try to get some of the reforms put in the right way. The IMF seems to stand firm with the standard medicine, no matter what the situation demands."

Just how far apart were the two sides was best illustrated by a comment from one of the President's sons, Hutomo Mandala Putra, "Tommy." He was quoted as saying: " We have fulfilled the letter of intent. Why does the IMF still delay the fund disbursement?" On the other hand, the IMF was saying that there was a "long list" of things still not done. The Deputy Chairman of KADIN, Iman Taufik said that Indonesia should question whether the IMF's move to withhold funds "is purely the IMF's or the United States.'" Culminating in the visit of Walter Mondale, the US had played a high profile role in backing the IMF and there were still lingering fears in some people's minds that the real target was not reform but toppling the New Order Government. In a few days time, with a new Government unanimously elected, this would become a very hard thing to do.

By no means everyone, even in Indonesia, agreed that the Government had implemented the IMF package in full. In a leader published on March 10, the 'Jakarta Post' said: "It is futile for the Government to keep asserting its self-righteousness, claiming that it has fully implemented the reforms as scheduled. It previously back-tracked on agreed reforms and can ill afford any more policy flip-flops right now. Our currency has fallen more than 75 percent since July, inflation is at its highest in over three decades, most companies are already technically bankrupt, trade is at a virtual standstill and massive unemployment is looming. Asserting now that the reform package is not in line with the basic principle of our economic system could be seen as another blatantly capricious excuse on the part of the Government." The 'Jakarta Post' saw little to complain about in the IMF package, describing it as a continuation of Indonesia's reforms of the 1980s but with the caveat: "The only slight changes needed in the IMF package seem to be related to the urgent need for rescheduling the measures that will directly affect the lives of the common people such as the reduction of subsidies on basic staples and fuel oil. The establishment of social safety nets through massive labour intensive works also needs to be speeded up." Surely, this was the President's point! But the changes didn't seem so "slight."

Indonesia was divided over the IMF. Awed by its 'magic', its status and its power, most felt that its recommendations should be carried out - with the exception of subsidies. Some were doubtful because, after all the measures tried, there had still been no improvement in the economy.

Australian Prime Minister, John Howard, was now quoted as saying that: "We believe that the IMF's package (for Indonesia) must be implemented with care and sensitivity towards the impact of that package on social stabilities and social cohesion within in Indonesia." Referring to the ongoing IMF review leading up to a hoped-for disbursement of a second tranche of US$3 billion, Howard was quoted as saying: "I hope that the IMF review can be quickly concluded and that a productive partnership between the IMF and the new Indonesian Government can be developed as quickly as possible." The message was clear. Howard thought that the IMF had not established a "productive partnership" with the outgoing Government. The world thought so, too, and the international media continued to refer to a square-off between the two 'sides' - Indonesia and the IMF.

Later, Australia's Deputy Opposition leader, Gareth Evans supported Howard by saying: "The requirements are just too tight in terms of their potential to cause civil unrest - the winding back of fuel subsidies, the very tight budgetary outcome standards being set. Former Australian Reserve Bank Governor, Bernie Fraser was quoted as saying that the IMF bailout for Indonesia "lacked sensitivity and should have been tailored to suit Indonesia's needs rather than modelled on similar packages for other countries." The Deputy Governor of the Reserve Bank of Australia, Stephen Grenville, was quoted as saying that the "situation in Indonesia was now so desperate that immediate pressure for structural reform had to be set aside for emergency measures - a feeling long held deeply by the Indonesian Government. However, Grenville did not deny that reform was necessary. It was a matter of timing.

Philippine President, Fidel Ramos, was quoted by Malaysia's 'New Straits Times' as saying that IMF "conditionalities" should help countries recover quickly, instead of pushing them " to the depths of depression." Malaysian, Deputy Prime Minister, Anwar Ibrahim, sent an urgent message to the IMF calling on the Fund to speed up the disbursement of a rescue loan to Indonesia. While Malaysia's gesture was appreciated in Jakarta, it was also motivated by strong self interest. Flotillas of Government patrol boats were on the high seas around Malaysia night and day stemming the tidal waves of economic refugees flooding out of Indonesia. Scores of new coastal lookout posts were hastily put in place. The number of illegal immigrants held in Malaysian detention centres, 70 percent of them from Indonesia, had risen from 5,000 to 11,000 between February and March alone. The Indonesian navy had also stepped up its patrols and had prevented thousands more from leaving Indonesian waters. Singapore also increased marine patrols. Hong Kong's Chief Executive, Tung Chee-Hwa, feared a ripple effect around the world from Indonesia's economic crisis and he called on the international community to solve the turmoil.

In Washington, Michel Camdessus was quoted as again warning that Indonesia must carry out all its recommendations, including a reduction of subsidies, financial sector reform and the abolition of politically driven monopolies - hardly a "long list." The monopolies had gone: the subsidies could not go without risking national anarchy. The banking system was deep in the mire and to get it out Indonesia demonstrably needed lots of help - not threats. As usual opinion was divided about how to solve the problem of bank insolvency, on one side those who favoured drastic surgery, on the other those who feared that surgery would do more harm than good by spreading panic, as it had when 16 banks had been closed the previous year. In other words there were those who wanted to kill off ailing banks in a drastic bid to restore sector health and confidence and those who favoured an approach of slowly nursing them back to health. To date, the Central Bank was reported to have spent approximately US$6 billion in its 'nursing' activities. The IMF was on the side of drastic surgery, suspecting that cronyism more than anything else was the real reason for Government procrastination.

The division of opinion about the usefulness of the IMF was even present in the minds of single individuals. The 'Jakarta Post' quoted the Chief Economist at Danareksa Securities, Rino Agung Effendi, as saying that implementing the IMF reforms was the only way for Indonesia to stave off economic collapse. He criticised the Government for weak political will in implementing the programmes. But, then, he added: " The IMF's package does not state any solution to the country's mounting private debts and to the sufferings of the common people." While agreeing that the "pills" prescribed by the IMF were, in some cases "bitter", some people added that, since measures introduced by the Government of Indonesia to try to contain the crisis had failed, the country may as well try out those proposed by the IMF. The 'Jakarta Post' quoted had Soesastro, a Senior Economist at the Center for Strategic and International Studies as saying that if the IMF cut off its assistance to Indonesia: "The impact would not only affect the economy, it would also completely destroy confidence in the country." While most people agreed with this, there were certainly those among Indonesia's nationalists who would dearly have liked to tell the IMF to 'go to hell' - a stock phrase on the lips of Indonesians who feel unduly or unfairly pressured by foreigners. The freezing nature of the relations between the IMF and Indonesia was summed up by the Deputy Secretary General of the Economic and Monetary Resilience Council, Fuad Bawazier, who said that a special team would soon be sent to Washington to argue for a continuation of IMF help so that consultations between the IMF and the Government of Indonesia "will not be terminated." It had come to that! The prospect loomed of an open breech!

Or did it? On March 10, the day Soeharto was elected President for a seventh term, within the People's Consultative Assembly, members called on the soon-to-be-formed cabinet to maintain a "cooperative stance" with the IMF. "Like it or not the IMF is an international financial institution with major funds and influence," the 'Jakarta Post' quoted Hamzah Haz, from the PPP, as saying . Regional countries whose economies were threatened by a collapse in Indonesia kept up their pressure. There seemed a spark of new hope and a willingness to work mutually for acceptable solutions. Washington was now odd man out, with another tough warning being issued by White House spokesman Michael McCurry. President Clinton's spokesman was quoted as saying: "We believe that the Government of Indonesia needs to demonstrate through its actions and through the work of its leadership that it remains fully committed to the IMF programme, that it understands the importance of promulgating and moving forward with the economic reform measures that have been a condition for IMF assistance."

Many statements critical of Indonesia included the word "leadership" rather than a direct reference to President Soeharto. Because of the power vested in the President by the Constitution, because no major decisions could be taken, or not taken, without his direct involvement and because the Currency Board seemed very much a pet project of President Soeharto, foreigners had the impression that what the President wanted, or didn't want, would automatically be the case. Just as power was focused on the Indonesian President, so, too, was international criticism. If there was foot dragging it seemed to foreigners to be the President's foot dragging, engaged in for his own purposes. The full extent to which the President, his role and his family had become mixed up in the minds of foreign observers was made clear on March 19, by 'The Far Eastern Economic Review' when it said: "Indonesia's leader has reasons to cling to the old order, which has also enriched his family and friends. Despite the IMF's call to dismantle them, family and crony-run monopolies are still in place, and new ones are being created. What's more the Central Bank continues to provide liquidity to dozens of near-insolvent banks. Implementing IMF reforms would restore confidence, but it would also destroy the Soeharto family's economic empire."

If the friends and family of the President have been enriched and if he himself has become enriched, this enrichment was no part of the cause of Indonesia's crisis, a crisis to which some companies in which family and friends held interests had fallen victim. The decision had been taken to disband monopolies and no new ones were intentionally added by the Government. In the case of plywood a new toll system which looked remarkably like extortion was rapidly withdrawn. As we have seen, there were genuine difficulties in regard to BULOG, which even the IMF subsequently admitted. The Government had wanted to disband it since August, 1997 but then pressure on the supply of basic items and on prices plus the failure of substitute private sector companies to come forward to replace the agency made the administration nervous to proceed. Perhaps it was needed after all. In the case of the clove monopoly, it was true that the previous marketing regime had been left in force, minus the President's son. This was a grey area and possibly one in regard to which the critics were right. The Government, or the President himself, would have been best advised to take the strong action to eliminate this monopoly which had been constantly promised.

Implementing the IMF reforms might restore confidence or it might not. No aspect of the implementation of the reforms would in any way affect the business interests of the Soeharto family which, like everyone else, had everything to gain and nothing to lose from the restoration of a healthy economy.

CHAPTER ELEVEN

New Government - New Resolve

Undoubtedly, President Soeharto was sincere in wanting to cooperate with the IMF, if he could. When he couldn't, he would feel it his duty to explore other options - and there appeared to be several. A Currency Board was one, another was pegging the rupiah to a basket of currencies. To obtain the additional foreign exchange reserves required in any pegging scenario, there was still hope that, if the IMF turned its back on Indonesia, friendly countries might advance the funds. Also, there is always a strong undercurrent of feeling in Indonesia that the country is too big and too strategically important to be allowed to collapse. In Washington and other influential world capitals there was the same underlying feeling. Could the US and the world really afford to let Indonesia collapse? The problem was that foreigners had blind sided themselves with their obsession with President Soeharto and his leadership. A quite unreal battle line had been drawn between President Soeharto on one side and the IMF, the US and others on the other side. As 'The Far Eastern Economic Review' commented on March 19: "They (the US) can cut off Indonesia, possibly tipping the world's largest Muslim state into an ocean of civil unrest. Or they can succumb and bail out Soeharto on his terms...."

The President was by no means alone in his doubts about the efficacy of the IMF's programmes. Long-time Government critic, Kwik Kian Gie wrote in March: "President Soeharto...was right when he said that strengthening the rupiah value was an undebatable must. We must have a serious discussion with the IMF, asking for its support to stabilise the rupiah's value as soon as possible. If the IMF does not agree to support us in this way we could abandon our agreement with it. The most important un-solved factor is how to obtain an adequate level of foreign exchange reserves to support our rupiah strengthening meas-ures. Looking for an adequate amount of foreign loans would be very difficult, but not impossible if the newly established cabinet is regarded as credible by the international community."

For whatever reason and in response to whatever pressures, on March 11, the IMF blinked. IMF First Deputy Director, Stanley Fischer was quoted as saying that the IMF was now prepared to "tailor its economic programme to Indonesia and to take human suffering into account." Fischer was quoted as saying: "There is reason for flexibility." Fischer was even quoted as going so far as to say that a Currency Board could be implemented in Indonesia within six months if the right precondi-tions were met. And an IMF team would travel to Jakarta instead of an Indonesian team travelling to Washington. This made heaps of sense because it would enable the Fund's team to assimilate hefty doses of local reality.

Hours later, US Treasury Secretary, Robert Rubin, echoed closely the IMF's new "flexibility." In reality the Fund was making no concessions in respect of its opposition to a Currency Board in Indonesia - only commenting on its timing. Michel Camdessus was quoted by Reuters as saying in Washington that the IMF still opposed a Currency Board. " We have not dropped at all our opposition to a Currency Board, introduced now in Indonesia's present capacity. This country, with its very limited stock of reserves now with an extremely vulnerable banking system, with a corporate debt which has not yet been stabilised or rescheduled, cannot afford to manage a Currency Board." Of course, all of this was true.

In July, 1997, the Indonesian Government seemed not to have understood the crisis, had hoped it would somehow go away. When steps had been taken, it was true that they had been taken half-heartedly, inconsistently and without adequate follow-up and enforcement. There was a deep-rooted hope that busi-ness would soon return to normal and an equally deep rooted suspicion that it was probably not necessary to do too much or go too far. Even in November, few realised the cataclysmic nature of the crisis tearing through Indonesia. Few yet realised that many of the the old ways of managing and running the economy could go on no longer. Few foresaw the real scope of the reforms which would be required.

When the storm burst in full over the economy after Christmas, Indonesia was woefully unprepared. Because of the extreme urgency of the situation the attention of the Government was riveted on the rupiah, and on reversing its fall. Steve Hanke appeared like a messiah but it was too late. Tumbling confidence had pulled down Indonesia's once high-flying economy to dangerous levels of actual or near insolvency. Its legal, regulatory and institutional unpreparedness - exposed largely by the IMF - depressed confidence further. The slowness built into the "Indonesian Way" of doing things, increased by holidays and elections, brought confidence to rock bottom. By February, the Government claimed to be committed to total economic revolution but the pace of its progress was constantly overtaken by the pace and scale of the damage inflicted on the country by the undervalued rupiah.

By March, there was no way out. The currency could no longer be pegged - even if it had ever been possible. Reserves were depleted. The IMF wouldn't agree to a Currency Board and so would not commit funds to augment the reserves. The banking system was seriously unstable. Not only had no solution been found to the problem of repaying the private sector's offshore borrowings but there was no legal framework to reassure lenders who would now in all probability be faced with dealing with bankrupt borrowers. The wheel seemed to have turned full circle. Indonesia's economic problems had begun with loss of confidence among international market participants and this was still the critical issue in March. Indeed, it had always been the issue. Outgoing Minister of Industry and Trade, Tunky Ariwibowo was quoted as saying: " Our main problem now is that we have lost the confidence of the global community because of the crisis and it is hurting our industries." he might have added that the Government had also lost the confidence of large sections of the population. Standard & Poor slashed Indonesia's credit ratings because of "Jakarta's uneven progress in implementing economic reforms."

At 30 campuses throughout Indonesia, up to 20,000 students kept up their demands for political change. They were warned not to stray from the campuses. While the 'new' President and Vice-President were now known, there were high expectations of the incoming cabinet. The new ministers would be crucial in rebuilding confidence in Indonesia.

President Soeharto's speech in acceptance of his new term was greeted well at home and abroad. Currency and stocks did not move up - but at least they didn't go down. The President was painfully aware that Indonesia's crisis was the worst it had faced for decades and he said that he welcomed constructive advice and assistance from all quarters. He spoke sadly and perhaps with undue pessimism when he commented: " We will never enjoy again an economic growth such as we have experienced for more than the past quarter of a century." The use of the word "never" was perhaps over-strong, but clearly it reflected the depths of the President's concern and sadness. Equally, his oath reflected the seriousness with which he took his responsibilities, especially during a time of great suffering for the people of Indonesia. He said: "I have solemnly taken the oath. It was witnessed by the Honourable Assembly, by all the guests and audience present here. I have implanted the oath at the innermost part of my heart. I shall materialise the oath with concrete deeds. I have taken the oath in accordance with my religion, Islam. The oath starts with the words: In the name of Allah, I hereby swear. As a Moslem I am well aware of the true meaning of these words. At judgment day later on, I have to account my responsibility over all my deeds in leading this nation before The Most Knowing and The Almighty God." The President was also well aware that Muslim critics had been reminding him that one day he must face a 'higher accountability'. His willingness was spelt out.

President Soeharto had been a man with a mission since the day he became President of Indonesia. His speech showed that he had not faltered. He wanted his people to know that he had not faltered. 'The International Herald Tribune' quoted Assemblyman, Lieutenant General Yunus Yosfiah as revealing that President Soeharto had said that "with a fighting spirit and adherence to the Indonesian soldiers' oath he was prepared to devote his soul, not to mention his possessions, to the country."

Part of the President's vision for Indonesia, a vision with echoes and reflections in the hopes and dreams of the founders of modern Indonesia, was that Indonesia should improve its human resources and raise living standards through modernisation and industrialisation. Some US commentators had advised Indonesia to give up its hopes of industry and high technology and return to farming and resource extraction. The IMF had not only targeted aircraft and national car production in Indonesia but the President's dream of transforming his people and his country.

Everybody knows that the problem with agricultural produce and products is low prices and, while certain resources hold out the prospect of reasonable revenue from exports, it could never be enough to bring the living standards of 200-over million people up to the level of those in the developed world. This has always been Indonesia's problem. How to reduce poverty, raise living standards and, above all, to provide the jobs to achieve this. Industry was seen as the answer. Without it Indonesia would indeed be a "basket case" with a rising population of poor people doomed to live forever in the mud of their paddy fields and, incidentally, offering little opportunity for the sale of foreign made products.

The criteria for selecting a new vice-president had been that he should be a man of vision. The President's protege, B.J. Habibie, was certainly that. President Soeharto almost certainly feared that after his death, the grand dream of creating a new Indonesian human being with new capabilities and able to reap the just rewards of knowledge, skill and hard work would be left to wither on the vine. B.J. Habibie was duly chosen as the Republic's new vice-president.

Elements of his acceptance statement were pointed. He stressed his personal commitment to the President's and the New Order Government's vision of an educated and industrialised Indonesia as the road away from ignorance and poverty. He talked about a country with an industrial base and a strong agricultural sector - not about an agricultural country with patches of industry. He spoke about the need to tap into science and technology. Intentionally or unintentionally he defined how far foreigners could go in seeking to influence the Government's strategic economic plans. The market, previously said to be hostile to the appointment of Habibie as vice-president moved neither up nor down.

Liquidity in the banking sector was a bigger problem than ever. In February, the Central Bank had tried to impose some order on interest rates by decreeing that rates at 20 top banks could only be fixed at 0.25 percent above the Jakarta Interbank offered rates. Now, on March 9, in a further bid to control interest rates, Bank Indonesia announced that domestic time deposit interest rates would be pegged, not to the interbank rate but to its own short-term promissory note rates (SBI). The ceiling for time deposit rates was identified at 1.25 times the SBI rate. The formula for calculating the dollar deposit ceiling would remain at 1.5 times the Singapore interbank offered rate. SBI rates were raised from between 2 percent to 5 percent with the highest rate being 35 percent and the lowest 16 percent. The Central Bank set April 15 as the date of compliance with the new interest rate ceiling. Banks which had set rates higher than the Central Bank's would be allowed to continue until deposits matured. Banks which broke the ceiling would have the Government's guarantee of deposits at their banks withdrawn. In the wake of the massive public with-drawal of funds from the banking system, the banks needed new money, especially some of the smaller ones. Sky-high interest rates made the acquisition of additional liquidity very expensive and, for ailing banks, was more of a help than a hindrance. The Central Bank was itself continuing to pump liquidity into ailing banks - a serious bone of contention with the IMF. The corporates too were near-paralysed by high interest rates. Many could not keep up with their payments on existing loans nor could many afford new loans even if any were available - which they were not. On March 13, the 'Jakarta Post' quoted former Bank Indonesia director, economist Nyoman Moena, as saying that the Central Bank should do more to help create corporate liquidity by chan-nelling it through special credit lines to needy productive sectors such as, staple goods producers, distributors and exporters. He said that the credit lines could be made available through the commercial banks. Indonesia's Central Bank policy vis-a-vis interest rates can hardly have pleased the IMF, still committed to the policy of using high interest rates to restore confidence in the currency. Of course, the IMF was not responsible for Indonesia's corporate problems on the day-to-day basis on which they had to be dealt with by Bank Indonesia and by the Government.

In Indonesia and overseas, all eyes were now on President Soeharto. Who would be in the new cabinet? Would they be capable men and women? Would they be the exceptionally capable men and women the crisis seemed to call for? Would their appointment herald new hope? Would it instil new confidence at home and abroad? The 'Jakarta Post' quoted the Chairman of the Indonesian Footwear Association, Anton Supit, as saying: "The new cabinet must have a clear vision and be professional. The bottom line is integrity and capability. After that, everything will follow and we won't have to worry about corruption and collusion any more." Sri Mulyani Indrawati, a Senior Economist at the University of Indonesia, was quoted as saying: "What we have now is not merely a currency crisis but a crisis of public (and international) confidence in the Government."

Around the world, Indonesia and foreigners interested in Indonesia waited with baited breath for the news to break.

When it came, the international media was appalled. The line-up included one of the President's daughters, Siti Hardiyanti Rukmana and his long time friend, "Bob" Hasan, a man most asociated with the foreign media's favourite targets of monopolies and cronyism. The President's daughter was quoted as saying: "I asked Bapak (Soeharto) to skip my name from the cabinet lineup yet he insisted that I accept his wish. She was quoted as saying that her father told her: "You cannot refuse my request because the country is now in crisis. I want all my family members to help me perform my state duties and settle the crisis."

Behind the media hysteria, the President had recruited men and women, often with relative youth on their side, frequently foreign educated, occasionally because some faction or interest had to be represented, but in majority of cases because the candidates had a track record of achievement as well as commitment to stability, development and self reliance. Naturally, as their leader, the President wanted people around him that he could work with and who broadly agreed with his general thinking, though they may disagree on details. His and the new cabinet's objectives were no secret: stability, development, self -reliance and resilience. With an eye to the campuses and other sources of demands for 'clean' Government, the President asked his new cabinet members and their spouses to declare all fixed or liquid assets. The reports would not be made public except if ministers faced corruption charges. The President also asked his ministers to donate their first year's salaries to the poor, relying instead on ministerial allowances and benefits. Provincial governors were also obliged to declare their wealth.

The emphasis on stability seemed to promise little hope of political change to Indonesia's still demonstrating students and those who thought like them. Some of the students vowed to "monitor" the new cabinet's performance. The coupling of self-reliance with development, while traditional for the New Order, did nothing to calm the anxieties of those who thought that Indonesians would be better off as farmers and resource gatherers rather than the builders of aircraft and cars. The new line-up also fuelled their fears that "cronyism" was alive and very well in Indonesia.

Yet the new cabinet reflected precisely what the President felt Indonesia needed, as well as his own need to be surrounded with friends and even family who he thought could best help him lead Indonesia through the current crisis and into the next millennium. While condemned in some quarters, his choice of businessmen "Bob" Hasan and Tanri Abeng were hailed in others as bringing to the cabinet an element of hard-headed business expertise as well as channels to private sector support and even funds. The new Finance Minister and Central Bank governor were well qualified, with proven track records, but were perhaps more inclined to back Indonesia's perceived interests than to follow foreign doctrine and ideology.

While a pragmatic businessman, the new Minister of Industry and Trade, Mohammad "Bob" Hasan, could be counted on to take a tough, even abrasive line, with those thought to be trying to push Indonesia in directions its Government preferred not to go. The new Coordinating Minister for the Economy, Finance and Industry, Ginandjar Kartasasmita, was a pragmatist as well as a nationalist, capable of building bridges to the world beyond Indonesia's borders as competently as demolishing them. Among his initial statements he was quoted as saying: " ..I regret that the heated debates on the CBS (Currency Board) have caused some misunderstandings with the IMF which are now trying to be mended." He was quoted as saying also: " However, we will go ahead with our reform programme with or without IMF assistance." One of the President's sons, Bambang Trihatmadjo, was quoted by 'The International Herald Tribune' on March 11, as saying that: "Indonesia would go it alone rather than submit to foreign dictate. If necessary, we can rebuild this country starting from ground zero."

Opinion about the new cabinet overseas was near uniformly negative. It was said to be made up of friends and cronies of the President - dashing all foreign hopes of an end to so-called cronyism. It was also said to be a slap in the face for the IMF. Within Indonesia, opinion was divided. There were those like University of Indonesia Economist, Faisal Basri, who was quoted as describing the new cabinet as "incompetent", those like Adi Sasono, Secretary General of the Association of Indonesian Moslem Intellectuals, who thought that the inclusion of "Bob" Hasan and Tanri Abeng would "restore popular confidence in the Government," or Miriam Budiardjo, Professor of Politics at the University of Indonesia, who was said to be "hopeful" that the new cabinet would be able to solve the economic crisis and many others who felt and said that, at the very least, Indonesia's new Government must be given a fair chance to prove itself. The dominant attitude was that the deed was done; now it was a case of wait and see.

The appointment of Tanri Abeng was an interesting one. A former chief executive officer of the Bakrie Group with a reputation for being Indonesia's foremost manager, Tanri had been created State Minister for Empowerment of State Enterprises. Tanri's mission was to ensure that all the enterprises were healthy or could be restored to health and to privatise. There were 164 state enterprises. Some analysts claimed that 70 percent of them were 'unhealthy;' Government said that 100 of the total could be made healthy. Tanri was also to plug any illegal leaks of funds from the enterprises into bureaucratic or other pockets. His appointment and job description was a clear indication that the Government had had no change of heart about privatisation and Agreement with the IMF that the state companies would be best run efficiently and profitably. Indeed, the Government of Indonesia had agreed previously with the IMF that 12 state enterprises would be privatised during the first year of the programme. In fact only two were ready. Aside from any that were an unnecessary drain on the Government's budget (and this was hardly of concern to the investors who had turned their backs on Indonesia for wholly unrelated reasons) it was hard to justify the IMF's interest in the state companies except from the standpoint of ideology: they were state owned and by definition therefore badly run and should be privatised or closed.

When the President signed the Agreement with the IMF he may have genuinely believed that 12 companies could be successfully prepared for privatisation within a year, or, more plausibly, that they must be. If the IMF had know Indonesia better, they would have known how extraordinarily difficult such an undertaking would be, how extraordinarily difficult it would be to get people to act quickly, how extraordinarily difficult it would be to push privatisation through complex bureaucratic processes involving multiple ministries and overlapping jurisdictions, how extraordinarily difficult it would be to inspire and motivate the people involved, how very, very long it would all take. Privatisation involves the whole of Indonesia's business culture and could be the subject of a book in its own right. In fact it is. Those who wish can read my 'Culture of Business in Indonesia.' Before his appointment, Tanri Abeng was asked whether he thought that the economic crisis would lead to any changes in the cultural attitudes of Indonesians to work and business. Diplomatically he replied that every crisis was probably a blessing in disguise (a familiar stock phrase) and that he was sure Indonesia would learn something.....

Tanri Abeng moved quickly. The devaluation of the rupiah, the downward movement of oil prices, and the expectation that, while state revenues declined costs would rise, now gave the privatisation process urgent impetus. Government needed money. The sale or flotation of state companies could provide some. Almost at once Tanri set up a holding company to take charge of the state firms which would manage and restructure them. Previously, each state firm had been answerable to two different ministers. The new minister acknowledged that progress had been slow to date and promised to do his best to accelera-te the process. If he couldn't do it, probably nobody could. As many state companies as possible would be allowed and encouraged to continue as privatised entities, if necessary with foreign participation. Others would be allowed to die.

Other new ministers seemed to swing equally quickly into action, at least in terms of their statements. Agriculture Minister, Justika Sjarifudin Baharsjah vowed immediately to slash imports and to try to increase local production of such items as rice, corn and soybeans. The crisis had the potential to be a truly huge blessing in disguise for Indonesian industry if will and ways could now be found to try to quickly make as much as possible in Indonesia of what had formerly been imported. Here was a unique opportunity to fill the shelves of the shops in the shopping malls with Indonesian goods as well as an opportunity to generate more exports.

The new Finance Minister, Fuad Bawazier, vowed to make his priorities stabilising the rupiah, continuing banking reform and generally to try to recover overseas confidence. The Social Services Minister, President Soeharto's eldest daughter, inaugurated and led campaigns to provide food and jobs to the needy. Conglomerate directors at Barito and Astra donated a total of Rps 3 billion to give her immediately usable funds. Minister of Justice, Muladi, was quoted as calling for a judiciary independent of the legislature and the executive. Muladi was formerly Rector at Diponegoro University, Semarang, and known as a "sought-after commentator on legal-political affairs." So on after his appointment the Justice Minister swore to resign if he failed to eradicate corruption and collusion. "Bob" Hasan was quoted as threatening to fire any of his officials found guilty of corrupt practices. Other ministers made similar statements. The new Environment Minister, Juwono Sudarsono was quoted by "The Indonesian Observer" as "slamming tycoons and officials for ignoring (forest) fires."

With a new Government in place, the IMF now sent a senior director to Jakarta. On March 17, Asia-Pacific Director, Hubert Neiss, arrived, briefed to review progress and prospects. Despite having staff in Jakarta since well before Christmas, somewhat incredibly, special teams now had to be set up - at this eleventh hour - to undertake the review: for monetary policy, banking, the 1998-99 budget, structural reforms and debt restructuring. Had reviews and reports not been made to IMF headquarters by its staff on the spot? Had they not been called for by the IMF directorate? And, to the lay observer, none of the subjects to be reviewed had a single hint of any practical role for what the IMF was most valued - its money. If it wasn't going to give any money (assuming Indonesia actually needed this kind of help) why was it involved in Indonesia at all? One day after Neiss's arrival, Ginandjar Kartasasmita was quoted as saying: "On the Currency Board system, we will not adopt that for the time being because for that there are some requirements that we haven't been able to fulfil, especially sufficient foreign exchange reserves to support it." The IMF had won this round.

With a senior IMF official in Jakarta, in the preferred face-to-face environment, Indonesia now officially asked the IMF to be more flexible in its approach to the country's problems. Fuad Bawazier was quoted as saying that the Government would continue certain subsidies on basic items and that private companies had not come forward with available warehouse space to enable BULOG to end its activities as planned on February 1. He confirmed that, basically, the Government was still prepared to implement its agreement with the IMF in full.

It was not only President Soeharto and leading members of his new cabinet who feared that Indonesia was being pushed around too much. From two academics, Professor Peter Sheehan and David Ray, of Melbourne's Center For Strategic Economic Studies, came the recognition that the "one central failure of the IMF package, (is that) it tries to address a current crisis mainly by long-term reforms which will take 5-10 years to have full effect." The authors published a long advisory to the Government of Indonesia in the 'Jakarta Post', recommending that Indonesia:

1) Be given a respite from financial market pressures:- "Indonesia is one of many countries which have been pushed into this open world system without being fully prepared. It needs to retreat temporarily, returning to full open markets when it has a more robust financial system and better controls."

2) Continue most long-term reforms.

3) Regain control of national affairs - " a control that it has ceded to other parties as a result of the overhang of foreign currency debt."

4) Give priority to exports.

5) Introduce a fixed exchange rate for current account and foreign direct investment.

6) Restrict capital account convertibility.

7) Establish a debt restructuring agency.

8) Control price increases:- " Contrary to the IMF proposals, measures which contribute to rising prices, or perhaps more importantly to expecta-

tions of rising prices, should not be implemented at the present time. This includes the abolition of BULOG and the phasing out of subsidies on certain items."

9) Embark upon an expansionary fiscal policy:- "..contrary to the IMF proposals, Indonesia's current need is for an expansionary fiscal policy, to assist the economy to recover from the trauma of the last six months."

10) Firm policy to control inflation:- "With capital controls controlled and the exchange rate pegged, there will no longer be a need for high rates of interest to protect the currency."

All this was written by Australians! Much of it could have been written by Indonesians. Almost none of it by the IMF which was supposed to be rescuing Indonesia.

The phrase "regain control of national affairs" was laden with meaning not only in Indonesia but throughout the region. A developing country like Indonesia had the duty to ask itself how far it was desirable to open up to the penetration of foreign investors. The IMF's advice was "go all the way. Free up everything" In the 'Far Eastern Economic Review' of January 15, Malaysia's Martin Khor wrote: "The IMF "is forcing those affected (by the crisis) countries to open up to greater foreign ownership and probable domination in the financial sector and the economy as a whole. Malaysian Prime Minister, Mahathir Mohamad, recently warned that powerful nations had been given the opportunity to force open East Asia's developing economies, and in particular the IMF conditions would enable large foreign banks to take over the financial sector. These predictions are coming true." The developing countries of southeast Asia felt that they were being raped by the IMF. They still needed time to develop their institutions and their industries but the IMF seemed to be saying: "enough time. Now let foreigners do it." Foreign domination of the banking and financial services industry could lead to foreign domination of whole sectors of the economy so that, for example, if foreigners disagreed that Indonesia should build aeroplanes, cars or anything else, the funding weapon could always be wielded. Was Indonesia destined only to continue to provide cheap labour to make products for export to the rich, developed countries and to buy from the developed world things that it needed but now had no chance to make itself? Could its economy really be developed in this way? Could its people be developed in this way? Was free trade really the road forward for Indonesia?

These thoughts had long been in the minds of many Indonesians. To some extent, they may have slowed down the pace of implementation of the full IMF programme. But who could blame Indonesia for wanting to save something of its own? Who could blame it for not wanting, overnight, to wake up and find its high streets suddenly filled with the signboards of foreign operated companies? Indonesia had escaped 350 years of enslavement to a colonial power. Would it now be right for it to sacrifice its hard won sovereignty and enter into a new and perhaps endless period of slavery to foreign capital and foreign business?

On March 17, Australia again warned the IMF "not to lead Indonesia deeper into crisis." The Australian Foreign Minister was quoted as saying: "There is no point in imposing reforms on Indonesia in such a way that they tear apart the social fabric of the country, because, if that happens, the reforms will end up never taking place."

The US announced that it would provide US$25 million in food aid to Indonesia to make good shortages caused by the prolonged drought and to help head-off social unrest. At the same time the World Bank announced a food aid programme for Indonesia which would be given mid-year, regardless of the outcome of negotiations with the IMF. At least the milk of human kindness was now flowing through the arteries of the World Bank. The US Agriculture Department was quoted as recognising that poultry production in Indonesia had dropped by at least 70 percent and that supplies would likely run out by the end of March - " a scenario which possesses extreme stability concerns." Poultry supplies virtually all the protein intake of Indonesia's 200 million-over population.

Now suffering serious economic hurt from Indonesia's crisis, yet another Aussie voice weighed into the debate about whether or not the IMF had been useful to Indonesia in its time of economic trial. Ross McLeod from the Indonesia Research Project at the Australian National University was quoted by Reuters as saying: "As long as the IMF has been there (in Indonesia) the crisis has gone from bad to worse to really terrible.

I think that we can now say that the (IMF) package has failed in the sense that the rupiah has not recovered and there is no end in sight. What began as a financial crisis......has been very badly mismanaged. It has now become a fully fledged political crisis. The resolution of the crisis must involve the rupiah strengthening a great deal. Somehow that needs to be made to happen ... It seems to me that the IMF has seen in this crisis an opportunity to hit Indonesia, or specifically the President, while he's in a weak position. The IMF has virtually imposed a whole stream of macr-oeconomic reforms on Indonesia which it has been asking for for many years." Ah! So!

A few days later, former Australian Prime Minister, Paul Keating, made a spirited additional defence of Indonesia against the IMF. He was quoted by the 'Jakarta Post' as saying: (In Indonesia) "The IMF has done its job with good intentions, but I agree with those who argue that it has been the wrong job. The international goals for dealing with the crisis ... were expanded and restructured to include, explicitly, wholesale economic and social reform and, implicitly, a change in the political leadership."

Indonesians had been speculating that perhaps it was the CIA which was trying to topple President Soeharto. Here was Paul Keating apparently levelling a similar charge at the IMF.

Commenting on the impact of the crisis as a whole on Indonesia, Keating went on: "Indonesia was disproportionately punished because a grossly inaccurate view had taken hold in some quarters in Europe and North America that is was some sort of rogue state. The future of the Indonesian economy became caught up in judgments about its political system. The current rate of exchange is quite unreal, a fiction which bears no relationship to the strengths of the Indonesian economy." While defending Indonesia, the former prime minister said that that reforms of Indonesia's banking and finance sectors and a rescheduling of its debt were urgent necessities and he regretted that the Govern-ment of Indonesia had sometimes sent out "confusing signals" and been less than clear in making its intentions known. He was quoted as saying: "The regrettable truth is, that times like this require directness and clarity rather than the Javanese oblique-ness. Indonesia has not been good at telling its own story."

They also required replies to urgent faxes and tel-ephone calls. Traditionally, Indonesia prefers to do business face to face. It is very poor at answering any written communication and not much better at handling telephone voice traffic. On April 9, the 'Far Eastern Economic Review' reported that queries winged down from Hong Kong to official bodies concerned with Indonesia's banking and finance failed to receive a single reply.

At the end of the third week of March, there was good news for the poor people of Indonesia. According to BULOG Chairman, Beddu Amang, the IMF had at last accepted that subsidies must continue and that in the absence of other suppliers BULOG must go on with its work of buying and selling basic items of daily use. Fortuitously, at about the same time, David Ray, from the Center for Strategic Economic Studies at Australia's Victoria University was writing in the 'Jakarta Post:' "For many Indonesian producers and consumers, the dismantling of the very institution charged with the responsibility of providing food security and price stability could not have come at a worse time.. Moreover, there is widespread skepticism that removing the Government's monopoly over the distribution of food will lead to more competitive conditions and therefore lower prices. This is because food production and distribution networks have long been dominated by large Indonesian business groups. By removing the Government monopoly there is a real fear that such monopoly power will simply move into the hands of a few large business groups. While the operations of BULOG have long been exploited as a tool for rent-seeking activities by politically well connected business groups, it has nevertheless served to hold down or stabilise prices for ordinary Indonesians.There is no doubt that Indonesia's food distribution is badly in need of reform, quite independently of the financial crisis. However, the first step must be to abolish the monopolies through effective legislation and implementation of anti-trust laws and to introduce genuine competition into the system Only then will it make sense to phase out BULOG, the mechanism for protecting ordinary people from the monopolies."

In insisting on scrapping BULOG before any anti-monopoly legislation was in place, was the IMF putting the cart before the horse again - this time with the dangerous possibility of leading to even higher prices for basic items and the very real prospect of wholly unnecessary social unrest? A few days later, Hubert Neiss was quoted by the 'Jakarta Post' using words about subsidies which could have been spoken by the President himself. He was quoted as saying: "Subsidies cannot be abolished quickly, they have to be abolished gradually, including the ones on staple foods."

At last! Common sense from the IMF!

Incredibly, he was quoted by 'The Indonesian Observer' as going on to say that an immediate lifting of fuel subsidies would "not do any good" at the present time when Indonesia is facing very serious economic difficulties. Why, then, had the Fund pressed for it and, faced with Indonesia's very understandable reluctance to scrap them, made Indonesia look so bad in the eyes of the world press? 'The Indonesian Observer' carried the quote on its front page above the sarcastic statement: " ....yeah, Mr Camdessus. You should know by now."

The Government now announced that unemployment stood at almost 9 million. The number of people working less than 35 hours per week had doubled to over 18 million.

Even though the rupiah had found a new equilibrium, the Government was still concerned about the activities of currency speculators and, on March 20, announced that to discourage speculators, especially those buying and selling US dollars, from March 24, a 5 percent tax would be imposed on foreign exchange purchases. One can imagine that the announcement sent an electric shock through the heart of the directors of the IMF. Critics immediately doubted whether such a tax would be effective. On the very day of its planned enactment, the tax was cancelled. Finance Minister, Faud Bawazier was quoted as saying that the IMF package should be given a chance to work in full before other measures were applied. "There wasn't any pressure from the IMF," he was quoted as saying.

More importantly, interest rates were raised. The Central Bank raised interest rates on its short-term promissory notes (SBIs) for all terms except overnight to as high as 45 percent in a new effort to tighten liquidity and curb rising inflation. Commercial banks raised one month deposit rates to as high as 67.5 percent. Governor Sjahril was quoted as saying that on both definitions, M1 and M2, money supply had "expanded tremendously" during December and January. He was quoted as saying that it had "plateaued" in February. In December M1 increased 12.15 percent and M2 by 7.59 percent, month on month. More worryingly: "Early indications show a relatively high increase in both monetary aggregates for this March. Therefore, the Government feels it necessary to contain the growth of those monetary aggregates by quickly increasing SCBI rates," the Governor was quoted as saying. Sjahril added that it was the Bank's policy to continue to slash money supply in an effort to keep annual inflation below "40 percent." On April 2, inflation during the first quarter was said to have reached 25 percent, but on a declining trend. Inflation in January was 6.88 percent, February 12.76 percent and March, only 5.49 percent. The decease was attributed to market operations by BULOG and to the onset of the rice harvest. Food, clothing and house prices were the biggest contributors to the consumer price index. For 1996-97 the annual inflation rate had risen to 34.22 percent, the highest of any year of the New Order's administration. The rupiah strengthened to Rps 8,500 to one US dollar.

The IMF's, Hubert Neiss, was quoted as predictably welcoming the interest rate hike. Local banks and industry were plunged into deeper gloom. Banks were especially concerned. The short-term hope was that domestic commercial banks would now be able to attract back a portion of the funds they had lost, especially to foreign banks, now said to be "awash" with liquidity. As ever, throughout the crisis, whether it was or wasn't the IMF's advice, the Government had to balance the interests of Indonesia's corporates with the need to push up the value of the rupiah. This time the rupiah won. Shahril promised to reduce rates again as soon as practical. The 'Jakarta Post' warned in a leader: "Bank Indonesia cannot maintain such prohibitively high interest rates for some time without crippling economic activities."Within a week, after the unleashing of an unsustainable interest rate war among the private banks, the Central Bank persuaded state and private bank associations to jointly agree to push commercial deposit rates down again to 47.5 percent. Private Bank Association Chairman, A. Subowo said the week-old rates war could have "killed the banking sector."

Students were maintaining their sporadic demonstrations. Leaders said that whereas their protests could be characterised as a moral movement, since they had failed to influence events at the recent People's Consultative Assembly, some of them felt that "moral force alone was no longer adequate. We need something more permanent, some organisations which include other elements in society." Political observer, Emha Ainun Nadjib was quoted by the 'Jakarta Post' as saying: "There should be a synergy between the students and other elements in society...to establish a people's power movement."

In their harping on corruption, collusion and nepotism, the students were reflecting widely held disenchantment with the morality of the New Order Government. Unleashed beyond the campuses, their campaign might enjoy widespread public support, especially from Muslim communities emboldened by a new sense of rightness and even power. Amien Rais articulated these beliefs and frustrations and after the conclusion of the People's Consultative Assembly he was quoted as saying that he would give the new Government six months to "prove itself." Student leaders had latched onto his comment and were saying the same thing. A clock appeared to be ticking, a new time-bomb smouldering.

Concerned about the ongoing demonstrations, the Indonesian Armed Forces offered the students a dialogue and the first meeting took place in Bandung on March 25. Some student leaders demanded a dialogue with President Soeharto and the President was quoted as saying that he had no objection to meeting their leaders, just as he frequently met with other groups, as diverse as farmers. fishermen and athletes. He looked forward to any "concrete proposals on how to boost development." The Rector of Gadjah Mada University, Ichlasul Amal, was quoted as saying that neither the students nor the military were ready to dialogue. "The students were often not ready to defend and describe what it was that they meant by political reform. The military officers were not ready (to respond to the students) either." A further dialogue between the military and the Gadjah Mada students was refused by the demonstrators on the grounds that the agenda had been prearranged and therefore precluded free and open discussion.

In Yogyakarta, demonstrations turned ugly when students tried to march off campus and take their demonstrations to the streets. On April 2, 88 people were injured in scuffles with security forces. There were smaller demonstrations at other campuses. On April 7, the Government called on university rectors to control their students. Minister of Education and Culture, Wiranto Arismunandar, was quoted as reaffirming that stu-

223

dents were prohibited from engaging in "practical politics."

Meanwhile, military leaders confirmed that they still intended to try to have a dialogue with the students, talking to them as "equal partners" in Indonesia's development process. Minister of Defence and Security, Armed Forces Commander, General Wiranto, was quoted as saying: "The dialogue has not been cancelled or postponed. The dialogue is of national importance for mutual understanding." Another attempt was made at dialogue on Saturday, April 18, when no fewer than 15 ministers attended a meeting with students arranged by the Armed Forces. Unfortunately, according to the 'Jakarta Post', "only about 50 students" turned up with no one at all from the University of Indonesia, the Bandung Institute of technology and Gadjah Mada University, Yogyakarta.

The day before, 10,000 students had rallied at Surabaya, allegedly marching three kilometres through kampongs, where they were joined by members of the public sharing their concern to lower prices. The students demanded a new national leadership and an end to corruption, collusion and nepotism. More than 16,000 students were reported as rallying in Ujungpandang, the capital of South Sulawesi. Groups numbering from a few thousand to a few hundred rallied elsewhere. A pattern became established of daily students rallies at various campuses across the country, typically involving around 30,000 students and typically with the indulgence of at least some members of administration and faculty.

Significantly, Muslim leaders at Jakarta's, Istiqlal Mosque, celebrating Idul Adha, the Islamic Day of Sacrifice, called on Indonesian Muslims to be patient. President Soeharto had earlier described the crisis as a test from God, a stock phrase meaning that it was something that had not been invited and would have to be endured.

Rumours that the problem of Indonesia's offshore debt was about to be solved caused the rupiah to strengthen to Rps 7,800 to one US dollar. The principal rumour was that the IMF was smiling on a proposal from Indonesia to use a Mexico-style solution to its private debt problem. Under the Mexican scheme, indebted companies were granted an eight-year grace period during which interest payments were maintained during the first four years and the principal repaid during the ensuing four years.

Companies were given permission to make their payments in local currency to a Government institution which then made offshore payments in US dollars. In anticipation on the implementation of some such scheme, the reporting of private sector offshore borrowings to the Corporate Foreign Debt Settlement Team was made compulsory. According to the 'Jakarta Post,' to date, Radius Prawiro's team had secured debt data from only 180 out of a total of 800 companies. In the first week of April, Indonesia's debt restructuring team announced that it had completed the first phase of its negotiations with creditors in Singapore and would undertake a second phase in New York later in April.

The sharp downturn in Indonesia's economy had sent waves of 'boat people' to neighbouring countries. An incredible 12,000 illegal immigrants were now shipped home to Indonesia from Malaysia. At four camps, some refused to go, fighting ensued and people died, including a Malaysian guard. Critics of Malaysia's repatriation policy said that Kuala Lumpur was taking advantage of the situation to send home Indonesians who had been in Malaysia long-term, helping to build the country during the "good times." Others were even more critical of the Malaysian Government's refusal to recognise that some of those sent back might be genuine political refugees.

April 1 was the first day of a new financial year and there was widespread anticipation that Indonesia must reach a new agreement with the IMF around that time. Hopes were raised further by the arrival of Stanley Fischer who was quoted as saying: "It is understood by everybody that it is a crucial moment for Indonesia's economy and the carrying out of the (IMF) programme is essential for its success." Of course, the Agreement would still leave many even leading companies in a shaky business situation but, at the very least it would boost confidence. The 'Jakarta Post' quoted GK GOH Ometraco Analyst, Joko Santoso, as saying: "..most investors base their investment (decisions) on market sentiment rather than fundamentals." Another wheel had almost turned full circle. A crisis which had begun as 'sentiment,' had spun through currency to economic to political now promised to end on 'sentiment.'

If companies rushed to recapitalise there was hope of a resurgence in the securities market and agreement with the

IMF promised to further restore confidence in the rupiah. According to State Minister of Investment, Sanyoto Sastrowardoyo, direct investment to Indonesia had held up well during the first quarter of 1998 with commitments of US$5.2 billion, compared with US$ 6.5 billion the previous year. The Minister said that he expected the total for the year to still be in the region of more than US$20 billion. The average for the past four years of exceptionally high direct investment had been US$32 billion. Such flows should be seen in perspective because, in all preceding years, the level of annual direct investment was US$10 billion or less. Increased portfolio investment was also needed by Indonesia but some observers criticised the Government for appearing to try to attract capital by the policy of high interest rates. Economist Rizal Ramli was quoted by the 'Jakarta Post' as saying that such flows were essentially "short-term." Rizal called on the Government to go further, faster, in opening up the economy to foreign direct investors to "strengthen the economy and the currency" - especially the resource-based sectors.

In the banking sector, meanwhile, in the wake of the losses expected at Bank Expor-Impor, Bank Niaga Director, Arwin Rasyid was quoted by the 'Jakarta Post' as warning that banks may have engaged in up to US$20 billion of forward US dollar contracts. He was quoted as describing the effect of the devaluation of the rupiah on these contracts as a "time bomb." Perhaps in anticipation of problems to come in the banking sector, on advice from the IMF, President Soeharto ordered a new bankruptcy law to be prepared to replace a law inherited from Dutch times. Neither debtors nor creditor felt well served by the existing law, which was said to be "opaque" and almost impossible for companies to use, especially foreign lenders.

On the eve of a new agreement with the IMF, a blistering attack on the Fund appeared in the 'Jakarta Post.' Using extremist analogies and language, T.J. Addati wrote: "Make no mistake, while untold thousands of the working poor in America (once) "owed their souls to the Company Store," as the popular song goes, what the IMF is after is not your soul, but your economy - labour, natural resources and any spare cash you happen to have lying around. The IMF is not a charitable organisation or an aid agency prepared to rush in and altruistically rescue a struggling country. Whatever its original mandate, it has become an instrument dominated by financial interests with no interest in, or patience with, archaic national borders. Furthermore, it is completely inured to ignoring the aspirations of ordinary people in society. It acts on behalf of people who want their money back....."

Another writer of extreme views, Ram Ramanathan, went so far as to advise that Indonesia simply withdraw from the globalisation process and concentrate instead on achieving self-reliance behind a wall of controls on imports and foreign currency dealings. This way, he wrote, at least "national pride will be retained."

In Malaysia's 'The Star', Harvard Professor, Robert Lawrence, also slammed the IMF's programme for Indonesia. He was quoted as saying: "The IMF should have had fewer conditions attached that dealt with critical and specific situations. There are now too many conditions, of which some might not be useful."

Like the so-called Asian economic miracle, such was the power and imagery of the IMF that it, too, was expected to work a miracle on the rupiah. With new days of the new financial year ticking past and expectations that the IMF team, which had now been in Jakarta for three weeks, would complete its work any day, expectations rose, even stock prices rose. At the same time, new rumours began to circulate that more banks might be closed. The markets had already seen a hike in interest rates and a curtailment of the money supply, favourite hobby horses of the IMF. The Agency was also well known for its view that insolvent banks should be merged or shut. Bank mergers seem to have come to a standstill and there was little sign that many banks would be able to meet the new minimum capitalisation requirement set by the Government. B.S. Kusmuljono, an executive of the Federation of Private Domestic Banks was quoted by the 'Jakarta Post' as saying that bad debt had risen to 30 percent of outstanding bank loans. Like all generalities these global statements could be misleading. For example, Bank Niaga reported that its bad debt was only 0.3 percent of total loans and that in 1997 it had booked a profit of Rps 60 billion. Not all banks, then, were in such bad shape.

Without denying the possibility of more bank closures, Central Bank Governor, Sjahril, confirmed that 54 banks had been brought under the direct supervision of the Indonesian Bank Restructuring Agency. Next day, April 4, seven banks were closed, including two of the so-called "well connected" ones. According to 'Media Indonesia', the banks had received liquidity credits in excess of 500 percent of their equity. Moreover, 75 percent of their total assets were funded with these credits. The paper said: " It does not take a banking expert's knowledge to discern that this means that public money has been irresponsibly used, through Bank Indonesia."

The former Chairman of the Indonesian Bank Restructuring Agency, Bambang Subianto, had been replaced over this issue after he planned to convert the equity into bonds. On April 10 the subject of bonds was raised again in the media. This time by a Government announcement that the Bank Restructuring Agency would be issued with bonds which it was expected would be sold "largely" to the Central Bank, but also to the general public, the proceeds being used to fund the Agency's operations. When ailing banks had been restored to health and were subsequently sold, part of this money would be recovered. A new Asset Management Company was also announced to try to recover "troubled assets." Doubts were soon raised about whether buyers for the bonds could be found with inflation and interest rates rising.

The suspended banks were: Centris Bank, Deka Bank, Hokindo Bank, Bank Kredit Asia, Bank Pelita, Bank Subentra and Bank Surya. In closing the banks, Finance Minister, Faud Bawazier reminded the public that all bank deposits were still guaranteed by the Government. "There is no need to rush to withdraw your money," he was quoted as saying. Government owned, Bank Negara Indonesia was assigned to handle all the liabilities of the closed banks. Depositors could either withdraw their funds or open new accounts.

Additionally, seven banks were brought under the management of the Bank Restructuring Agency including, Bank Ekspor-Impor Indonesia, Bank Danamon Indonesia, Bank Dagang Nasional Indonesia, Bank Umum Nasional, Bank Tiara Asia, Modern Bank and Bank PDFCI. It was announced that a new company would soon be set up to manage the assets of suspended or ailing banks.

Subsequently, the names of all the banks were made public, to the distress of many of those on the list who hoped that their banks would soon be restored to health. Merely being seen to be on the list would not be helpful. A statement from Fitch IBCA said: "A likely scenario would involve most of the Indonesian banking sector being brought under IBRA's management."

Interviewed by state television on the eve of the announcement of a new agreement between the IMF and Indonesia, Stanley Fischer stressed that the new deal was the key to a recovery of confidence in Indonesia. And he underlined that it was not the signing of a new deal that mattered so much as its implementation. The Fund had compromised on its demand for a budget surplus, compromised on its demand that subsidies be scrapped immediately, compromised on its demand that BULOG be terminated but otherwise its position remained unchanged, particularly that no funds would be disbursed until the agreed reform programme was carried out. Fischer spoke in an opinionated, school masterly and even condescending manner, as if the Fund was really doing Indonesia a very big favour. But was it?

So far, only US$3 billion had been disbursed under circumstances in which the public at large were not even convinced that Indonesia needed money. In his interview, Fischer made it clear that the Fund would not be paying any of the offshore debts. If there were to be bankruptcies, the Agency had recommended a new bankruptcy law. If banks became insolvent, the Fund supported their closure. If the closure of insolvent companies instilled confidence, high interest rates would generate even more and these also the Fund supported. On the ideological side, far removed from an actual solution to the current crisis, Fischer insisted that monopolies must not be reinstated and that there should be a new anti-monopoly law to prevent it. Indonesia he said, faced the prospect of recovery with the IMF or inflation and disorder. On April 8, when the new agreement was announced by the Coordinating Minister for Economy, Finance and Industry, Ginandjar Kartasasmita, the impression persisted that, for the time being the Fund was playing a strictly advisory role, with the promise of funding but with no actual disbursements.

CHAPTER TWELVE

Prisoner Of
Global Forces

A new, third Agreement, was announced between Indonesia and the IMF on April 10. The budget had been revised again, forecasting a growth contraction of 4 percent, inflation at 17 percent and the barrel-price of oil at a more realistic US$14.50 instead of US$17.00. There would be a budget deficit of 3.2 percent which would be partly made good by foreign loans and partly from revenues from the sale of state companies. Subsidies were allowed on rice, soybeans and fuel while those on food-stuffs, drug raw materials, animal feed and energy were to be removed by October, 1998 - six months after the new Government took office. Ginandjar confirmed that to help companies pay offshore loans Indonesia would implement a Mexico-style solution with the Government guaranteeing debtors access to foreign currencies to repay their debts at a "reasonable" rate. He stressed: "There's not going to be a Government bailout or a Government subsidy." He was quoted as saying that the Government was looking at a three to four year time-frame within which the debts would be settled rather than the eight years applied in Mexico. A new bankruptcy law would be available to those who could not settle. The policy of high interest rates was confirmed but small and medium sized companies and cooperatives would be offered credits at subsidised rates. A number of taxes with revenues going to local Government were increased by as much as 5 percent but all local levies, official and unofficial, were abolished. There was no mention of a Currency Board.

The 'Jakarta Post' quoted Ginandjar Kartasasmita as saying: "Restoring the economic situation is not a simple and easy task. Recovery, as reflected in the rupiah's exchange rate, interest rates or inflation, will not occur instantly." Central Bank Governor, Sjahril Sabirin, confirmed that the Government was still looking at various exchange rate mechanisms but he was quoted as saying that the basic hope was that: " ..through the current system and with the support of the IMF, we can restore public confidence and the rupiah will gradually strengthen."

Few things illustrate how complete a surrender to the IMF was this third agreement than the decision to maintain high interest rates. The question of whether rates should be high or low was not just a matter of the balance the Government felt it needed to maintain between the interest of the rupiah and the interests of the corporates, it was not just a matter of disagreement between the Government of Indonesia and the IMF. Interest rates were a genuinely contentious issue.

On March 27, 'Asiaweek' had quoted World Bank chief, Joseph Stiglitz, as saying: "...our econometric studies tend to support the view that high interest rates have more deleterious effects on financial systems than do devaluations." He went on: " Many believe that you need to increase interest rates to sustain exchange rates. Still, the evidence of that in the current situation is much more ambiguous. In Latin America, raising interest rates showed that Governments were doing something about macroeconomic imbalance. Here (in Asia) the economies were in macro-balance. In that context, excessively tight monetary policy could lead to high levels of unemployment and bankruptcy, undermining the overall strength of the economy."

Indeed, it could. Indonesia had become the living proof!

A few days earlier, Harvard economist, Jeffrey Sachs had been quoted in 'The Straits Times' of Singapore as saying: "High interest rates and fiscal austerity will impose widespread bankruptcies. This approach won't work. You don't stabilise exchange rates by killing the economy."

In a leader, the 'Jakarta Post' described the April deal with the IMF as "Our last chance." Ginandjar Kartasasmita was quoted as saying that President Soeharto himself had ordered that "all agreements and commitments should be honoured to the letter." Stanley Fischer was quoted as saying that the "jury was still out" on whether Indonesia would implement the programme agreed with the IMF in full and on time. He was quoted by Reuters as saying: "We have measures in place and if they are not implemented, the programme (of funding) will not go ahead. We have no assurance. We cannot have assurance, given history, that it will be done."

The history he referred to we have seen to have been deeply characterised by initial disbelief that Thailand's crisis would effect Indonesia; then a new belief that, since Indonesia's fundamentals were strong, the market would soon realise that Indonesia's currency had become undervalued, a correction would take place. After a temporary fall it would be back to business as usual. Such was the Government's confidence, fuelled by long years of praise from organisations such as the IMF and the World Bank, that not only was it slow to introduce major corrective measures and reforms but some of those introduced were subsequently withdrawn when the markets seemed to improve. It was only the near total collapse of the rupiah that finally brought the Government to the shocking realisation that it faced an immensely serious crisis to cope with which it would have to take action on a scale and in a timeframe never before experienced in Indonesia.

The markets and the media, especially, called all this shilly-shallying and foot dragging and suspected that needed measures were withdrawn or not undertaken to protect vested interests, so-called crony capitalism. When it was realised that the chips really were down cronies and even family went out of the window. Nobody was silly enough to put vested interests before national survival. It was better to live to fight another day than to die on the deck of Indonesia's sinking economy. The Government wanted to preserve from the crisis projects it regarded as strategic, such as aeroplanes and cars but the IMF, foreign Governments, and observers generally disagreed that these were legitimate targets at which Indonesia should aim, creating a further poor impression of Indonesia as the Government struggled to maintain them.

Those highly sensitive emotions, pride and dignity were involved in these issues, not to mention national sovereignty. The world seemed to care little about pride, dignity and sovereignty, creating further bad public relations for Indonesia the more the country clung to what it felt were its rights. There is always an inertia factor in Indonesia resulting in changes taking place very gradually and slowly. As the crisis unfolded the Government was doubtless genuinely daunted by the magnitude of the reforms the IMF said must be made. To complicate matters still further there were major holidays, elections and a complete change of Government.

Plus, Indonesia, unlike the US, is not a legalistic, rules-and-regulations-type society but a high contextual society from which there can emerge a thousand different solutions to the same problem, which all involved will be very happy if it can be solved in whatever way people want to solve it so long as everyone ends up happy. The Indonesian Way of doing things is always to find a way - never mind what the rules say. Now Indonesia was being asked to pin its hope for survival on rules alone, on reforms. There was a comprehension gap. Things had worked well before. Why not now? Indonesia had misunderstood and underestimated the crisis. The world misunderstood Indonesia and its media attributed only the worst motives to all that the Government did. In the end, there can be absolutely no doubt that the Government was totally committed to carrying out the programme agreed with the IMF - even though it had not worked to date. Even carrying it out posed challenges. In Washington, it could all have been done in a trice. But in Indonesia! Did they have the experience? Did they have the people? Did the people have the will? Nothing was easy. Ironically, if rapid and widespread change was to happen it would only happen with strong leadership, the leadership of a man like President Soeharto, the very man the Western press said should step down.

Paul Keating had said that Indonesians were not good at telling their own story. Mahathir Mohamad was better at telling his, and there were startling similarities. Asked by 'Asiaweek' on March 27, what had gone wrong in Malaysia in 1997 (as well as throughout much of the region) he was quoted as saying: "We have been doing the same thing all this while. We haven't changed. Suddenly, on a certain day, there was a loss of confidence. I don't know what we did that was different from what we had been doing. It's not as if suddenly we say, "We reject the free market" or "We reject democracy the way we have been practising." You can look back. What was the difference in June and July? In June, everything was fine; in July, everything was not. Even before what happened in Thailand, whatever it is that you find under the microscope has been there all the time. Why do you take a microscope and look and then suddenly say, "We have no confidence." You know, when you devalue a currency, you make people poor. You undermine a perfectly good country with a good economy. You undermine perfectly good companies and businesses. The businesses fail and you say, "There you are. (I told you so) " It reminds me of somebody who tells you, "You cannot run that fast." You keep running and he shoots you in the leg and says, " I told you, you cannot run." Currencies devalue because somebody does something to devalue them." Many Indonesians would have agreed with all of this.

At the end of 1997, when it was believed that the crisis had been triggered by offshore debts owed by Indonesia's conglomerates, some people said that 200 million Indonesians were being made to pay the price of the mistakes and greed of 200 companies. By the end of the first quarter of 1998, as Dr Mahathir had said, it was clearly funds and speculators which had brought down the rupiah. And, as Dr Mahathir had said, the misery of millions was now on their hands, if not their consciences.

Malaysia's 'The Star' quoted Hong Kong economics professor, Tsang Shu-Ki as saying that: " ..although international financial speculators did not create the fundamental problems....they smelt blood, took part in speculative activities and ignited a massive financial panic, and they must bear responsibility for this."

By the beginning of April, once booming Indonesia, was in need of very substantial supplies of food and medicines from overseas. Bilateral donors, the United Nations and even the Red Cross became involved. Speculators, drought, the IMF - now lives and health were at risk. Where before Indonesia had won praise, now it earned pity.

Dr. Mahathir now spoke about the new sense he had of somehow being a prisoner of global forces. He was quoted as saying: "...the problem we have now is that we cannot even talk freely. Because if you say something that is not quite right, it will cause what is known as loss of confidence. And, when there is a loss of confidence we suffer. We have to pay a price. I've been told many times that if I say certain things, the currency will devalue. That will cause poverty for millions of people, not only in Malaysia but also in neighbouring countries...The Prime Minister has lost his voice, the right of free speech. I find that I am actually not allowed to explain. I must say the correct things."

Thailand, Korea and Indonesia, to varying degrees, all felt that they had been pushed around by the IMF and there was smouldering resentment. In both countries the attitude was: "We'll do it because we have to, not because we like it." Prime Minister Mahathir and President Soeharto now found their every word and act under global scrutiny and capable of global censure by the markets if what was said and done was disliked. The issues of sovereignty raised by the actions of the IMF will not go away soon. In April, Dr Mahathir spoke about the threat to Malaysia's way of life posed by globalisation and called upon Malaysians to defend it. Who could see where these lines of thought would lead - away from total globalisation, perhaps, away from the notion of total free trade and capital movements, perhaps, towards even deeper cultural exclusiveness, perhaps, towards a more widespread commitment to Islam, perhaps, the dominant religious force in Malaysia and specifically mentioned on April 7 by Dr. Mahathir.

While we cannot say that Indonesia's Muslims are in any way opposed to the modern sector, during Lebaran there was much depiction on television of the simple agriculture-and-fishing-based traditional lives of many Indonesians. As the war clouds of the urban-originating economic crisis rolled over Indonesia's countryside it wasn't difficult to imagine that, so long as they had land or a job and enough to eat many of Indonesia's sons of the soil were happy being just that. Looking at the streams of people flooding into Jakarta looking for work, some people could easily deny this. Because of the inevitably uneven nature of development in a country as large as Indonesia, there are almost two Indonesias - the Indonesia of the farms and villages and the sophisticated Indonesia of the cities, chic, modern, high-tech, affluent. The sophisticats once lived in the villages and still make the pilgrimage home on highdays and holidays. Many of these people value the new, modern lifestyle and hope that the economic crisis will soon be solved so that they can continue to enjoy it. Many of them are also Muslims.

A fear was developing in parts of the region that the global world would also be a standard world and that the standard would be Western or more probably, American. Loss of sovereignty and loss of cultural identity had been placed firmly on the table as possibilities in the years ahead. In Indonesia, in one of its March issues,'Ummat' magazine said: "We have pawned our institutions to foreign banks, the IMF and the World Bank but, for the long-term, it is best for our national economy to be independent. We cannot afford to open our doors to a form of naked imperialism. This doesn't mean that we are opposed to foreign investors in Indonesia; we want to work together with foreign investors and institutions. But, first, we want to focus on matters important to our country and not subordinate this to matters which are important to foreigners." When complete details of the new and, hopefully, final agreement with the IMF were known, after the Easter holiday, even Government critic, Amien Rais, said that the turn to the IMF had made Indonesia "surrender its soul."

At the end of March, Malaysia's 'New Straits Times' quoted Dr. Mahathir Mohamad as saying in Germany that southeast Asian countries should be "allowed to choose their own way to resolve their economic problems and restore confidence among foreign investors." Malaysia had done just that and its head was high. The country sympathised with the plight of its neighbours, seemingly being bullied by the IMF and the West.

If the third Agreement with the IMF failed to halt the slide in the rupiah, a combination of desperation, hurt national pride and outrage that so many things were apparently not functioning properly could explode in new demands for political reform. Throughout Easter, up to 25,000 students held rallies demanding such change.

The fine details of the IMF April deal reflected both the determination of the Government of Indonesia to please the IMF and the markets and also its desperation. It also seemed to reflect a new approach by the IMF based on a better understanding of Indonesia's needs. The new IMF Agreement - a Letter of Intent - reminded the Government to more fully implement changes the Government thought it had made but the IMF thought it hadn't and set out a timetable for the accomplishment of reforms, old and new. It reminded the Government to implement reforms promised but so far not delivered. This time, the IMF would not be satisfied with promises. It wanted action. Its funds providers wanted action. The timetable was extremely ambitious by Indonesian standards. The fact that firm dates were inked in beside each reform was a measure of the Government's desperation as well as of the IMF's distrust.

The detailed consultancy, legislative and administrative work described in the Agreement hopefully reflected new awareness in the IMF that, without friendly but informed guidance, many of the changes the Fund and the markets wanted to Indonesia's institutional, legal and regulatory environment might be slow in coming and ineffective in implementation. The tight timetable certainly posed the very real risk that new laws and regulations might not be well formulated. Observers could not be sure how far the timetable reflected mistrust and how far it reflected helpfulness. The closer to the former, the less chance of success. The closer to the latter the more chance of success. If the Fund and its officials worked collaboratively with the Indonesians the reforms had a chance. Any return to confrontation and criticism would slow them down. The recommendation to appoint high level foreign officials to assist Indonesia with its now urgent banking reforms seemed a step in the right direction.

The 117-point Agreement covered bank reforms, financial and fiscal reporting, measures to further free-up foreign investment in Indonesia, steps to smooth the flow of trade, proposals for diminishing state costs and boosting revenues, enhancing overall economic efficiencies, such as by the dismantling of monopolies, privatisation of state enterprises and, subsidies. There was now an ambitious programme of privatisation but, in a deep recession, it remained to be seen who, other than foreigners, would still have funds to buy into them. Government would retain 51 percent of each entity and hoped to raise around US$2 billion. The opportunity was also taken by the Fund to press for a reform of the procedures for procurement and contracting for private sector involvement in the provision of infrastructure and even for accelerated programmes for converting to cleaner fuels. The former would be widely welcomed by foreigners but one really wondered how the latter, highly desirable though it might be, could help halt the slide of the rupiah.

In general, the Fund's recommendations were sound and badly needed after the ravages on the economy by the crisis. In the past, its advice had been sweeping and vague, for example, 'reform the banking system.' Now, the steps said to be required were spelt out in great detail. And there were more requirements and steps than ever before, partly reflecting new apparent needs thrown up by the crisis as it went on. Many of the suggestions and much of the advice must have been welcomed by ministers still very new to their portfolios. The IMF's advice was now so broad and its timetable so tight that foreigners had instant doubts as to whether everything could really be carried out as planned. And, if it wasn't? Would the IMF again lambaste Indonesia, again fuelling negative media coverage? Again undermining the confidence so vital to Indonesia's recovery? Some of the items stipulated to be done the Government of Indonesia was under the impression had been done. Would the Fund ever agree? Could it ever be pleased? And if not?

It was evident from the package details that the IMF believed that the Government had been moving slowly in the areas of banking reform and privatisation of state enterprises and had found that it was still far from having the necessary plans and tools in place. Partly, this was due to the elections and the appointment of a new cabinet. A long list of legal and regulatory work was now listed as being necessary to achieve the agreed real sector changes. By itself, the Government of Indonesia may not have been able to devise the network of often related procedures, probably plucked so effortlessly from its stock of economic models by the IMF. Clearly, the Fund wanted reconfirmation of things it had wanted done earlier but which it still suspected hadn't been done. And, equally clearly, it also felt that work had progressed too slowly on measures to further free-up foreign investment. There were a number of new measures, reflecting the needs and opportunities of the moment, aimed at smoothing the flow of trade as well as for diminishing state costs and boosting revenues,

On whosoever advice it had come about, the fixing of minimum bank capitalisation at US$30 million (Rps 250 billion) by the end of 1998 for banks which had cleared their balance sheets of non-performing loans removed industry fears that they would not be able to meet the new targets and diminished the threat of seriously widespread closures. Banks with high levels of bad debt would still be required to meet the high targets set previously.

The Fund's willingness to compromise with Indonesia on the timing of the removal of subsidies was now seen to be limited to October, 1998. After that, it said, subsidies on corn, wheat flour, sugar, soybean and fish meal must go. Time would tell whether this would be practical or not. If it turned out to be not practical..........?

Offshore debt had been central to Indonesia's problems since the crisis began. Now the Fund said that credible progress should be made in solving this problem "by April 22." That the Agreement, for the first time, confirmed the Fund's willingness to try to help solve the problem of offshore private debt should have been greatly welcomed by markets which had been waiting for a solution to this problem since the beginning of the crisis way back in June, 1997. Of course, a commitment to help was far from being a solution. Still, better late than never, perhaps.

At first sight, "By April 22" seemed like advice given by an impatient schoolboy with all the arrogance and naivete of youth, rather than a headmaster, even. As if the Government of Indonesia had not been trying for months to solve the problem. As if the steering committee had not been trying for weeks. Lenders were not under the control of the Government of Indonesia; they could not be forced. Until now, lenders had shown no signs of wanting anything less than their money back. Were they waiting to see how the rupiah would perform? Were they pressing borrowers for financial details so as to be in a better position to assess what had to be or could be done about the unpaid loans? Rumour had it that lenders might be prepared to write-off 30-40 percent of the sums outstanding. Was this what the debtors were waiting for? Were they cooperating fully with their respective lenders in providing full information about finances and assets? The only sure thing was that both sides seemed to be trying to out wait the other. Of course, if a solution could really have been found "By April 22" there was every chance that the rupiah would have begun to rise. If that had happened what an irony it would have been. Debt had been the problem since June, 1997. The Indonesian people had gone through untold suffering and humiliations only to find that paying the bills solved the problem. Had it been done in the first place, maybe there would have been no need to involve the IMF. By 'April 22" everyone, other than the players in the debt drama, was still firmly in the dark about that was happening.

While the IMF was engaged in its Spring meeting in Washington, the committee of bankers representing Indonesia's private sector debtors was meeting in New York - a follow-up to the Singapore meeting. The New York meeting was a larger one and, while some banks had been added, others had dropped out. Banks represented on the committee in New York included: Standard Chartered Bank, ABN-AMRO, Citibank, Bank of America, Deutsche Bank, Societe Generale, Bank of Tokyo-Mitsubishi, Chase Manhattan Corporation, Deutsche Morgan Grenfell, Hong Kong & Shanghai Banking Corporation Holdings, Sanwa Bank, Sumitomo Bank. Korean Development Bank, Overseas China banking Corporation and Banque Nationale de Paris. Radius Prawiro represented the Government's external debt team, Anthony Salim, represented private sector debtors and Bank Indonesia Governor, Sjahril Sabirin also attended.

The IMF's "By April 22" deadline seemed to suggest that this meeting would result in great progress. Even before it began, however, the 'Jakarta Post quoted bankers as saying that " their initial task will be to assess the extent of the Indonesian corporate sector's US$74 billion debt stockpile, and to evaluate the implications of Jakarta's reform package." None of this sounded overly promising, or even new.

The joint statement issued, after the meeting ended, suggested that lenders and borrowers were playing hardball. There seemed to be no evidence that banks were willing to write-down the debt. The bankers were said to have insisted on being given a complete breakdown of each companies financial position and also a report card for the economy as a whole. On the issue of debt restructuring, the 'Jakarta Post' quoted a banking source as saying: "We would insist that they (the Indonesians) are in complete compliance with the IMF programme before we agree to any debt restructuring." So, there had been no agreement on a write-down and no agreement on restructuring repayments. In fact, Radius was quoted as saying: " We did not discuss any grace period for the repayment of the debt." He was also quoted as saying that he and his team would have to return to Jakarta to obtain the data requested by the bankers, a step which held out little hope of any quick solution to the debt problem. Providing data about the health of the economy should have been feasible but getting the corporate data was likely to be comparable to pulling dragons' teeth. Knowledgeable bankers said that the debtors had taken tough positions, insisting that repayment would largely have to wait for the rupiah-US dollar exchange rate to return to a more equitable position. Press reports indicated that they were hoping for a write-down of anything from 40 to 70 percent of the funds owed. At the same time, in the context of possible bankruptcy, they were said to be refusing to acknowledge the new market value of their assets, expecting asset values to recover with the exchange rate.

So, what had been agreed? Very little, it appeared. Really, it seemed to be implied, only that, if and when agreement could be reached by debtors and creditors, borrowers could make use of Government facilities to use rupiah to buy the needed foreign exchange. There was no indication of what exchange rate would be used and no indication of what rate of interest would be charged. However, there was important additional information. Indonesia's Legal Counsel, Mark Walker, of Cleary Gottlieb, Steen and Hamilton was quoted as saying that such facilities could take the form of funds provided by "the IMF, the World Bank, the G-7 countries or Japan." With official foreign currency reserves down at US$ 13.3 billion this would ensure that the Government had enough foreign currency to cover the debts. Of course, the exchange rate would be crucial, otherwise, despite all prior denials, the Government would end up shouldering some of the debt. Walker said that these new facilities were expected to be available by the second half of 1998. Corporate participation in the scheme would be voluntary, implying that some or perhaps even many of the debtors would not take part, preferring to simply wait for better times. For those who did take part a six-month timeframe was put on negotiations leading to a resolution of their debt problems. This hardly looked like sufficient progress to please the IMF but it was hard to tell because April 22 came and went and the Fund made no comment. The IMF's own involvement in the committee's proceedings did not seem to have extended much beyond a briefing from Michel Camdessus. Later, the IMF's Chief Economist, Michael Mussa confirmed that the Fund had only been "watching closely." He was quoted as saying: "It's not something where...we are going to be the authors or underwriters of the plan."

However, private sector comment was instructive and illustrative. The 'Indonesian Observer' quoted Ascanio Martinotti, Managing Director for Hong Kong-based, Regent

Pacific Group Ltd, as saying of the New York joint statement: " It gave no specifics. it doesn't mean a thing." Commenting on the possible role of the Indonesian Government Martinotti went on: " It's just shifting the responsibility from the public sector from the private sector and could push the Government to print money to help repay the debt."

The committee's next meeting was planned for May in Tokyo and was expected to focus on measures related to Indonesia's access to trade finance and interbank lines, including the resolution of payment arrears. On April 22, to unblock credit lines, the Government announced that it would immediately settle the US$500 million bill and recover the funds from involved banks at a later date. The intervening time would presumably be used by Radius to gather additional data and information and would include the announcement of new regulations relating to bankruptcy - crucial if foreign lenders were to have a chance of recovering their loans through the forced sale of assets. On April 21, the Government announced that amendments to Indonesia's bankruptcy law would be enacted within 120 days, after deliberation by Parliament. The time would also be needed to set up a commercial court and train judges. Meanwhile, the amendments were issued in the form of a Government regulation which had the force of law. While it was good to see progress being made, it was disappointing that full implementation would take another four months, bringing the date to September. And foreigners still had questions relating to the law, about, for example, indemnity for trustees, the problem of court deadlines being ignored, the rights of unsecured creditors and measures to prevent the fraudulent transfer of assets. While the bankruptcy law would not be in operation until September the Government let it be known that it hoped that a framework for the restructuring of the offshore debt could be agreed by the steering committee no later than June 30.

Another section of the April Agreement with the IMF which gave pause for thought was that relating to the state companies. Given the pace at which life is lived in Indonesia could there really be "action plans for all 164 public enterprises by September?" Was the Fund once again drastically overestimating the will and ability of Indonesians to get things done quickly? In any case, other than satisfying ideological purity and, possibly, giving the Government some extra cash, would it really make any difference in terms of halting the slide of the rupiah? As if to set doubting minds at rest, the Government announced very quickly indeed that, in line with the new Agreement with the IMF, seven state companies would be ready for privatisation before March, 1999, with five others in which state interest would be reduced.

The seven were port management companies, PT Pelindo I and II, palm oil plantation firm PT Perkebunan Nusantara IV, construction company, PT Jasa Marga, coal mining firm, PT Tambang Batubara Bukit Asam, PT Krakatau Steel and airport management company, PT Angkasa Pura II. The five were PT Telkom, satellite operator, PT Indosat, PT Semen Gresik, mining firm, PT Aneka Tambang and tin mining company, PT Tambang Timah. The Government confirmed that it expected to earn US$ 1.9 billion. It also revealed that the state companies as a whole had incurred offshore debt of US$12.5 billion. It now seemed clear that Indonesia's uncharacteristic swiftness in pushing along the process of privatisation of state companies probably had much to do with the repayment of this debt - additional to the private sector borrowings of over US$80 billion.

Although a promising start appeared to have been made, looking at the new Agreement, with its 117 action points, each one in reality backed by an IMF threat to withhold funds if it wasn't implemented in full by the due date, it is easy to imagine that the average Indonesian Government official would gasp with dismay at the work involved, work which he would probably think should take a decade at least.

Weaknesses notwithstanding, even critics of the IMF must surely have agreed with the Fund that, if all the suggested reforms were implemented, the 'new' Indonesian economy would indeed not only be much stronger but also much more hassle-free as a place for foreign companies to do business. The Government and the IMF now had their hopes pinned exclusively on the reputation of the IMF and the effectiveness of the reform programme being sufficient to restore that nebulous emotion known as 'confidence.' If the IMF had got it wrong, Indonesia could very well be heading for disaster. If the Government backed away from the reforms, Indonesia could be heading for disaster.

The elements still pointing in this direction were numerous.

There was the ongoing unsolved problem of the

private sector offshore debt - the issue that had sparked the initial collapse of confidence. Even in April, almost a year after the crisis broke, the Government of Indonesia had still not managed to track down all the private debts. The latest report, on April 15, was that private debt had now been identified as being US$ 80.2 billion, up from US$73.96 billion; Government debt had fallen to US$ 53.5 billion, down from US$63.46 billion. Of the private debt US$ 15.6 billion were short-term with a further US$ 7.4 billion in commercial papers - a total of US$23 billion - down from US$ 35.6 billion. If previous figures were not wrong, somebody had been paying their bills. Bulk of the debt repayment was on near-standstill while all the parties involved, Government, debtors and lenders, waited for the time to come when their respective positions would be optimal to resolve the problem.

There was the ongoing problem of Indonesia's shakey banking industry, which, despite skeptics, seemed to be slowly being dragged back to proper diligence, if not solvency.

There was the ongoing and related problem of dishonoured Indonesian letters of credit, about which much had been promised but little had happened - pending IMF approval of Indonesia carrying out the agreed reforms. Even some of the help promised was sometimes highly focused and targeted and did not represent a solution to the overall problem. The LC logjam spawned a container crisis which the Government moved to solve by importing empty boxes.

There was the phenomenon of sky-high interest rates which were still said to be crippling the business sector. Care had to be taken with this. Although 80 percent of the companies listed on the Jakarta Stock Exchange were said to be technically bankrupt they seemed to be still trading. And, of course, not all companies had gone public. Many listed companies were but fragments of much larger, unlisted, parent companies. Indonesians and visitors to Indonesia could see substantial levels of business continuing, despite the gloom and doom on every side. It was known that one reason was that many companies were simply not paying their debts. Another was that there had to be very formidable sums of money outside the banking system. Still, despite the seeming continuance of business activity construction was largely stopped, new projects were halted and many factories were idle.

As the end of April neared, there were still too many negatives about Indonesia to impress foreign investors or to push the value of the rupiah up drastically. Direct investment was expected to slump by at least 40 percent while overseas investors waited for the economy to recover and for the political risk posed by ongoing student demonstrations to diminish. Portfolio investors might have an interest in bankrupt companies so long as they did not have to pay large debts and so long as the economy looked set for growth. A bankrupt company in a contracting market hardly seemed like much of a deal.

The 'Jakarta Post' quoted the Minister of Manpower, Theo Sambuaga, as warning that by March 1999, in the wake of a severe corporate shake-out, unemployment was likely to reach 13.5 million or 15 percent of Indonesia's work force of 90 million. Another 40 million people worked less than 35 hours per week - more than half the work force. Many of the workers laid-off to date had been given three months severance pay before Lebaran. In May it would run out. Then what? In its leader on April 14, the 'Jakarta Post' forecast "tough times ahead." The editorial said: "The nation is in for the roughest stretch of the reform programme over the next six months as all price subsidies for essential commodities, except rice and soybeans, will be eliminated by October. "This means that for most households the economic crisis will get much worse before it starts to stabilise and eventually recover. But higher prices for essential goods are not the only source of economic suffering. More companies may have to fold, with the consequence of massive layoffs and bigger bad debts, as the Government is required to maintain or even to further raise the already punitively high interest rates during the stabilisation period." (- estimated by the IMF as requiring up to three years.) The banking industry, also, may be in for bigger jolts as the operation of more banks, battered by high interest rates and huge sums of bad loans, may have to be suspended. Cumulative inflation for the calendar year is projected at 50 percent."

Asked if he thought that the new IMF package would help the Indonesian economy, Kwik Kian Gie wrote in the 'Jakarta Post:' "Not in the short-term." Asked if carrying out the IMF programme was a guarantee that Indonesia would not suffer a similar crisis of confidence again Kwik wrote: " No." The money market didn't seem too impressed either. The rupiah rose slightly and fell slightly and was predicted to stabilise at between Rps 7,500 and Rps 8,500 to the US dollar - hardly an improvement worth talking about.

The markets were still said to be concerned about the debt hangover. Next day, while Michel Camdessus was saying in Washington that his team had at last got to the "root of the problems" in Indonesia, the rupiah fell again, to close to Rps 9,000 to one US dollar. The stock market also edged down. What was there to be bullish about? Many of the problems remained. The 'Indonesian Observer' was quoted as saying: " The sentiment was weak today. Many investors stayed on the sidelines amid uncertainties over the Government's commitment to the IMF reform package and the outcome of the debt negotiations." Continuing student demonstrations coupled with no sign of a rapid solution to the debt problem and deepening economic hardship as a result of the IMF's 'rescue' ensured that 'sentiment' stayed deeply negative - not only in Indonesia but overseas, in countri Ces interested in Indonesia.

As April ticked away, and the rupiah failed to register any dramatic progress against the US dollar, once again, from Indonesia's point of view the IMF 'medicine' seemed not to have worked. With the economy being driven into recession, if not bankruptcy, would it ever work? Even the IMF was not optimistic. Michael Musa, Research Department Director of the IMF, was quoted by "The Indonesian Observer" as saying that "there remains great uncertainty at this time over Indonesia where it is too early to perceive when the turnaround of the economy might come." Informed speculation put it at least three years away.

In Indonesia, one of the uncertainties was whether there actually was an Agreement between the Indonesian Government and the IMF. Unlike the second Agreement, no one had been seen to sign this one. Plus, according to media reports, the deal would be discussed at the IMF's April 20 meeting in Washington, the clear suggestion being that the meeting would include ratification - or otherwise. After the meeting, there was still no confirmation and the media held out the prospect of no additional funds until; at least the end of May and then only in tranches of US$1 billion per month, depending on Indonesia's progress. Not encouraging.

1997's problems were all still there and had even

been aggravated - high foreign and domestic debt, high interest rates, high levels of corporate insolvency. The April Agreement talked of only 17 to 20 percent inflation: there were many skeptics.

The new IMF Agreement featured a budget deficit of 3.2 percent of gross domestic product, to be covered from foreign funds and basically to allow subsidies and social programme to continue until October. But after that? Asked this question, IMF directors inclined their arms upwards to signify recovery. But were they really right? Especially when the Fund's agreement called for 4 percent negative growth in the current fiscal year - 5 percent in the calendar year!

Exports and tourism were two sectors which promised to help Indonesia weather the storm, Exports were rising but tourism seemed in the doldrums, pushed down by a combination of perceived economic and political uncertainties as well as international perceptions of the affect of the ongoing drought - most dramatically in the form of the forest fires but also in terms of rising health risks etc. Dengue fever was reported as having reached epidemic proportions in some areas, including Jakarta.

With so much misery forecast and so few bright spots, it was hardly surprising to find the students pressing on with their campaign for political reform - not that any amount of reform could have solved the crisis, which still seemed to hinge firmly and exclusively on solving the country's debt problem - offshore debt, bank debt and corporate debt. Even a brand new Government was likely to paralysed until this issue worked itself out. Nevertheless, on April 13, 'The Indonesian Observer' reported the Chairman of the Executive Board of the Indonesian Muslim Students Movement, Chatibul Umam Wiranu, as saying: " If the masses want to strengthen the creation of a people power movement, my group will support them." It was unlikely that "the masses" would respond to this, unless rising prices forced their backs to the wall. Off campus, at this stage, the students had no active supporters or patrons. What they did, they did alone. Movement member Sulthon was quoted as qualifying Chatibul's statement with another saying: "We would reject any unconstitutional political changes." In a statement, the group was alleged to have called upon Indonesia's armed forces to "announce where it stands." By April 15, the demonstrators were still calling for political reform but also demanding that the Government did not raise prices of essential items - one of the many key insistencies of the IMF.

On Tuesday, April 21, still concerned about price rises and inflation, Bank Indonesia announced that its interest rates on short-term promissory notes would be raised from between 3 to 5 percent on all maturities. The highest rate was 50 percent. Commercial bank deposit rates were once again up at 55 percent. The stock market nosed downwards. As always, and understandably, the Chamber of Commerce and Industry asked that the rate hike be short-term. But, in a statement KADIN said that it understood the necessity of keeping interest rates high to "avoid monetary and banking instability. The statement added that the steps were "unavoidable." The rupiah seemed to strengthen marginally but by no means dramatically at close to Rps 8,000 to one US dollar. It seemed that the markets doubted that rates could go higher or even be maintained and, in any case, the underlying problems of the offshore and domestic debt and the still looming spectre of bank insolvency provided no grounds for greater confidence in the rupiah. After the end-of-March- hike in interest rates Bank Indonesia had been successful in selling Rps 29 trillion (US$3.6 billion) of its promissory notes to investors, around 20 percent of them to foreigners. Clearly, the Bank hoped for a similar, if not better, result from the latest rates increase. Observers believed that, if truth be told, interest rates would have to remain high for "one to two years."

As April closed, student demonstrations continued, involving greater numbers, the use of Molotov Cocktails by the protesters and tear gas by the security forces, the Government raced to keep up with the IMF timetable for reform and the markets trod water. It seemed that everybody in Indonesia was now waiting. Waiting to see if the Government would carry out the new IMF reform package, awaiting the IMF's response, waiting to see what effects the reforms would eventually have, waiting to see what plan would emerge for the repayment of the offshore debt, waiting to see whether lenders really would be able to gain access to debtors' assets, waiting to see what would happen to the rupiah, waiting to see what would happen in the economy generally, waiting to see what would happen in politics if the trauma of economic change became unbearable. There seemed to be a kind of calm. No one could predict how things would turn out. Everyone hoped for a happy ending - but everyone knew that this still might not be the case.

CHAPTER THIRTEEN

On Roles
And Rules

The IMF's role in Indonesia's crisis promises to be the subject of de bate for years to come. In April, 1998, one thing was for sure: much of the the world outside Indonesia - the parts that counted - so to speak, attached cardinal importance to Indonesia being seen to put its economy in order along lines agreed with the respected, influential and powerful IMF. Like it or not, by this time, Indonesia had no choice but to do what it was told. As in the past, time would tell.

However, the Fund did not enjoy a blemish-free reputation. According to the 'Asian Wall Street Journal' of March 5: "Eight months before Mexico's economy imploded in 1994, the Fund's Managing Director wrote to the US Treasury praising Mexico for "pursuing fundamentally sound economic policies." In May, 1997, the 'Asian Wall Street Journal' said that the World Bank had published a report praising "Thailand and Indonesia as "exceptions to the boom-bust cycle of bank lending" - just a few months before their banking systems were seized by panic. Like ex-Indonesian Central Bank governor, Soedradjad, before them, in his efforts to identify private borrowings, according to the 'Journal,' "the World Bank's Asian staffers say they struggled to keep abreast of events by combing through economic papers and the daily press." In the IMF's September, 1997, annual report the 'Asian Wall Street Journal' said that the IMF "praised (South Korea) for its "continued macroeconomic performance" just as the country was headed towards financial disaster."

On February 7, the 'Asian Wall Street Journal' had quoted Harvard IMF critics Jeffrey Sachs and Steven Radelet as saying that: "The IMF had to redesign its programmes for   Thailand,

South Korea and Indonesia, within weeks of signing the original letters of intent." The 'Journal' noted: "The multinational agency, however, is already learning from its mistakes." In an article in the 'Jakarta Post' Hong Kong-based writer, Andrew Higgins, wrote: "The IMF has conceded in an internal report that it misjudged the Asian crisis."

Despite an eventual seemingly more sophisticated approach to Indonesia's problems, based on improved conversance and information, one of the questions which would doubtless be asked in the months ahead, as experts analysed the Asian currency crisis, was the appropriateness of Thailand, South Korea and Indonesia asking the IMF for help - not to mention the appropriateness of the IMF giving it, unless it really was acting as an "agent for the West." Lack of ability to disburse funds to meet debts, lack of expertise, especially in the vital banking sector (in Indonesia delegated to the World Bank), lack of adequate data and information, especially from the unfamiliar territory of the private sector and, finally, strong doses of free market ideology, ensured that much of the IMF's advice to Indonesia was irrelevant or more damaging than helpful.

As has been said many times, the IMF's mandate is basically to assist countries whose Governments have spent too much and where inflation threatens. Its standard prescriptions are belt-tightening, a Government surplus, high interest rates and the closure of insolvent institutions. It typically works with Governments, not with the private sector. The IMF duly applied the□{se 'medicines' in Indonesia - but to a completely different problem.

The Government had not overspent, until after mid-year inflation did not threaten, before Christmas banks were not so close to insolvency and interest rates at a bearable level were maintaining corporate health. Trade was in surplus. Reserves were 400 percent more than the sum of the current account deficit. The only element in Indonesia's fundamentals that Indonesians might have agreed it was legitimate to doubt, was the ability of corporate borrowers to repay their short-term debt. They couldn't know for sure because no records were kept. If excessive private sector debt really was behind the collapse of confidence, there was no point in going to the IMF because there was never any way that the Fund could use its public money to pay debts. And it was an area in which the Fund's experience was extremely limited.

As the Asian crisis progressed, the Fund was under heavy pressure from elements in the US Congress, who felt that it was handing good money to bad people. According to the March 23 issue of 'Time' magazine: "The Republican leadership on Capitol Hill considers the idea of approving billions of dollars in added funding to bail out Indonesia to be a total non-starter as long as President Soeharto, his family and cronies remain in place, lining their pockets. Soeharto, their thinking goes, is right up there with the late kleptocrats Mobutu Sese Seko of Zaire and the Philippines' Ferdinand Marcos in the category of skimming national funds and salting away fortunes in offshore banks. They will not sign on to a Soeharto strategy if the primary goal, as it now looks, is to save Soeharto."

The White House finally negotiated US$18 billion in new funding with the US Senate but only on condition that the IMF agreed to undergo reforms aimed chiefly at better "helping US interests." There were, and still are, loud calls for the IMF to be more accountable so that Americans can be sure that their money is being spent wisely. A special monitoring force has been established to check on the use of funds and the success of IMF programmes in South Korea and Indonesia.

But if the IMF was unable to solve the problem at the heart of Indonesia's crisis should it have been involved at all? Was it the right institution for the job? At the end of April, US Republican Congressman, Doug Bereuter asked this very question. Chairman of the House Sub-commitee on Asia-Pacific Affairs, Bereuter was quoted as saying that he was "not convinced that the Agency (the IMF) has sufficient knowledge" of the complex problems facing the crisis-hit economies (of Asia). He was quoted as saying that because the IMF usually assists countries with more straight-forward Government fiscal crisis, together with the international community, the Fund had "run into trouble attempting to force wide-ranging reforms.

What Indonesia needed was sophisticated help with its macro and micro-economic management, at a time of acute crisis, and sophisticated advice on strengthening its economy so as to be better able to resist any new losses of confidence in the future. During his many telephone calls to President Soeharto, culminating in the visit of Walter Mondale, ignorance about Indonesia and its needs drove President Clinton and many others to the view that President Soeharto was personally somehow torpedoing the reforms. There was little understanding that Indonesia's managers simply didn't know what to do, couldn't move fast enough and, as usual and as per culture, were trying to identify 'ways' of redoing old things as well as identifying new ones. There was little understanding of the unity of opinion in Indonesia that, above all, what was needed was stabilisation of he rupiah in the immediate term.

Back in February, Singapore's 'The Straits Times' had even quoted Steve Hanke as saying that if the rupiah could be stabilised using a Currency Board President Soeharto planned "a new package of steps that go far beyond previous commitments made to the IMF." In April, 1998, the IMF appeared to have learned from its experience in Indonesia and the right kind and amount of advice was finally forthcoming. High level foreign advisers were to be appointed to assist Bank Indonesia formulate and implement reforms quickly. It could be argued that, for short spells, Indonesia would benefit from the appointment of such advisers wherever new rules and frameworks needed to be devised. In the past, xenophobia, rooted in Indonesia's independence battle, had kept foreigners largely out of the corridors of power. In the early years of the New Order Government, President Soeharto's Harvard trained experts had to keep quiet about their educational backgrounds, as Michael Vatikiotis says in his book 'Indonesian Politics Under Suharto,' in order not to "provoke nationalist sentiment." Fund officials now seemed to realise that they had been demanding the impossible but that the impossible could still be delivered if Indonesia was helped by being given proper and adequate advice. It can only be hoped that they briefed the US President on their findings. Rather late in the day, it seemed that some good things could at last be said about the IMF.

In the US, prior to Congress's agreement to allocate new cash to the Fund, the issue of bailouts (wasting taxpayers money) seemed to call into question the very future of the Fund. It survived that hurdle. Now its continuance and what it is permitted to do will probably be measured against its perceived success or failure in solving the Asian crisis. It had not helped solve the crisis that, just as the Government of Indonesia was under pressure so, too, was the IMF. In its March 19 issue, 'The Far

Eastern Economic Review' had said: "With its credibility increasingly under question, the IMF can't afford to step down and give Jakarta money without hard evidence of reform."

While the IMF fought its battles with the US Congress and Senate, while President Soeharto fought his battles with the IMF, the people of Indonesia had been caught in the middle. In March, it was clear to the IMF that, as an institution the Fund must either limit its global role to dollars and cents bailouts of erring Governments or go forward to a new plateau of activity along the lines being developed in Indonesia. Michel Camdessus reportedly told 'Time' magazine at the end of March: " ...now we are going far beyond fiscal issues, to governance, banking structure, dissemination of information to the market. We must go in this direction. But this is only feasible if we have the appropriate human and financial means. The IMF is a small institution. We have a fine staff, but we must retrain staff to absorb the new disciplines." Indonesia had changed the IMF. Had anybody noticed? Had Washington noticed? Would its members support the Fund's directorate in its self-chosen more ambitious global role? Was the IMF right for this role? Many people in Asia didn't think so, especially those affected by its policies.

At a conference organised by Consumers International in Malaysia in March, participants from Thailand, South Korea and Indonesia said that the Fund's policies had fuelled inflation, spread panic among the public, caused shortages of essential items, triggered bankruptcies, pushed up unemployment and made it difficult for poor people to have access to basic necessities, including health care. Delegates slammed the IMF for its "bad advice" on financial market liberalisation and called on Governments to impose controls on short-term speculative funds and on capital account transactions. Finally, reflecting a substantial rage against the IMF a communique said: " Unless the IMF changes its present policies...., there will be increasing public pressure for it to be closed."

Just as the IMF's role in Indonesia and throughout the Asian region was unlikely to be easily forgotten nor was the role of the hedge and investment funds in increasingly open and unregulated markets. In Washington, reflecting the US and Western view, in March, IMF chief Camdessus was quoted as calling for still more open global financial markets and systems. If there were problems, he was quoted as saying, the way to address them was not by "clamping new controls" but through Governments "maintaining sound economic and regulatory policies." In Bangkok, reflecting the Eastern view, Adrianus Mooy, Under Secretary General of the United Nations Economic and Social Commission for Asia and the Pacific (ESCAP) was quoted as saying that destabilising speculative global capital flows should be controlled. "Some rules need to be set up to guide these capital flows, what we refer to as global governance." Hong Kong economics professor, Tsang Shu-Ki, was quoted in Malaysia's 'The Star' as saying that "financial liberalisation had to go hand in hand with regulatory safeguards because if the safeguards are not put in place in an effective way, liberalisation could lead to serious problems."

It seemed that yet another battle line was being drawn between the IMF and its Asian clients.

In a survey, ESCAP commented on the role of the IMF in Asia's monetary and economic crisis. The report raised concerns about " ....the appropriateness of the prescribed 'medicine' mandated by the IMF," questioning in particular the Fund's requirements for "reduced Government spending, high domestic interest rates and bank closures."

In London, at the Asia-Europe Meeting at the beginning of April, in a statement regarding Asia's financial crisis, Prime Minister, Mahathir Mohamad, won support for the inclusion of a clause citing currency speculation as a cause of economic instability. Italian Prime Minister, Romano Prodi was quoted by Reuters as telling reporters: "One of the lessons that we must learn from the Asian crisis is that speculation, and currency volatility, will be a big problem for the future of economies." Dutch Prime Minister, Wim Kok, was quoted as saying: "It is important for the international monetary and financial institutions to have a close look into whether they are sufficiently equipped to follow what is happening and to prevent certain events. No less a person than US Federal Reserve Chairman, Alan Greenspan, was quoted as saying that a "review of the international financial system was needed to avoid future crisis."

At Davos, Switzerland, during the first week of February, world political and business leaders had also been shaken by Asia's turmoil. Referring to a revolutionary change of heart, one report from the British Guardian News service concluded: "The havoc wrought in the Far East by the crisis of the last nine months has led to a significant change of heart. At the Davos forum of world political and business leaders .... the talk was not of whether free market fundamentalism should be reined in but how." The world market suddenly found itself labelled the "casino economy." Though the fundamentalists still ruled the day, loud voices were raised against the suffering created by unbridled free marketeering - once the market went wrong.

In the end, it seemed that the one man in Asia that Westerners most love to hate, Malaysia's, Dr. Mahathir Mohamad, was actually right. Not only right but the leader of one of the few countries in the region not to ask the IMF for help; the leader of a country which seemed to be one of the first to bounce back. On February 3, 1998, unthinkable of the unthinkable, World Bank President, James Wolfensohn, even said that he would be asking Dr Mahathir for advice. He said he thought that the issue of currency speculation now "deserves serious attention." If he read this, Dr. Mahathir must surely have chuckled to himself if not laughed heartily. In Paris, World Bank Senior Economic Advisor, Pieter Bottelier, was quoted as saying: "The rapid and uncontrolled movement of capital around the world can cause economic damage as severe as war and its consequences should be thoroughly debated."

A month later, last in the field, the IMF entered the funds debate, suggesting that the wings of the hedge funds be clipped by raising the margin and collateral requirements so that their ability to take positions in financial markets could be limited - taking positions being a euphemism for speculating.

Quoting the University of Hong Kong's Professor Tsang Shu-Ki, Malaysia's 'The Star' had said on March 19: "The East Asian financial crisis has exposed the failure of international markets, the lack of international governance on finance and the dangers to developing countries of financial liberalisation and manipulation. Governments that have already liberalised have to exercise great caution and plug existing loopholes that now enable major international market players and speculators to exploit newly introduced financial instruments for their own benefit at the expense of the economy." Professor Tsang slammed private funds for "seeking quick returns on the basis of incomplete information, or worse, hearsay. The frightening aspect of international capital is that it is so difficult to control and it is not transparent in its movements and operations." He said that the IMF and the World Bank were "lamentably lacking in funds and authority" to address pressing problems of global finance and warned that even if this was not the case they were " entrenched in the economic orthodoxy of the West and therefore not particularly sympathetic to non-Western countries problems, constraints and difficulties."

An article in Malaysia's 'The Star' exposed a weakness in the actual use of regional financial markets by local business people which, while, hopefully, not relevant to Singapore, the writer thought true of other neighbouring countries. Dr Ong Hean-Tatt wrote: "The Asian stock exchange turmoil reflects one thing Asians should suspect: the Westerners were more familiar with stock exchange mechanisms than us. We need to know more than the foreigners about the mechanisms of our own stock exchanges."

Having witnessed the financial power of the funds, especially investment funds, Singapore announced plans to make the island Republic Asia's "premier fund management centre" over the next 5 to 10 years - of course, within a suitable and suitably prudent regulatory environment being worked out even as the announcement was made. Singapore had said many times that no one should be at the mercy of financial "gunslingers."

The crisis had roared through Indonesia with the force of a hurricane, leaving the economy stripped bare and exposing every weakness. A similar thing had happened in global capital and currency markets. Globalisation was the direction and goal now set for much of the world. But which would be the world bank? Who was lender of last resort? Who could provide buffer funds against speculators or credit insurance for trade? Who was mandated to set up such institutions? If they were mandated to whom would they be accountable? Should truly enormous capital sums be free to move more or less instantly in and out of markets around the world? (Ironically, in the light of events, back in December, Indonesia had tabled an offer to the WTO to further liberalise its banking and insurance industries.) Was it true that exchange rates work best when floated? Wasn't it true that world experts and politicians had now been shown weaknesses even more serious than those detected in Indonesia? Couldn't the entire global economy be at risk from the people Dr Mahathir called 'gunslingers?"

If things went wrong, as they had in 1997, was the IMF the right organisation to deal with the crisis? Did it have the mandate? From whom? To do what? Was it accountable? To whom? Did it have the requisite staff and more importantly, the requisite detailed micro as well as macro economic information about the economies it was allegedly rescuing? Were its staff sufficiently knowledgeable about the world's diverse business cultures in addition to textbook economics. Did it have the requisite money? Were the purposes for which its funds could be used extensive enough? Should they be extended or was a whole new organisation needed with fresh terms of reference, wider functions, more funds, more staff, better information, greater transparency and public accountability? The IMF wrestled with these issues in Washington, in April, at its annual Spring meeting with the World Bank.

Critics wanted the Fund to explain in more detail where their money had been spent; others wanted to know "what had gone wrong" with the Fund's rescue activities in Asia. The Fund said that it wanted to survive, to expand its activities and to try to do better in future. Italian Foreign Minister, Lamberto Dini, a former director of the Fund, was quoted as saying in Rome that the Asian crisis had shown that the IMF was in need of extensive reform. He said: "Profound reform is needed as is a revision of the entire logic behind it." In the event, the Fund signalled its understanding that private debt could not be allowed to be turned into public debt, as usual, called for further strengthening of domestic financial systems and asked members to provide much more information and data, particularly about the private sector, to facilitate IMF monitoring and assistance.

The massive loss of investor confidence in Indonesia had brought the Indonesian economy to its knees. In doing so it had revealed that deficiencies acceptable in good times could become serious liabilities in bad times. Indonesia was like someone who had been sick for a long time but who could have nevertheless have survived under normal circumstances. When the currency plague hit, Indonesia was too sick to withstand it. The crisis had revealed the organisation and supervision of the entire banking sector to be dangerously inadequate and business-related laws were either antiquated or non-existent. There was need for massive reform of substantial portions of Indonesia's business-related legislative and legal environment. Coherence and transparency were seen to be a must. If it could be done, modernising and strengthening these areas boded only well for Indonesia.

The crisis had also activated dangerous social and political currents which would work themselves out in the months ahead alongside and depending on improvements in the economy. Desperate times make desperate people and the public temper was only likely to be contained if the drawn out crisis was finally solved and there was a recovery in business and work prospects, revenues and salaries and in living standards generally. While it persisted, people on the street said that the Indonesian people were "crying." The policy of Indonesia's new Government vis-a-vis stability remained unchanged. The question for observers was how far and for how long social and political currents could now continue to be stabilised. Time alone would tell. On the Government's side was the fact that it had just been resoundingly endorsed, not only by the Assembly, but, as it were by proxy, by majority of the middle class, business and bureaucratic, which owed its new wealth and position to the New Order. Despite the students, the Government, in fact, faced no organised or effective political opposition. It was not in anyone's interests to 'make trouble,' especially if the troublemakers had no more a solution to the crisis than the Government itself.

Although the people of Indonesia were suffering, there was nevertheless a feeling of helplessness, a feeling that no one had an answer to the pestilence which had inexplicably befallen the country and set it back so far. Like the Government itself, the people felt that their country was at war with an invisible enemy. It was:- with speculators who were no more than electronic entries on dealer's computer screen and with the completely intangible factor of 'confidence' a factor so rightly respected by a man like George Soros, the king of 'feelings.'

The crisis had not begun as an Indonesian crisis; it had been imported from outside. It could only be solved from outside. What could anyone in Indonesia do, in the streets or in the President's palace, against forces outside - except create conditions under which confidence in Indonesia could return. Fighting each other would be no solution. Sure, many people continued to resent what were regarded as the unfair advantages allegedly enjoyed by the President's family, many people resented what they saw as blatant crony capitalism in the new cabinet - there were even student calls for the dismissal of "Bob" Hasan - many people were convinced that lack of morality in their country's leadership was massively to blame for the weakness of Indonesia's institutions and corporations. But few seemed to feel that President Soeharto had caused the crisis or was somehow preventing its solution.

In action, the new cabinet line-up looked good, their statements more promising than usual, their actions along the right lines. President Soeharto seemed to be taking a less conspicuous position, in the background, leaving more of the daily work to his newly appointed ministers, including to his vice-president who some thought might be the long awaited successor. Of course, no one was under any illusion that this was a foregone conclusion nor that President Soeharto could not step forward every bit as quickly as he appeared to be stepping back. There was no suggestion and, given the President's role in the 1945 Constitution, there could be no suggestion, that President Soeharto was anything less than in complete control of his Government.

The crisis and the President's age made the new cabinet a Government with a difference. Within it might be the seeds not only of a solution to the present crisis, not only of a programme of much needed reform but also to the political crisis which might face Indonesia when President Soeharto retires or dies. Indonesians generally were not so concerned with the long-term issues. Day by day they read their newspapers and listened to news reports about the rupiah. Could it be stabilised? Could people afford to live normally again? As Stanley Fischer had said: the jury was still out...........

CHAPTER FOURTEEN

What
next ?

As April led into May, there was a new sense of hope abroad. The rupiah had 'stabilised' at between Rps 7,500 to Rps 8,500 to the US dollar and there were hopes that it would rise further on the back of growing confidence and high interest rates. The new cabinet had moved fast to implement the Government's third Agreement with the IMF. On April 23, press headlines screamed: "Indonesia meets reform deadline." The usually implacable foreign media was forched to acknowledge that progress appeared to have been made. In Washington, Finance Minister, Fuad Bawazier had been quoted as saying: "Indonesia is determined to regain the confidence of the international community through a more open economic system." His promise seemed to be being fulfilled. There was momentum and there seemed to be a new openness regarding economic matters. A new cabinet had been sworn in. There were new ministers. Ginandjar Kartasasmita was singled out for praise; he cut a crisp, authoritative figure. There was the prospect of change; the prospect of reform. To promote economic transparency, Bank Indonesia announced that monetary indicators would henceforth be published weekly. The Central Bank seemed to be on the move, too. Rains had come removing the spectre of famine and dousing forest fires raging in Kalimantan. People spoke about a corner having been turned.

The new ministers involved with the economy, had, of necessity, been highly sensitive to the IMF's timetable for reform - reforms which had now been taken very securely on board by Indonesians as a whole. Whether or not the IMF reforms worked was now beside the point. Inside and outside of Government, there was wide and broad agreement that Indonesia had not been able to weather the monetary crisis because of the weakness of its institutions and irregularities in their operation. Most people believed firmly that domestic and international confidence would not return unless the IMF agreed reforms were implemented in full and on time. Aware that the opinions of both its domestic and international audience had coalesced, the Government almost daily repeated that it was utterly committed to carrying out the reform programme. The public sensed that this would involve pain and had braced themselves to take it - up to a point. the Government knew that it was up against a tidal wave of skepticism and cynicism and seemed to be trying extra hard.

Nevertheless, at the end of April, Indonesian society was an incipient powder keg. If the reforms worked, if job opportunities reappeared, if prices could be held down, or better still reduced, the touch match might not be lit. If unemployment and prices continued to rise, desperation might provoke some as yet unknown hand to plunge a flaming brand into the flames of discontent. At this stage, the most likely hand was that of a student. Campus demonstrations continued almost daily calling for political reform and lower prices of basic necessities. In Denpasar, Medan, Semarang and Jakarta students tested the security forces by attempting to march off campus. A few non-students joined them. The People's Consultative Assembly, incredibly, was in recess and its members on vacation. Unsurprisingly, toward the end of April, the students demanded that it be recalled to discuss the economic crisis. There was an undercurrent of opinion that while the poor suffered the rich played. However, between the rich and the poor was the middle class, until now, it seems, able to weather the storm. By the end of April, there was widespread media reporting of middle-class suffering as mortagages could not be maintained, payments on durable items fell by the wayside and spending had to be cut back, especially on non-essential items such as entertainment, dining out and even fashion clothes. If their cars and hand-phones began to be repossessed would the middle-class continue to stay quiet. In Jakarta the number of suicides rose.

As Indonesians tightened their belts, in some quarters, resentment deepened against the President, his family and those who were alleged to have grown rich in dubious ways under the New Order. Many people, on and off campus, responding to rumours that First Family companies were among the offshore debtors, wondered whether Family companies would be allowed to go bankrupt. There was a growing thirst for fairness and transparency. From the highest to the lowest, the New Order Government had become the target of frustrated, largely repressed, rage. On April 13 'Newsweek' reported "Yogyakarta student, Victor, as saying: " We will keep fighting until Suharto steps down." Amien Rais was quoted as saying: "The students have reached the point of no return." To prevent student unrest from spreading outside the campuses, the Government had taken the unprecedented step of dialoguing with the demonstrators but the dialogues seemed to have little support among the students. The Armed Forces led the dialogue initiative and maintained a position of neutrality bordering on tolerance. As events unfolded the tolerance might be expanded - or contracted.......

Aware of the impact of drastically raised prices on its millions of poor people, the Government had taken steps to maintain subsidies and other controls over the price and supply of basic items. It was still an open question whether all these controls could, in fact, be removed at the IMF's insistence without provoking widespread dissatisfaction. Rigorous measures had been taken to control inflation. Make-work programmes continued in a bid to provide some income to some of the unemployed. In Singapore, toward the end of April, an advisory council to the APEC Forum urged that Pacific Economic Cooperation Council member countries to assemble emergency loans worth US$3 billion to assist Indonesia's small and medium-sized industries. Implementation of the IMF reform programme was expected to unleash more funds for food, medicine and emergency assistance. In many parts of Indonesia, rains had come at last, increasing food availability and enabling the Government to say that it was optimistic in meeting its targeted annual production for rice of 53 million tons. (Just as a fortuitously strong rupiah had disguised institutional weaknesses the rains disguised the fact that Indonesia had still been doing too little to quell the fires, provoking the United Nations, no less, to call on the Government to take stern measures against fire raisers.) Improved food security also made it possible for at least some of the unemployed to remain in their home villages with food to eat and perhaps even some part to play in cultivating it. Life in the countryside and in the market towns seemed oddly normal against the backdrop of the crisis in the economy. Even in the cities, there was a semblance of normality as people went about their daily routines. The Government continually stressed the desirability of discipline and calm.

The one issue that disturbed the tranquillity of seemingly everyone was that of rising prices. Whether in town or village, opinion was united that prices must be held down. On the campuses the students demanded political change if this could not be done. Many of them wanted political change anyway. For the time being, the students' complaints were loud while their objectives remained vague. By the end of April the numbers of students engaged in demonstrations had increased to over 40,000 and there were reports of Molotov Cocktails thrown at security forces and of tear-gas used in retaliation. While responsive and allegedly receptive to non-Government opinion, the Administration stressed the need for gradualness. Dialogue was the intermediary.

Meanwhile, affects of the economic crisis were still working themselves out in the form of unemployment, loss of wages and purchasing power, a spurning of credit in favour of cash transactions, a general business downturn, truncated foreign trade, business closures, rising costs and prices and the still looming threat of bank and corporate bankruptcy. The 4 percent economic contraction forecast in the 1998-99 budget would not help. Major new projects could be expected to be few and far between. The construction industry alone expected full recovery would take five years. Against this background, foreign investors were very much on the sidelines, although a major Government hope was that there would soon be a significant increase in indirect and even direct investment, as foreign investors saw opportunities and bargains. While there was hope of foreign investment, there was also deep rooted fear that too much investment, too many open doors, might lead to Indonesia being dominated by foreigners, as it had been during colonial times.

Once again, there was a sense of waiting, waiting to see not only if the reforms would be carried out but if they would work; waiting to see how much more serious the impact of the crisis would become and, finally, waiting to see what political developments might ensue if the economy refused to resuscitate. In the minds of many there was hope and there was despair. Only time would tell.

Publications about Indonesia from Gateway Books

BUSINESS TITLES

Directory of Indonesian Exporters 1998
(In collaboration with the National Agency For Export
Development, Ministry of Industry and Trade,
Government of Indonesia.

Economic Crisis In Indonesia
The Full Story

Guide To Indonesia's Industrial Exports
(In collaboration with the Ministry of Industry and Trade,
Government of Indonesia)

Guide to British Business In Indonesia 1997, 1998
(In collaboration with the Indonesian British Business
Association
and the
Government of the United Kingdom.)

Indonesia Comes Of Age
50 years of Independence

Expats in Indonesia
1996. 1997

Guide To Industrial Estates
In Indonesia 1995, 1997
(In collaboration with the Indonesian Investment Coordinating
Board, (BKPM), and the
Ministry of Industry and Trade, Government of Indonesia.)

The Culture Of Business In Indonesia
(Asia Pacific Economic Conference, (APEC) 1994, 2nd edition
1996, 3rd edition, 1998)

Opportunities For Australian Investment In Indonesia
(In collaboration with the Indonesian Investment Coordinating
Board, (BKPM), Government of Indonesia.

Women's Role In Development
(In collaboration with the State Minister for the Role of Women,
Government of Indonesia and
with a special introduction by
late First Lady, Ibu Tien Soeharto.)

A Guide For British Investors
(In collaboration with the Indonesian Investment Coordinating
Board, (BKPM), Government of Indonesia and
the British Embassy.

United States Investment In Indonesia
(In collaboration with the Indonesian Investment Coordinating
Board, (BKPM), Government of Indonesia.

**Dutch Investment And Trade In Indonesia
Building A New Era**
(In collaboration with the Indonesian Investment Coordinating
Board, (BKPM), Government of Indonesia and
the Royal Netherlands Embassy.)

Business Travellers Guide to Indonesia
(For Garuda Indonesia)

1992-93/1995-96 Directory of Indonesian Exporters
(In collaboration with the National Agency For Export
Development, Ministry of Industry and Trade, Government of
Indonesia.)

1992-93 Guide To Batam Real Estate